In the same
**INTERNATIONAL
FILM GUIDE SERIES**
edited by Peter Cowie

a dictionary of the

CINEMA

by Peter Graham

A. ZWEMMER LIMITED, LONDON

A. S. BARNES & CO. INC. NEW YORK

Cover designed by Sebastian Carter. Photograph shows Louise Brooks in Pandora's Box (1928)

First Published October 1964
Reprinted November 1964
REVISED AND RESET 1968

Author's Note

THE filmographies that follow each director, actor, scriptwriter, etc., listed in the dictionary are *complete*, unless there is an indication (i.e. 'Main films') that a selection has been made. For reasons of space, the dates which are attributed to each film in the dictionary are given by the last two digits only: thus 09 is an abbreviation for 1909, 67 for 1967, and so on. The dates of films are given under the entries for their directors and are not given again when the title appears under other entries (actors, directors of photography, scriptwriters etc.). If however a film whose director does not have an entry in the dictionary is cited, the director's name and the film's date are given in brackets after the title in the index. Titles of foreign films are as a general rule translated into English where accepted translation exists. But French, Italian, and Spanish titles are left in the original, except where this might cause confusion (e.g. *Ladri di biciclette* is referred to as *Bicycle thieves*). The following abbreviations have been used in the dictionary:

Assist.	*Assistant*
Co.	*Co-directed, co-scripted, co-produced, etc.*
Collab.	*Collaborated on, or in collaboration with*
Doc.	*Documentary*
Scr.	*Scripted, wrote the screenplay of*

I would like to thank the following for their help: Robert Benayoun, Susan Beresford, Stig Björkman, Albertine Bui, Sebastian Carter, Elisabeth Cowie, Peter Cowie, John Gillett, Pierre Philippe, Bertrand Tavernier, Jean-Paul Török Bibliothèque de l'I.D.H.E.C., British Film Institute Library. The Paris offices of Unifrance, Unitalia, Sovexportfilm, 20th. Century-Fox, Paramount, Gaumont, and Metro Goldwyn Mayer were very helpful in providing illustrations, as were Europa Film and Sandrews of Stockholm.

Note to Revised Edition

I would like to thank the following for their help: Lynette Trotter, Peter Cowie, Robert Weingarten, and Allen Eyles.

Publisher's Note

Owing to exigencies of time and budget, such a book as this can be accused of being outdated almost before it appears on the market. Every effort, therefore, has been made to include major films begun by January, 1968.

A

1 Aldo, G. R., Italian director of photography. 1902-53. Main films: *Les derniers jours de Pompeii, Cielo sulla palude, La terra trema, Miracolo in Milano, Othello* (52), *Umberto D, Tre storie proibite, Stazione termini, La provinciale, Senso* (completed by Krasker).

2 Aldrich, Robert, American director, b. 1918. Assistant to Losey, Milestone, Renoir, Wellman, and Chaplin. Since 1951: also producer. Films: *The big leaguer* 53; *World for ransom, Apache, Vera Cruz* 54; *Kiss me deadly, The big knife, Autumn leaves* 55; *Attack!, The garment jungle* (completed by V. Sherman) 56; *Ten seconds to hell* 58; *The angry hills* 59; *The last sunset* 61; *Sodom & Gomorrah* 62; *Whatever happened to Baby Jane?, Four for Texas* 63; *Hush, hush, sweet Charlotte* 64; *The flight of the phoenix* 65; *The dirty dozen* 66; *The legend of Lylah Clare* 67.

3 Alessandrini, Goffredo, Italian director, b. 1904. 1929-30: assistant to Blasetti. Also scripted some of his films*. Main films: *La diga di Maghmod* (doc.) 29; *La segretaria privata* 31; *Seconda B* 34; *Don Bosco* 35; *Cavalleria* 36; *Caravaggio* 40; *Nozze di sangue* 41; *Giarabub*, Noi vivi** 42; *Ebreo errante** 47; *Camicie rosse* (completed by F. Rosi) 52.

4 Alexandrov, Grigori, Russian director, b. 1903. Collaborated with Eisenstein on: *Strike, Battleship Potemkin, October, The general line.* Acted: *Gloumov's diary, Strike, Battleship Potemkin.* Main films: *Romance sentimentale* (short) 31; *Jolly fellows* 34; *The circus* 36; *Volga-Volga* 38; *Spring* 47; *Meeting on the Elbe* 49; *Glinka* 52; *Russian souvenir* 60; *Lenin in Switzerland* (doc.) 67. Also co-scr. and co-prod. *Ten days that shook the world.*

5 Alexeïeff, Alexandre, French animator, b. 1901. Also stage set-designer and book illustrator. See *animation.* With his wife, Claire Parker, who has collaborated on many of his films, invented the "pin screen". Credit titles: *The trial.* Main films: *Une nuit sur le Mont Chauve* 32; *La belle au bois dormant* (puppets) 35; *En passant* 43; *Fumées* 51; *Masques* 52; *Nocturne, Pure beauté, Rimes* 54; *Le buisson ardent, Sève de la terre* 55; *Bain d'X* 56; *Quatre temps, Cent pour cent* 57; *Cocinor, Constance, Anonyme* 58; *Le nez* 63.

6 Allégret, Marc, French director, b. 1900. Assistant to Florey. Main films: *Voyage au Congo* (short) 26; *Le blanc et le noir* (co-dir. Florey), *Mam'zelle Nitouche* 31; *La petite chocolatière, Fanny* 32; *Les beaux jours* 35; *Sous les yeux de l'occident* 36; *Gribouille, La dame de Malacca* 37; *Entrée des artistes, Orage* 38; *Parade en sept nuits* 41; *L'Arlésienne* 42; *Blanche Fury* (in Engl.) 47; *Blackmailed* (in Engl.), *Avec André Gide* (short) 51; *Futures vedettes* 55.

7 Allégret, Yves, French director, b. 1907. Brother of above. Assistant to Renoir. 1935-40: shorts. Main films: *Les deux timides* 41; *Les démons de l'aube* 45; *Dédée d'Anvers* 47; *Une si jolie petite plage* 48; *Manèges* 49; *Les miracles n'ont lieu qu'une fois* 50; *Les*

7

sept péchés capitaux (one episode) 51; *Les orgueilleux* 53; *Oasis* 54; *La meilleure part* 55; *Quand la femme s'en mêle* 57; *Le chien de pique* 60; *Germinal* 63.

8 Amidei, Sergio, Italian scriptwriter, b. 1904. All his scripts written in collaboration. See *neo-realism*. Main films: *Roma, città aperta, Paisa, Sciuscia, Anni difficili, La macchina ammazzacattivi, Sotto il sole di Roma, Domenica d'agosto, Stromboli, Ragazze di Piazza di Spagna, Cronache di poveri amanti, Angst, Il generale della Rovere, Il momento più bello, Era notte a Roma, Viva l'Italia, Il processo di Verona.*

9 Anderson, Lindsay, British director, b. 1923. From 1946: film critic. See *free cinema*. Also stage producer. Supervised: *Together, March to Aldermaston.* Produced: *The pleasure garden.* Main shorts: *Three installations* 51; *Wakefield Express* 52; *O dreamland, Thursday's children* (co-dir. G. Brenton) 53; *Trunk conveyor* 54; *Foot and mouth* 55; *Every day except Christmas* 57. Films: *This sporting life* 63; *Red white and zero* (one ep.) 66; *Come the revolution* 68.

10 Andersson, Bibi, Swedish actress, b. 1935. Also stage actress. Main films: *Smiles of a summer night, Last pair out, The seventh seal, Wild strawberries, So close to life, The face, The devil's eye, Lustgården, The mistress, Now about these women, The island* (64), *Duel at Diablo, My sister, my love, Persona, Le viol, The black palm trees, The girls.*

11 Andersson, Harriet, Swedish actress, b. 1932. Since 1949: also stage actress. Main films: *Medan staden sover,*

Ubåt 39, Trots, Summer with Monika, Sawdust and tinsel, A lesson in love, Journey into autumn, Smiles of a summer night, Last pair out, Through a glass darkly, Siska, A Sunday in September, To love, Now about these women, Adventure starts here, Loving couples, The vine bridge, The deadly affair, Rooftree, Stimulantia (J. Donner episode), *People meet and sweet music fills the heart, The girls.*

12 animation. General term applied to films which are shot "frame by frame" (as opposed to being shot "live"). It includes: (a) animated cartoons, and (b) films in which puppets or other objects are animated. Those who made important contributions to the development of animation include: (Canada) **Norman McLaren** (q.v.); (Poland) **Walerian Borowczyk** (q.v.); **Jan Lenica** (q.v.); (Germany) **Hans Richter** (q.v.); **Lotte Reiniger** (q.v.); **Oscar Fischinger:** *Studien 1-11, Komposition in Blau* 28-33; *Optical poem, Allegretto* 41; **Wolfgang Urchs:** *The pistol* 63; *Contrast* 64; *The machine* 66.

13 animation (cont.) (Czechoslovakia) **Jiri Trnka** (q.v.); **Karel Zeman** (q.v.); **Jiri Brdecka:** *Love and the dirigible* 47; *Clementine* 59; *Our Red Riding Hood* 60; *Sentiment and reason* 62; *Gallina Vogelbirdae* 63; *The letter M* 64; *Why do you smile, Mona Lisa?* 66; **Zdenek Miler:** *Red Riding Hood, The millionaire who stole the sun* 48; *Lenora* 49; *The cock and the hen* 54; *The ghost bear* 55; *The story of the moon* 58; *The rich sparrow* 60; *The red stain* 63; **Bretislav Pojar:** *The gingerbread cottage* 51; *The little umbrella* 57; *The orator* 62; *Romance* 63; *The ideal* 65.

14 animation (cont.) (France) **Emile Cohl** (q.v.); **Alexandre Alexeieff** (q.v.); **Paul Grimault:** Go chez les oiseaux 39; L'épouvantail 43; Le petit soldat 47; La bergère et le ramoneur (full length) 52; La faim du monde 58; **Henri Gruel:** Martin et Gaston 54; La Joconde 58; Monsieur Tête (co. Lenica) 59; **Peter Foldes:** Animated genesis 52; A short vision 55 (both in Engl.); Un garçon plein d'avenir, Appétit d'oiseau 65; Eveil 66; **Jean-François Laguionie:** La demoiselle et le violoncelliste 64; L'arche de Noé 66.

15 animation (cont.) (England) **Richard Williams** (q.v.); **Len Lye:** Colour box, Birth of a robot 35; Rainbow dance 36; Trade Tattoo 37; Musical poster 41; Bells of Atlantis 52; Colour cry 55; Free radicals 57; **George Dunning:** The wardrobe 59; The apple, The flying man 62; Charley 65; The ladder 67; **Bob Godfrey:** Polygamous Polonius 60; The do-it-yourself cartoon kit 61; The plain man's guide to advertising 62; The rise and fall of Emily Sprod 63; Alf, Bill, and Fred 64; L'art pour l'art 65; Whatever happened to Uncle Fred? 67; **John Halas** and **Joy Batchelor:** The owl and the pussycat 53; Animal farm 54; Speed the plough 55; History of the cinema 56; Automania 2000 64; Ruddigore 67.

16 animation (cont.) (Jugoslavia) **Vlado Kristl** (q.v.); **Vatroslav Mimica:** Happy end 58; The inspector goes home 60; Perpetual motion 63; **Dusan Vukotic:** Cowboy Jimmy 57; Concerto for sub-machine gun 59; Piccolo 60; Ersatz 61; Play 62.

17 animation (cont.) (U.S.A.) **Walt Disney** (q.v.); **John Hubley** (q.v.); **Winsor McCay:** Gertie the dinosaur 09; How a mosquito operates 10; Little Nemo 11; Jersey skeeters 16; **Max Fleischer:** Out of the inkwell 21; Koko the clown series from 22; Betty Boop series from 32; Popeye series from 33; **Stephen Bosustow,** who formed UPA in 1945, and for whom **Pete Burness** (Mr. Magoo series from 50), **Bob Cannon** (Gerald McBoing Boing and Christopher Crumpet series 50-55; Madeline 52; Fudget's budget 54), and Hubley have worked; **Chuck Jones:** Bugs Bunny, Daffy Duck, Mimi, Beep-Beep, and Coyote series 47-67; **Tex Avery:** Kingsize Canary, Slap-happy Lion, Half-pint Pigmy, Lucky-Lucky, Chilly-Willy, and Droopy series 47-52; **Friz Freleng:** Speedy Gonzales and Tweety Pie series 54-58; **Joseph Barbera** and **William Hanna:** Tom and Jerry series 44-60; **Ernest Pintoff:** Blues pattern 56; Flebus 57; The violinist 60; The interview 61; The critic, The old man and the flower 62; **Robert Breer:** Form phases 55; A man and his dog out for air 58; Blazes 61; Horse over tea kettle 63; **Teru Murakami:** The insects 63; The top 65; Breath 67; **Saul Bass:** credit titles of the following feature films: Carmen Jones, Cowboy, The big knife, The man with the golden arm, The seven year itch, Around the world in 80 days, Edge of the city (A man is ten feet tall), Saint Joan, Bonjour tristesse, The pride and the passion, The big country, Vertigo, Anatomy of a murder, Johnny Concho, North by Northwest, Psycho, Storm centre, Ocean's eleven, Nine hours to Rama, Spartacus, Walk on the wild side, It's a mad, mad, mad, mad world, Advise and consent,

Bunny Lake is missing, Seconds, Grand Prix, 2001: A Space Odyssey.

18 Antonioni, Michelangelo, Italian director, b. 1912. At first film critic. 1943: assistant to Carné. Co-scripted: *Un pilota ritorna, Caccia tragica,* and all his own films. Dir. of second unit: *La tempesta.* Shorts: *Gente del Po* 43-47; *N.U.* 48; *L'amorosa menzogna, Superstizione, La funivia del Faloria, Sette canne un vestito* 49; *La Villa dei Mostri* 50. Films: *Cronaca di un amore* 50; *I vinti* 52; *La signora senza camelie, L'amore in città* (one episode) 53; *Le amiche* 55; *Il grido* 57; *L'avventura* 59; *La notte* 60; *L'eclisse* 62; *Deserto rosso* 64; *Blow-up* 66; *Zabriskie Point* 68.

19 Arletty, French actress. b. 1898. Since 1920: also stage actress. Main films: *Pension Mimosas, Faisons un rêve, Les perles de la couronne, Hôtel du Nord, Le jour se lève, Fric-Frac, Madame Sans-gêne, Les visiteurs du soir, Les enfants du paradis, Le père de mademoiselle, Le grand jeu, Huis clos, L'air de Paris, The longest day.*

20 Armendariz, Pedro, Mexican actor. 1912-1963. Main films: *La isla de la pasión, Maria Candelaria, La perla, Enamorada, The fugitive, Maclovia, Fort Apache, Three godfathers, La Malquerida, We were strangers, Viva vuelve, Rosauro Castro, The torch, El bruto, Manuela, Les amants de Tolède, La cucaracha, The wonderful country, From Russia with love.*

21 Arnold, Malcolm, British composer, b. 1921. Main films: *The sound barrier, Hobson's choice, I am a camera, An island in the sun, Trapeze, The bridge* on the River Kwai, The key, The roots of heaven, The heroes of Telemark.

22 Asquith, Anthony, British director, b. 1902-1968. 1926: assistant, scriptwriter, editor. Main films: *Shooting stars* (co-dir. A. Bramble) 27; *Cottage on Dartmoor* 29; *Tell England* 31; *Pygmalion* 38; *French without tears* 39; *We dive at dawn, The demi-paradise* 43; *The way to the stars (Johnny in the clouds)* 45; *The Winslow boy* 48; *The woman in question (Five angles on murder)* 50; *The Browning version* 51; *The importance of being earnest* 52; *Carrington V.C. (Court martial)* 54; *Orders to kill, The doctor's dilemma* 57; *The millionairess* 60; *Guns of darkness* 62; *The V. I. P.s.* 63; *The yellow Rolls-Royce* 64.

23 Astaire, Fred, American actor, b. 1899. 1910-47: also stage actor (mainly musical comedy). Long collaboration with Ginger Rogers. Main films: *Dancing lady, Flying down to Rio, The gay divorcee, Roberta, Top hat, Follow the fleet, Swing time, Shall we dance, A damsel in distress, Carefree, The story of Vernon and Irene Castle, Holiday Inn, Yolanda and the thief, Ziegfeld Follies of 1946, Easter parade, The Barkleys of Broadway, Royal wedding, Belle of New York, The band wagon, Daddy Long Legs, Silk stockings, Funny face, On the beach, The notorious landlady, Finian's rainbow.*

24 Astruc, Alexandre, French director, b. 1923. 1945-50: film critic and theorist. See *caméra-stylo.* Scripted: *Jean de la lune* (48), *La p . . . respectueuse.* Films: *Aller retour, Ulysse ou les mauvaises rencontres* 48; *Le rideau cramoisi* 51 (all shorts); *Les mauvaises ren-*

contres 55; *Une vie* 57; *La proie pour l'ombre* 60; *L'éducation sentimentale* 61; *Le puits et le pendule* (for TV) 63; *La longue marche* 66.

25 Auric, Georges, French composer, b. 1899. Acted: *Entr'acte.* Main films: *Le sang d'un poète, A nous la liberté, Gribouille, Entrée des artistes, Macao, l'enfer du jeu, L'éternel retour, Dead of night, La symphonie pastorale, La belle et la bête, Queen of spades* (48), *Ruy Blas, Les jeux sont faits, L'aigle à deux têtes, Les parents terribles, Hue and cry, Passport to Pimlico, The galloping major, The Titfield Thunderbolt, The divided heart, La p . . . respectueuse, Father Brown, Orphée, Lola Montès, The wages of fear, Rififi, Gervaise, The Lavender Hill Mob, Moulin Rouge, Roman holiday, Next to no time, Le mystère Picasso, It always rains on Sunday, Les espions, Les aventures de Till l'Espiègle, Les sorcières de Salem, Celui qui doit mourir* (He who must die), *Heaven knows Mr. Allison, Bonjour tristesse, Les bijoutiers du clair de lune, La princesse de Clèves, The innocents, Thomas l'imposteur.*

26 Autant-Lara, Claude, French director, b. 1903. At first set-designer on many of L'Herbier's films. 1923-25: assistant to Clair. Main films: *Buster se marie* 31; *Ciboulette* 33; *Fric-Frac* (co-dir. M. Lehmann) 39; *Le mariage de chiffon, Lettres d'amour* 42; *Douce* 43; *Le diable au corps* 47; *Occupe-toi d'Amélie* 49; *L'auberge rouge* 51; *Le blé en herbe* 53; *Le rouge et le noir* 54; *Marguerite de la nuit* 55; *La traversée de Paris* 56; *En cas de malheur, Le joueur* 58; *Tu ne tueras point* 61; *Le meutrier*

62; *Le magot de Joséfa* 63; *Le journal d'une femme en blanc* 65; *Le plus vieux métier du monde* (one ep.), *Le Franciscain de Bourges* 67.

27 avant-garde: term used to describe films which, in content or form, have an experimental or abstract nature. The term strictly applies to a group of film-makers, with close connections with the other arts, who worked from about 1916 in France and Germany. It comprises the film experiments of the Dada and Surrealist movements. Films of the avant-garde include: *Perfido incanto* (A. Bragaglia; Italy, 16); most of the films of Louis Delluc and Germaine Dulac (q.v.); *La chute de la maison Usher* (Epstein); *Ballet mécanique* (Fernand Léger 24); *L'inhumaine* (Feyder; sets by Léger); *Entr'acte* (Clair and Francis Picabia 24); *Ménilmontant* 24, *Sylvie-destin* 26, *Brumes d'automne* 27 (all Dmitri Kirsanoff); *Le retour à la maison* 24, *Emak-Bakia* 26, *Le mystère du chateau de dés, L'étoile de mer* 29 (all Man Ray); *Un chien andalou, L'âge d'or* (Buñuel); *Le sang d'un poète* (Cocteau); *Vieux chateaux* 27, *La marche des machines* 28, *Les nuits électriques* 30, *Robots* 32 (all E. Deslaw); *L'idée* (B. Bartosch 32); and in Germany: *Vertikal-horizontale symphonie* 20, *Diagonale symphonie* 25 (both Viking Eggeling); all the films of Hans Richter, and those of Walter Ruttmann up to about 1933 (q.v.). The term avant-garde is also loosely applied to some modern American experimental film-makers, who include Stan Brakhage (q.v.), Kenneth Anger, Gregory Markopoulos, Andy Warhol, Ron Rice, Jack Smith, and Curtis Harrington (see *new cinema: U.S.A.*).

11

B

28 Bacall, Lauren, American actress, b. 1924. At first stage actress. Main films: *To have and have not, Confidential agent, The big sleep, Dark passage, Key Largo, Bright leaf, How to marry a millionaire, The cobweb, Blood Alley, Written on the wind, Designing woman, The gift of love, Northwest frontier (Flame over India) Shock treatment, Sex and the single girl.*

29 Bacon, Lloyd, American director. 1890-1955. 1911-21: actor *(The rink, The fireman,* and other Chaplin shorts). 1921: worked for Sennett. Main films: *The raspberry romance 25; The singing fool 28; 42nd Street, Footlight parade 33; Wonder Bar, Here comes the navy 34; In Caliente 35; Gold diggers of 1937 36; Marked woman 37; A slight case of murder 38; The Oklahoma Kid 39; The Sullivans, Sunday dinner for a soldier 44; Call me mister 51.*

30 Balcon, Sir Michael, British producer, b. 1896. 1919: distributor. From 1938: director of production at Ealing Studios (where he was responsible for the "Ealing comedies"). 1959: founded Bryanston Films. 1964: took over British Lion. Main films: *Woman to woman, The white shadow, The passionate adventure, The blackguard, The prude's fall, The pleasure garden, The mountain eagle, The lodger (26), Downhill, Easy virtue, Man of Aran, The man who knew too much (34), The 39 steps, The secret agent, Sabotage, Dead of night, The overlanders, Hue and cry, Kind hearts and coronets, Passport to Pimlico, Whisky galore, The Lavender Hill Mob,* The man in the white suit, The Titfield Thunderbolt, The galloping major, Secret people, The ladykillers, Nowhere to go, The scapegoat.

31 Ballard, Lucien, American director of photography, b. 1908. Main films: *The devil is a woman, Crime and punishment, The king steps out, The lodger, The house on Telegraph Hill, Fixed bayonets, O.Henry's full house* (with others), *Don't bother to knock, The magnificent matador, The desert rats, The killing, Buchanan rides alone, The king and four queens, Band of angels, Ride the high country (Guns in the afternoon), The sons of Katie Elder, The caretakers, Nevada Smith, Olle* (part), *Will Penny.*

32 Bardem, Juan Antonio, Spanish director, b. 1922. 1947: film school and criticism. Scripted with Berlanga: *¡Bien venido, Mister Marshall!, Novio a la vista.* Scripted all his own films. Films: *Esa pareja feliz* (co-dir. Berlanga) 51; *Cómicos 53; Felices Pascuas 54; Death of a cyclist 55; Calle Mayor 56; La venganza 57; Sonatas 59; A las cinco de la tarde 60; Los innocentes 62; Nunca pasa nada 63; Les pianos mécaniques 64.*

33 Bardot, Brigitte, French actress, b. 1934. At first model. Also stage actress. Main films: *Mio figlio Nerone, Futures vedettes, Les grandes manoeuvres, En effeuillant la marguerite, Et Dieu créa la femme, Les bijoutiers du clair de lune, Une Parisienne, En cas de malheur, Babette s'en va-t-en guerre, La vérité, La bride sur le cou, Vie privée, Le repos du guerrier, Le mépris, Une ravissante idiote, Viva Maria!, A coeur joie, Histoires extraordinaires (William Wilson ep.), Shalako.*

34 Barnet, Boris, Russian director, 1902-65. At first boxer and actor: *The extraordinary adventures of Mr. West in the land of the Bolsheviks, Storm over Asia, A living corpse.* Main films: *Girl with a hat-box* 27; *House on Trubnaya Square* 28; *Outskirts (Patriots)* 33; *By the bluest of seas* 36; *A night in September* 39; *Fighting film album* (No. 3: *Manhood,* and No. 10: *A priceless head)* 41-42; *One night* 45; *The scout's exploit* 47; *The poet* 57; *Alenka* 62.

35 Barrault, Jean-Louis, French actor, b. 1910. Since 1931: also stage actor, producer, and theatre manager. Main films: *Les beaux jours, Mayerling, Jenny, Sous les yeux de l'occident, Hélène, Un grand amour de Beethoven, Les perles de la couronne, Drôle de drame, Mademoiselle Docteur, Le puritain, Orage, Altitude 3200, Macao, l'enfer du jeu, Parade en sept nuits, La symphonie fantastique, Les enfants du paradis, La ronde* (50), *Si Versailles m'était conté, Le testament du Dr. Cordelier, Dialogue des Carmélites, The longest day, Chappaqua.*

36 Barzman, Ben, Canadian scriptwriter, b. 1912. Worked in U.S.A., but left in 1952 because of McCarthy. Main films: *The boy with green hair, Give us this day, He who must die, Time without pity, Blind date, The fall of the Roman Empire* (co.), *The visit, The heroes of Telemark, The blue Max* (co. adapt.).

37 Batalov, Alexis, Russian actor, b. 1928. Drama studies. Also stage actor. Main films: *The big family, The Rumiantsev case, Mother* (56), *The cranes are flying, The overcoat* (also dir., 58), *Lady with a little dog, Nine days of one year, A day of happiness, The doll of the heir Tutti (The three fat men)* (also co-dir. with J. Shapiro 66).

38 Bava, Mario, Italian director, b. 1914. At first dir. of photography for Monicelli, Leonard, Soldati, Emmer, Camerini, and Walsh. Films: *Black Sunday* (also co-scr.) 60; *Ercole al centro della terra* 61; *Gli invasori, Le meraviglie di Aladino, La ragazza che sapeva troppo* 62; *Incubo, I tre volti della paura* 63; *Sei donne per l'assassino* 64; *Le spie vengono dal semifreddo, Operazione paura* 66; *Danger: Diabolik* 67.

39 Bazin, André, French film critic and theorist. 1918-1958. One of the founders of La Revue du Cinéma (1947), which became Les Cahiers du Cinéma in 1950. In his four volumes of criticism, 'Qu'est-ce que le cinéma?' he contributed important studies on eroticism in the cinema, filmed theatre, neo-realism, the cinema and painting, Chaplin, Wyler, the ontology of the cinema, the Western and many other topics. His other works include a monograph on Orson Welles. His ideas strongly influenced the *nouvelle vague* (q.v.).

40 Becker, Jacques, French director. 1906-1960. 1932-37: assistant to Renoir. Films: *Le commissaire est bon enfant* 35; *L'or du Cristobal* 39; *Dernier atout* 42; *Goupi mains rouges* 43; *Falbalas* 45; *Antoine et Antoinette* 46; *Rendez-vous de juillet* 49; *Edouard et Caroline* 51; *Casque d'or* 52; *Rue de l'Estrapade* 53; *Touchez pas au grisbi* 54; *Ali Baba* 55; *Arsène Lupin, Montparnasse 19* 57; *Le trou* 60.

41 Bellocchio, Marco, Italian director, b. 1940. Films: *I pugni in tasca* 66; *La Cina è vicina* 67.

42 Belmondo, Jean-Paul, French actor, b. 1933. 1950-59: stage actor. Main films: *Classe tous risques, A bout de souffle, A double tour, Moderato cantabile, Léon Morin, prêtre, Une femme est une femme, Two women, Cartouche, Le doulos, L'aîné des Ferchaux, Dragées au poivre, L'homme de Rio, Les tribulations d'un Chinois en Chine, Paris brûle-t-il?, Pierrot le Fou, Le voleur, Casino Royale, Ho.*

43 Benedek, Laslo, Director, b. 1907 in Hungary. 1933: editor in Germany and France. 1935: scriptwriter in England. 1937: U.S.A. Films: *The kissing bandit* 48; *Port of New York* 49; *Death of a salesman* 51; *The wild one, Bengal Brigade (Bengal Rifles)* 54; *Kinder, Mütter, und ein General* (in Germany) 55; *Recours en grâce* (in France) 60; *Moment of danger (Malaga)* 61; *Namu, the killer whale* 66.

44 Benoît-Lévy, Jean, French director. 1888-1959. 1941-46: U.S.A. From 1946: worked for U.N.E.S.C.O., making documentaries and educational films. Main films: *Pasteur* (co-dir. J. Epstein) 22; *La maternelle* (co-dir. M. Epstein) 32; *Hélène* 36; *Altitude 3200* 37; *La mort du cygne* 38.

45 Bergman, Ingmar, Swedish director, b. 1918. Since 1940: also stage producer. 1963-66: director of Royal Dramatic Theatre, Stockholm. Scripted: *Frenzy, Woman without a face, Eva, Frånskild, Last pair out, Lustgården* (co.), and all his own films. Films: *Crisis* 45; *It rains on our love (The man with an umbrella)* 46; *A ship bound for India, The night is my future (Music in darkness)* 47; *Port of call, Prison (The devil's wanton)* 48; *Thirst, To joy,* 49; *This can't happen here, Summer interlude (Illicit interlude)* 50; *Waiting women, Summer with Monika* 52; *Sawdust and tinsel (The naked night)* 53; *A lesson in love* 54; *Journey into autumn (Dreams), Smiles of a summer night* 55; *The seventh seal* 56; *Wild strawberries* 57; *So close to life (Brink of life), The face (The magician)* 58; *The virgin spring* 59; *The devil's eye* 60; *Through a glass darkly* 61; *Winter light* 62; *The silence* 63; *Now about these women* 64; *Persona* 65; *Stimulantia* (one ep.) 66; *The hour of the wolf* 67; *The shame* 68.

46 Bergman, Ingrid, Swedish actress, b. 1915. From 1933: also stage actress. 1939: U.S.A. 1950: Italy. Main films: *Swedenhielms, Intermezzo, A woman's face, Intermezzo, a love story, Dr. Jekyll and Mr. Hyde* (41), *Rage in heaven, Casablanca, For whom the bell tolls, Gaslight, Saratoga trunk, The bells of St. Mary's, Spellbound, Notorious, Arch of triumph, Under Capricorn, Stromboli, Europa 51, Siamo donne, Voyage to Italy, Giovanna d'Arco al rogo, Angst, Eléna et les hommes, Indiscreet, The inn of the sixth happiness, Anastasia, Aimez-vous Brahms?, The visit, The yellow Rolls-Royce.*

47 Berkeley, Busby, American choreographer and director, b. 1895. 1920-30: worked in theatre. Films as choreographer only: *Whoopee, Kiki, Palmy days, Flying high, Night world, Bird of paradise, The kid from Spain, 42nd Street, Gold diggers of 1933, Footlight parade, Roman scandals, Wonder*

Bar, Fashions of 1934, Twenty million sweethearts, Dames, Go into your dance, In Caliente, Stars over Broadway, Gold diggers of 1937, Singing marine, Varsity show, Gold diggers in Paris, Broadway serenade, Ziegfeld girl, Lady be good, Born to sing, Girl crazy, Two weeks – with love, Call me mister, Two tickets to Broadway, Million dollar mermaid, Small town girl, Easy to love, Rose Marie, Jumbo. Films as director and choreographer: She had to say yes 33; Gold diggers of 1935, Bright lights, I live for love 35; Stage struck 36; The go getter, Hollywood Hotel 37; Men are such fools, Garden of the moon, Comet over Broadway 38; They made me a criminal, Babes in arms, Fast and furious 39; Forty little mothers, Strike up the band 40; Blonde inspiration, Babes on Broadway 41; Calling all girls (short), For me and my gal 42; Three cheers for the girls (short), The gang's all here 43; Cinderella Jones 46; Take me out to the ball game (Everybody's cheering) 49.

48 Berlanga, Luis, Spanish director, b. 1921. At first journalist. Scripted all his own films. Main films: Esa pareja feliz (co-dir. Bardem) 51; ¡ Bien venido, Mister Marshall! 52; Novio a la vista 53; Calabuch 56; Los jueves, milagro 57; Plácido 61; Les quatre vérités (one episode) 62; El verdugo 63; Las Pirañas 67.

49 Bernard, Raymond, French director, b. 1891. Also stage actor. Main films: Jeanne Doré (with Sarah Bernhardt) 16; Le petit café 19; Le secret de Rosette Lambert 20; Le miracle des loups 24; Le joueur d'échecs 27; Les croix de bois 32; Les misérables 33; Tartarin de Tarascon 34; Marthe Richard 37; J'étais une aventurière 38; Maya 49.

50 Bernstein, Elmer, American composer. Main films: The man with the golden arm, Men in war, Saddle the wind, The tin star, God's little acre, The ten commandments, Fear strikes out, Sweet smell of success, Desire under the elms, Some came running, The magnificent seven, Birdman of Alcatraz, The carpetbaggers, The Hallelujah trail, The world of Henry Orient, The sons of Katie Elder, The caretakers, Seven women, The reward, Hawaii.

51 Björnstrand, Gunnar, Swedish actor, b. 1909. Since 1933: also stage actor. Main films: Panik, Night in the harbour, Frenzy, Midwinter sacrifice, It rains on our love, The night is my future, Private Bom, Waiting women, Sawdust and tinsel, A lesson in love, Gabrielle, Journey into autumn, Smiles of a summer night, The seventh seal, Wild strawberries, The face, Fröken April, The devil's eye, Through a glass darkly, Lustgården, Lyckodrömmen, Winter light, Loving couples, My sister, my love, Stimulantia (G. Molander episode), Persona, Here is your life, The shame, The girls.

52 Blasetti, Alessandro, Italian director, b. 1900. 1924-28: film critic. Since 1932: also stage producer. Acted: Bellissima. See neo-realism. Main films: Sole 29; Nerone, Resurrectio 30; Palio 32; 1860, Vecchia guardia 34; Aldebaran 35; Ettore Fieramosca 38; Un'avventura di Salvator Rosa 40; La corona di ferro, La cena delle beffe 41; Quattro passi fra le nuvole 42; Un giorno nella vita 46; Fabiola 48; Prima communione 50; Altri tempi 52; Io, io, io e... gli altri 65.

53 Boetticher, Budd, American director, b. 1916. At first toreador. 1943: assistant. 1944-46: shorts. Also TV producer and novelist. Main films: *The bullfighter and the lady* 51; *Horizons West, Red Ball Express* 52; *Seminole, The man from the Alamo, Wings of the hawk* 53; *The magnificent matador* 55; *The killer is loose, Seven men from now* 56; *Decision at Sundown, The tall T* 57; *Buchanan rides alone* 58; *Ride lonesome, Westbound* 59; *Comanche Station, The rise and fall of Legs Diamond* 60; *Olle* (doc.; in Mexico) 67.

54 Bogarde, Dirk, British actor, b. 1920. At first stage actor and producer. Main films: *The blue lamp, The woman in question, Blackmailed, Hunted, Doctor in the house, The sleeping tiger, Ill met by moonlight, The doctor's dilemma, Song without end, Victim, I could go on singing, The servant, King and country, Darling, Modesty Blaise, Accident, Our mother's house, Sebastian, The fixer.*

55 Bogart, Humphrey, American actor. 1899-1957. 1920-30: stage actor. Married to Lauren Bacall. Main films: *Up the river, The petrified forest, Marked woman, Kid Galahad, Bullets or ballots, Men are such fools, Swing your lady, The Oklahoma Kid, The amazing Dr. Clitterhouse, Angels with dirty faces, Dark victory, The roaring twenties, They drive by night, High sierra, The Maltese falcon, Across the Pacific, Casablanca, Sahara, To have and have not, The big sleep, Dead reckoning, Dark passage, The treasure of Sierra Madre, Key Largo, Knock on any door, Tokyo Joe, In a lonely place, The enforcer, The African Queen, Deadline U.S.A., Battle circus, Beat the devil, The barefoot contessa, The Caine mutiny, Sabrina fair, We're no angels, The left hand of God, The desperate hours, The harder they fall.*

56 Bolognini, Mauro, Italian director, b. 1920. Assistant to Zampa, Delannoy, and Y. Allégret. Main films: *Gli innamorati* 55; *Giovani mariti* 57; *La notte brava* 59; *Il bell'Antonio, La giornata balorda* 60; *La viaccia* 61; *Senilità* 62; *Agostino* 63; *La corruzione, La mia signora* (one ep.), *I tre volti* (co. F. Indovini), *Le bambole* (one ep.) 64; *Mademoiselle de Maupin, La donna è una cosa meravigliosa* 65; *Le streghe* (one ep.), *Le fate* (one ep.) 66; *Le plus vieux métier du monde* (one ep.) 67.

57 Bondarchuk, Sergei, Russian actor and director, b. 1922. Main films as actor: *Young guard, The cavalier of the golden star, Unfinished story, The grasshopper, Othello* (55), *Era notte a Roma, Seryozha.* Films as both actor and director: *Destiny of a man* 59; *War and peace* 64-67 (four pts.: *Andrei Bolkonsky* 64; *Natasha* 65; *Borodino* 66; *Pierre Bezukhov* 67).

58 Borowczyk, Walerian, Polish animator, b. 1923. Art Studies. At first commercial artist. Since 1959: France. Films: (in collaboration with Lenica) *Once upon a time, Love requited* 57; *Dom* 58; (alone) *The school* 58; *Les astronautes* (co. Marker) 59; *Le dernier voyage de Gulliver* 60; *Le concert de Monsieur et Madame Kabal* 62; *L'encyclopédie de grand'maman* 63; *Renaissance, Les jeux des anges* 64; *Le dictionnaire de Joachim* 65; *Rosalie* 66; *Le théâtre de Monsieur et Madame Kabal* (full length) 62-67; *Gavotte, Diptyque* 68.

Grigori Alexandrov
Harriet Andersson
Michelangelo Antonioni

Lauren Bacall
Brigitte Bardot
Jacques Becker

Jean-Paul Belmondo
Ingmar Bergman
Ingrid Bergman

Gunnar Björnstrand
Alessandro Blasetti
Humphrey Bogart

Richard Brooks
Marlon Brando
Charles Boyer

James Cagney
Michael Cacoyannis
Luis Buñuel

Grigori Chukhrai
Marcel Carné
Renato Castellani

René Clément
Jack Clayton
René Clair

59 Borzage, Frank, American director, 1893-1961. From 1912: actor: *The ambassador's envoy, The battle of Gettysburg* etc. Main films: *Humoresque* 20; *Song of love* 23; *The lady* 25; *Seventh heaven* 27; *The river* 29; *Liliom* 30; *Secrets, Bad girl* 31; *A farewell to arms* 32; *A man's castle* 33; *No greater glory, Little man, what now?* 34; *Desire* 36; *History is made at night, The big city* 37; *Mannequin, The shining hour, Three comrades* 38; *Strange cargo* 40; *The Spanish Main* 45; *I've always loved you* 46; *Moonrise* 48; *China doll* 58.

60 Bow, Clara, American actress, 1905-65. Main films: *Beyond the rainbow, Down to the sea in ships, Eve's lover, Kiss me again, The plastic age, Free to love, Dance madness, Mantrap, It, Children of divorce* (27), *Wings, Hula, Red hair, Ladies of the mob, The wild party* (29), *Dangerous curves, Paramount on parade, Love among the millionaires, Call her savage, Hoopla.*

61 Boyer, Charles, French actor, b. 1897. Since 1918: also stage actor. 1934: U.S.A. Main films: *L'homme du large, Le capitaine Fracasse* (29), *Buster se marie, The big house, Liliom* (34), *Private worlds, Mayerling, The garden of Allah, History is made at night, Conquest, Orage, Love affair, When tomorrow comes, Tales of Manhattan, The constant nymph, Gaslight* (44), *Confidential agent, Cluny Brown, Arch of triumph, Madame de ...*, *The cobweb, Around the world in 80 days, The buccaneer* (58), *Fanny, The four horsemen of the Apocalypse* (61), *How to steal a million, Paris brûle-t-il?, Casino Royale.*

62 Brakhage, Stan, American director of experimental shorts, b. 1933.
See *avant-garde.* Main shorts: *Interim* 51; *Unglassed windows cast a terrible reflection, Desistfilm* 53; *In between, The way to shadow garden, Wonder ring, Reflections on black* 55; *Flesh of morning, Nightcats, Daybreak, White eye* 56; *Anticipation of the night, Loving* 57; *Colorado legend* 59; *Prelude* 61; *Thin line lyre triangular, Window water baby moving* 63.

63 Brando, Marlon, American actor, b. 1924. At first stage actor. Main films: *The men, A streetcar named Desire, Viva Zapata!, Julius Caesar, The wild one, On the waterfront, Désirée, Guys and dolls, The teahouse of the August Moon, Sayonara, The young lions, The fugitive kind, One eyed jacks* (also dir., 61) *Mutiny on the Bounty* (62), *The ugly American, The saboteur — code name Morituri, The chase, The Appaloosa (Southwest to Sonora), A countess from Hong Kong, Reflections in a golden eye.*

64 Brasseur, Pierre, French actor, b. 1905. Since 1920: also stage actor and playwright. Main films: *La fille de l'eau, Quai des brumes, Les deux timides* (41), *Lumière d'été, Les enfants du paradis, Les portes de la nuit, Les amants de Vérone, Le plaisir, La tour de Nesle, Oasis, Porte des Lilas, La loi, La tête contre les murs, Les yeux sans visage, Dialogue des Carmélites, Pleins feux sur l'assassin, Il bell'Antonio, Les bonnes causes, Un monde nouveau, La vie de château, La petite vertu.*

65 Braunberger, Pierre, French producer, b. 1905. Actor: *Nana* (25). Main films: *Nana* (25), *Rien que les heures, Voyage au congo, Tire-au-flanc*

(29), *La p'tite Lili, Un chien andalou, L'âge d'or, On purge bébé, La chienne, La petite chocolatière, Mam'zelle Nitouche, Une partie de campagne, Paris 1900, Van Gogh, Gauguin, Guernica, La course de taureaux* (also co-dir. with Myriam 51), *Avec André Gide, Toute la mémoire du monde, Les maîtres fous, Le chant du styrène, O saisons, ô châteaux, Une histoire d'eau, Cuba si!, La punition, Moi un noir, Tirez sur le pianiste, La pyramide humaine, Vivre sa vie, Muriel, ou le temps d'un retour* (co.).

66 Bresson, Robert, French director, b. 1907. Studied painting. Assistant to Clair. Films: *Les affaires publiques* (short) 34; *Les anges du péché* 43; *Les dames du Bois de Boulogne* 45; *Le journal d'un curé de campagne* 50; *Un condamné à mort s'est échappé* 56; *Pickpocket* 59; *Le procès de Jeanne d'Arc* 62; *Au hasard Balthazar* 65; *Mouchette* 67.

67 Broca, Philippe de, French director, b. 1935. Shorts in Africa. Assistant to Chabrol and Truffaut. Films: *Les jeux de l'amour, Le farceur* 60; *L'amant de cinq jours, Cartouche, Les sept péchés capitaux* (one episode) 61; *Les veinards* (one episode) 62; *L'homme de Rio* 63; *Un monsieur de compagnie* 64; *Les tribulations d'un Chinois en Chine* 65; *Le roi de coeur* 66; *Le plus vieux métier du monde* (one ep.) 67.

68 Brook, Clive, British actor, b. 1891. 1924-35: U.S.A. Also stage actor. Main films: *Woman to woman, The penalty, The white shadow, The passionate adventure, Underworld, Slightly scarlet, Tarnished lady, Shanghai Express, Gallant lady, Cavalcade, The loves of a dictator, On approval* (also dir., 44).

69 Brook, Peter, British director, b. 1925. Since 1945: also stage producer. Films: *The beggars' opera* 53; *Moderato cantabile* 60; *The lord of the flies* 62; *The persecution and assassination of Jean-Paul Marat, as performed by the inmates of the asylum of Charenton, under the direction of the Marquis de Sade* 66; *Red white and zero* (one ep.) 67; *Tell me lies* 68.

70 Brooks, Louise, American actress, b. 1906. At first ballerina then dancer in Ziegfeld Follies. 1929-30: Europe. 1938: retired. Films: *The street of forgotten men, The American Venus, A social celebrity, Love 'em and leave 'em, It's the old army game, The show-off, Just another blonde, The city gone wild, Rolled stockings, Evening clothes, Now we're in the air, A girl in every port, Beggars of life, The canary murder case, Pandora's box, Diary of a lost girl, Prix de beauté, It pays to advertise, Windy Riley goes to Hollywood, King of gamblers, God's gift to women, Empty saddles, When you're in love, Overland stage raiders.*

71 Brooks, Richard, American director, b. 1912. Since 1940: also stage producer. Also novelist (*Crossfire* was adapted from his first novel). Since 1956: also producer. Scripted: *My best gal, Brute force, To the victor, Storm warning, Key Largo, and**. Films: *Crisis** 50; *The light touch** 51; *Deadline U.S.A.** 52; *Battle circus**, *Take the high ground* 53; *Flame and the flesh, The last time I saw Paris* 54; *The blackboard jungle**, *The last hunt** 55; *The catered affair (Wedding breakfast)* 56; *Something of value** 57; *The brothers Karamazov**, *Cat on a hot tin roof** 58; *Elmer*

18

Gantry* 60; Sweet bird of youth* 62; Lord Jim* 64; The professionals* 66; In cold blood* 67.

72 Brown, Clarence, American director, b. 1890. 1915: assistant to M. Tourneur. Main films: Smouldering fires 24; The goose woman, The eagle 25; The flesh and the devil 27; A woman of affairs 28; Romance, Anna Christie 30; Possessed, Inspiration, A free soul 31; Chained 34; Anna Karenina, Ah! wilderness 35; Wife versus secretary 36; Marie Walewska (Conquest) 37; Intruder in the dust 49.

73 Browning, Tod, American director, 1882-1944. 1914: stage actor. 1916: assistant to Griffith. Scr. many of his own films. Main films: The wicked darling 19; The virgin of Stamboul 20; Outside the law 21; The unholy three 25; The road to Mandalay, The blackbird 26; The unknown, London after midnight 27; West of Zanzibar 28; Where East is East, The unholy three (remake) 30; Dracula 31; Freaks 32; Mark of the vampire 35; The devil doll 36; Miracles for sale 39.

74 Buñuel, Luis, Mexican director, b. 1900 in Spain. 1920: at Madrid University with Dali and Lorca. 1925: Paris. 1926-28: assistant to J. Epstein. 1938: U.S.A., shorts for the Armed Forces. Since 1947: Mexico. Acted: Llanto por un bandido. See avant-garde. Films: Un chien andalou (short, scr. Dali) 28; L'âge d'or 30; Land without bread (short) 32; Gran Casino 47; El gran calavera 49; Los olvidados (or The young and the damned), Susana 50; La Hija del engaño, Una mujer sin amor, Don Quintin el Amargado, Subida al cielo 51; El bruto, Robinson Crusoe, El

52; Abismos de pasión, La ilusion viaja en tranvia 53; El rio y la muerte 54; The criminal life of Archibaldo de la Cruz, Cela s'appelle l'aurore (in France) 55; La mort en ce jardin 56; Nazarin 58; Republic of sin (or La fièvre monte à El Pao) 59; The young one 60; Viridiana 61; The exterminating angel 62; Journal d'une femme de chambre (in France) 63; Simon del desierto 65; Belle de jour (in France) 67; La voie lactée 68.

75 Burel, Léonce-Henry, French director of photography, b. 1892. Long collaboration with Bresson. Main films: Mater dolorosa (17), La dixième symphonie, J'accuse (18), La roue, Crainquebille, Visages d'enfants, L'image, Napoléon, Baroud, Boudu sauvé des eaux, La mort du cygne, Le journal d'un curé de campagne, Un condamné à mort s'est échappé, Pickpocket, Le procès de Jeanne d'Arc.

76 Burton, Richard, British actor, b. 1925. Also stage actor. Main films: My cousin Rachel, The desert rats, Alexander the Great, Bitter victory, Look back in anger, Cleopatra, The V.I.P.s, Becket, The night of the iguana, The spy who came in from the cold, The sandpiper, Who's afraid of Virginia Woolf?, Dr. Faustus (also co. dir. and prod.), The taming of the shrew (66), Goforth.

C

77 Cacoyannis, Michael, Greek director, b. 1922. 1939-50: G.B., as radio and stage producer and actor. Films: Windfall in Athens 53; Stella 55;

A girl in black 56; *A matter of dignity* 57; *Our last spring* 59; *The wastrel* 60; *Electra* 61; *Zorba the Greek* 64; *The day the fish came out* 67.

78 Cagney, James, American actor, b. 1904. 1920-30: stage actor. Main films: *The steel highway, Public enemy, The crowd roars, Ceiling zero, Footlight parade, Here comes the navy, G men, A midsummer night's dream, Angels with dirty faces, The roaring twenties, The Oklahoma Kid, Each dawn I die, The strawberry blonde, Yankee doodle dandy, 13 rue Madeleine, White heat, What price glory? Run for cover, Mister Roberts, Tribute to a badman, Short cut to hell* (dir. only, 56), *Man of a thousand faces, Shake hands with the devil, Love me or leave me, One, two, three.*

79 caméra-stylo: (camera-pen) term invented in 1948 by Astruc, who said: "The cinema is becoming a means of expression like the other arts before it; it is no longer simply a spectacle, it is becoming an autonomous language". This concept of the cinema as a specific independent language influenced many *nouvelle vague* directors (q.v.).

80 Camerini, Mario, Italian director, b. 1895. From 1920: scriptwriter, assistant to Genina. Main films: *Gli uomini, che mascalzoni!* 32; *Il capello a tre punte* 34; *Daro un milione* 35; *Ma non è una cosa seria* 36; *Il signor Max* 37; *Grandi magazzini* 39; *Una romantica avventura, I promessi sposi* 40; *La figlia del capitano* 47; *Ulisse* 53; *Suor Letizia* 57.

81 Capra, Frank, American director, b. 1897 in Sicily. 1903: U.S.A. From 1921: gagman for Hal Roach. Scr.: *Tramp, tramp, tramp, Westward the women,* and*. Films: *Fultah Fisher's boarding house* 23; *The strong man* 26; *Long pants, For the love of Mike* 27; *That certain thing, So this is love, The matinee idol, The way of the strong, Say it with sables*, Submarine*, The power of the press* 28; *The young generation, The Donovan affair* 29; *Ladies of leisure, Rain or shine* 30; *Dirigible, The miracle woman, Platinum blonde* 31; *Forbidden*, American madness* 32; *The bitter tea of General Yen, Lady for a day* 33; *It happened one night, Broadway Bill* 34; *Mr. Deeds goes to town* 36; *Lost horizon* 37; *You can't take it with you* 38; *Mr. Smith goes to Washington* 39; *Meet John Doe, Arsenic and old lace* 41; *Why we fight* series 42-45: *Prelude to war, Nazis strike* (co. Litvak) 42; *Divide and conquer* (co. Litvak), *Tunisian victory* 43; *Two down – one to go, The battle of China* (co. Litvak) 44; *Know your enemy: Japan* (co. Ivens) 45; *It's a wonderful life** 46; *State of the Union (The world and his wife)* 48; *Riding high* 50; *Here comes the groom* 51; *A hole in the head* 59; *Pocketful of miracles* 61.

82 Cardiff, Jack, British director and director of photography, b. 1914. Main films as dir. of phot.: *As you like it, Caesar and Cleopatra, A matter of life and death, Black narcissus, The red shoes, Under Capricorn, Pandora and the Flying Dutchman, The African Queen, The barefoot contessa, War and peace, The prince and the showgirl, The legend of the lost, The Vikings, The diary of Anne Frank.* Films as director: *Intent to kill* 57; *Beyond this place* 58; *Sons and lovers*

59; *Scent of mystery* 60; *The lion, My geisha* 62; *The long ships* 63; *Young Cassidy* (started by Ford) 64; *The liquidator* 65; *Dark of the sun* 67.

83 Carné, Marcel, French director, b. 1909. At first film critic. 1929-35: assistant to Feyder and Clair. Long collaboration with Jacques Prévert. Main films: *Nogent - Eldorado du dimanche* (short) 29; *Jenny* 36; *Drôle de drame* 37; *Quai des brumes, Hôtel du Nord* 38; *Le jour se lève* 39; *Les visiteurs du soir* 43; *Les enfants du paradis* 44; *Les portes de la nuit* 46; *La Marie du port* 49; *Juliette ou la clé des songes* 50; *Thérèse Raquin* 53; *L'air de Paris* 54; *Le pays d'où je viens* 56; *Les tricheurs* 58; *Terrain vague* 60; *Trois chambres à Manhattan* 65; *Les jeunes loups* 68.

84 Cassavetes, John, American director and actor, b. 1929. Also TV actor. Main films as actor: *Crime in the streets, Edge of the city (A man is ten feet tall), Saddle the wind, The killers* (64), *The dirty dozen*. Films as director: *Shadows* (two versions) 60; *Too late blues* 61; *A child is waiting* 63.

85 Castellani, Renato, Italian director, b. 1913. 1940: assistant to Blasetti. Scripted: *La corona di ferro, Una romantica avventura* and *. See neo-realism. Main films: *Un colpo di pistola* 42; *Zazà* 43; *Sotto il sole di Roma* 47; *È primavera* 49; *Due soldi di speranza* 51; *Romeo and Juliet* 54; *I sogni nei cassetto* 57; *Nella città l'inferno** 59; *Il brigante** 61; *Mare matto** 63; *Tre notti d'amore* (one ep.), *Controsesso* (one ep.) 64; *Sotto il cielo stellato* 66; *Questi fantasmi* 67.

86 Cavalcanti, Alberto, Brazilian director, b. 1897. 1920: France. Set-designer: *L'inhumaine* (assistant to Léger), *Feu Mathias Pascal, Yvette.* 1934: G.B. 1934-41: worked with Grierson (q.v.), produced documentaries. 1949: returned to Brazil. Scripted many of his films*. Main films: *Rien que les heures** 26; *En rade** 27; *Yvette*, *Le train sans yeux**, *La p'tite Lili* 28; *Le capitaine Fracasse, Le petit Chaperon Rouge** 29; *Pett and Pott* 34; *Coal face* 35; *We live in two worlds* 37; *Film and reality* (anthology) 42; *Dead of night* (co-dir.) 45; *Nicholas Nickleby, They made me a fugitive* 47; *O canto do mar** 53; *Mulher de verdade** 54; *Herr Puntila und sein Knecht Matti* (E. Germany; * with Brecht) 55; *Les noces vénitiennes* (Italy) 59.

87 Cavalier, Alain, French director, b. 1931. Film school. Assistant to Malle. Short: *Un Américain* 58. Films: *Le combat dans l'île* 62; *L'insoumis* 64; *Mise à sac* 67.

88 Cayatte, André, French director, b. 1909. At first lawyer, journalist, and novelist. Scripted: *Entrée des artistes, Remorques.* Main films: *Les amants de Vérone* 48; *Justice est faite* 50; *Nous sommes tous des assassins* 52; *Avant le déluge* 53; *Le dossier noir* 55; *Oeil pour oeil* 57; *Le miroir à deux faces* 58; *Le passage du Rhin* 60; *Le glaive et la balance* 62; *La vie conjugale* (two films: *Jean-Marc* and *Françoise*) 63; *Les risques du métier.*

89 Cecchi d'Amico, Suso, Italian woman scriptwriter, b. 1914. At first journalist. All scripts written in collaboration. See *neo-realism*. Main films:

Vivere in pace, Roma, città libera, L'onorevole Angelina, Bicycle thieves, Fabiola, È primavera, Miracolo in Milano, Bellissima, Altri tempi, Processo alla città, Siamo donne, I vinti, La signora senza camelie, Senso, Proibito, Le amiche, Le notti bianche, La sfida, Kean, I soliti ignoti, Nella città l'inferno, I magliari, Estate violenta, Risate di gioia, Rocco e i suoi fratelli, Salvatore Giuliano, Boccaccio '70, The leopard, Io, io, io e... gli altri, Casanova '70, Vaghe stelle dell'Orsa, The taming of the shrew (66).

90 Chabrol, Claude, French director, b. 1930. Up to 1959: film critic. Also producer. See nouvelle vague. Acted: Paris nous appartient, Les jeux de l'amour, and *. Films: Le beau Serge 58; Les cousins, A double tour 59; Les bonnes femmes, Les godelureaux 60; Les sept péchés capitaux (L'avarice ep.), L'oeil du malin 61; Ophélia, Landru* 62; Les plus belles escroqueries du monde (one ep.) 63; Le tigre aime la chair fraîche 64; Marie-Chantal contre le Docteur Kah*, Paris vu par . . .* (La Muette ep.), Le tigre se parfume à la dynamite* 65; La ligne de démarcation 66; Le scandale, La route de Corinthe 67.

91 Chaney, Lon, American actor, 1883-1930. At first stage actor. Main films: The wicked darling, Outside the law (21), The penalty, Oliver Twist (22), The hunchback of Notre-Dame, He who gets slapped, The phantom of the opera, The unholy three (25), The tower of lies, The blackbird, The road to Mandalay, London after midnight, The unknown, West of Zanzibar, Where East is East, The thunder.

92 Chaplin, Charles, Director and comic actor, b. 1889 in London. From 1895: vaudeville actor. 1910: U.S.A. 1913: worked under Sennett (q.v.) with Mabel Normand as partner. Also composed music of *. Scr. all his own films and acted in all but one: A woman of Paris. Main films as actor only: Making a living, The rounders, Dough and dynamite, His prehistoric past, Tillie's punctured romance etc. 13-14. Films as director: The tramp, A night in the show, His new job, A night out, The champion, In the park, The Jitney elopement, By the sea, Work, A woman, The bank, Shanghaied 15; Carmen, Police, The floorwalker, The fireman, The vagabond, One a.m., The count, The pawnshop, Behind the screen, The rink 16; Easy Street, The cure, The immigrant, The adventurer 17; Triple trouble, A dog's life, The bond, Shoulder arms 18; Sunnyside, A day's pleasure 19; The kid 20; The idle class 21; Pay day 22; The pilgrim, A woman of Paris 23; The gold rush 25; The circus 28; City lights 31; Modern times 36; The great dictator 40; Monsieur Verdoux (co-dir. Florey) 47; Limelight* 52; A king in New York 57; A countess from Hong Kong* 66.

93 Chayefsky, Paddy, American scriptwriter, b. 1923. Also writer of short stories and TV playwright. Films: Marty, The catered affair, Bachelor party, The goddess, Middle of the night, The Americanization of Emily.

94 Cherkassov, Nicolai, Russian actor, 1903-66. Since 1918: also stage actor. Main films: Baltic deputy, Peter the First, Alexander Nevsky, Man with a gun, Lenin in October, Ivan the Terrible I & II, In the name of life, Pirogov, Spring, Academician Ivan Pavlov, Mussorgsky, Rimsky Korsakov, Don Quixote.

95 Chevalier, Maurice, French actor, b. 1888. Since 1901: also stage actor, music hall artist and singer. 1911-14: acted in shorts by Linder. Main films: *The love parade, Paramount on parade, The smiling Lieutenant, One hour with you, Love me tonight, The merry widow, L'homme du jour, Break the news, Pièges, Le silence est d'or, Love in the afternoon, Gigi, Pepe, Can-Can, Fanny* (60).

96 Christensen, Benjamin, Danish director, 1879-1959. 1900-07: operatic singer and producer. 1914: Germany. 1926-30: U.S.A. 1930: returned to Denmark. Acted: *Mikaël* and *. See expressionism.* Main films: *Det hemme-lighedsfulde X* 13; *Haevnens Nat* 15; *Witchcraft through the ages* 22; *The haunted house* 28; *The house of horror, Seven footprints to Satan* 29; *Children of divorce* 39; *The child* 40.

97 Christian-Jaque, French director, b. 1904. At first set designer. Assistant to Duvivier. Main films: *François Ier* 36; *Les perles de la couronne* (co-dir. Guitry), *Les pirates du rail* 37; *Les disparus de Saint-Agil* 38; *La symphonie fantastique* 42; *Boule de suif* 45; *La chartreuse de Parme* 47; *Souvenirs perdus* 50; *Fanfan la tulipe* 52; *Babette s'en va-t-en guerre* 59; *Les bonnes causes* 63.

98 Chukhrai, Grigori, Russian director, b. 1921. Worked under Romm and Yutkevitch. Main films: *Nazar Srodolia* 55; *The forty first* 56; *Ballad of a soldier* 59; *Clear skies* 61; *There lived an old man and an old woman* 64; *People!* 66.

99 cinéma-vérité: term invented by Jean Rouch (and derived from Vertov's *Kino-Pravda* — see Vertov), first used to describe his film *Chronique d'un été* (1961), and subsequently applied to any kind of documentary film where emphasis is given to the camera's power as a recording instrument and to its directness of impact through the use of impromptu interviews, hand-held sequences, direct sound recording etc. Directors who have sometimes been grouped under this heading include, apart from Rouch (q.v.): Marker (q.v.), Mario Ruspoli *(Les inconnus de la terre* 59; *Regards sur la folie* 61), François Reichenbach *(L'Amérique insolite* 59; *Un coeur gros comme ça* 61), Jean Herman *(Les chemins de la mauvaise route* 62), Bertrand Blier *(Hitler, connais pas* 62), Richard Leacock and his associates (q.v.), Albert and David Maysles *(The showman* 62, *The Beatles in New York* 64); William Klein *(Broadway by light, Le business et la mode),* and P. Perrault and M. Brault *(Pour la suite du monde* 61).

100 Clair, René, French director, b. 1898. At first journalist, then actor *(Parisette* and *L'orpheline* series). 1935-38: G. B. 1940: U.S.A. 1946: returned to France. Scripted: *Prix de beauté* and all his own films except *Entr'acte.* See *avant-garde.* Films: *Paris qui dort* 23; *Entr'acte* (scr., sets, and also act. Francis Picabia), *Le fantôme du Moulin Rouge* 24; *Le voyage imaginaire* 25; *La proie du vent* 26; *Un chapeau de paille d'Italie* 27; *La tour* (short), *Les deux timides* 28; *Sous les toits de Paris* 30; *Le million, A nous la liberté* 31; *Quatorze Juillet* 32; *Le*

23

dernier milliardaire 34; The ghost goes West 35; Break the news 37; Air pur (unfinished) 39; The flame of New Orleans 40; Forever and a day (one ep.), I married a witch 42; It happened tomorrow 43; And then there were none (Ten little niggers) 45; Le silence est d'or 47; La beauté du diable 49; Les belles de nuit 52; Les grandes manoeuvres 55; Porte des Lilas 57; La Française et l'amour (one episode) 60; Tout l'or du monde 61; Les quatre vérités (one episode) 62; Les fêtes galantes 65.

101 Clayton, Jack, British director, b. 1921. From 1945: assistant. Also producer. Films: The bespoke overcoat 55; Room at the top 58; The innocents 61; The pumpkin eater 63; Our mother's house 67.

102 Clément, René, French director, b. 1913. At first cameraman. Technical adviser on La belle et la bête. Main shorts: Soigne ton gauche 39; Chefs de demain, La grande pastorale 43. Films: La bataille du rail 45; Les maudits 46; Au delà des grilles 48; Le château de verre 50; Jeux interdits 51; Knave of hearts (in England) 53; Gervaise 55; Barrage contre le Pacific (The Sea Wall) (in Italy) 58; Plein soleil 59; Quelle joie de vivre 61; Le jour et l'heure 63; Les félins (The love cage) 64; Paris brûle-t-il? (Is Paris Burning?) 66; Ecrit sur le sable 68.

103 Clouzot, Henri-Georges, French director, b. 1907. At first journalist. 1932-38: assistant to Litvak and Dupont in Germany. Scripted: Les inconnus dans la maison. Films: L'assassin habite au 21 42; Le corbeau 43; Quai des Orfèvres 47; Manon 48; Retour à la vie (one ep.) Miquette et sa mère 49; Le salaire de la peur 52; Les diaboliques 54; Le mystère Picasso (documentary) 56; Les espions 57; La vérité 60; L'enfer (unfinished) 64; La prisonnière 67.

104 Cocteau, Jean, French director. 1899-1963. Also novelist, essayist, playwright and poet. Scripted: Les dames du Bois de Boulogne, L'amore (both dialogue only), L'éternel retour, Les enfants terribles. See avant-garde. Films: Le sang d'un poète 30; La belle et la bête 45; L'aigle à deux têtes 47; Les parents terribles 48; Orphée 49; Villa Santo Sospir (short) 51; Le testament d'Orphée 59.

105 Cohl, Emile, French animator. 1857-1938. Made some of the first important animated films. See animation. 1912-14: U.S.A. Main films: Fantasmagorie, Le cauchemar du fantoche, Un drame chez les fantoches 08; Les joyeux microbes, Les locataires d'à côté 09; Le retapeur de cervelles, Le tout petit Faust (puppets) 10; Les aventures d'un bout de papier 11; Les aventures de Pieds-Nickelés (series, co-dir. B. Rabier) 17; L'oreille 24.

106 Colman, Ronald, British actor. 1891-1958. 1914-24: stage actor. 1923: U.S.A. Main films: The white sister, Romola, Lady Windermere's fan, The dark angel, Stella Dallas (25), The winning of Barbara Worth, The magic flame, Bulldog Drummond, Raffles, Arrowsmith, Cynara, Clive of India, Under two flags, Lost horizon, The prisoner of Zenda, The light that failed, The talk of the town, Random harvest, Kismet (44), The late George Apley, A double life, Around the world in 80 days, The story of mankind.

107 Colpi, Henri, French director. b. 1921 in Switzerland. At first journalist. Author of book on film music. Edited: *Nuit et brouillard, Hiroshima, mon amour, L'année dernière à Marienbad, A king in New York.* Films: *Une aussi longue absence* 61; *Codine* 63; *Mona, l'étoile sans nom* 66.

108 Cooper, Gary, American actor. 1901-61. At first cartoonist. Main films: *The winning of Barbara Worth, Children of divorce, Wings, Half a bride, The patriot, Morocco, City streets, Paramount on parade, Devil and the deep, If I had a million, A farewell to arms, Today we live, Design for living, Alice in Wonderland, The wedding night, Lives of a Bengal Lancer, Peter Ibbetson, The plainsman, Desire* (36), *Souls at sea, The general died at dawn, Mr. Deeds goes to town, Bluebeard's eighth wife, The adventures of Marco Polo, Beau Geste, North West Mounted Police, The Westerner, Meet John Doe, Sergeant York, Ball of fire, For whom the bell tolls, Casanova Brown, The story of Dr. Wassell, Saratoga trunk, Cloak and dagger, Unconquered, The fountainhead, Bright leaf, Task force, High noon, Springfield rifle, Vera Cruz, The court martial of Billy Mitchell, Friendly persuasion, Love in the afternoon, The hanging tree, They came to Cordura, Man of the West.*

109 Corman, Roger, American director. b. 1926. 1950-52: literary agent and writer. Also producer of almost all his own films. Also acted in *. Has directed over 50 films since 1955. Main films: *The day the world ended* 56; *Attack of the crab monsters, Not of this earth, She-gods of Shark Reef* 57; *The gun-slinger, The undead, Machine Gun Kelly* 58; *War of the satellites*, I mobster (The mobster)* 59; *A bucket of blood* 60; *The fall of the house of Usher, The pit and the pendulum, The premature burial, Tales of terror, The little shop of horrors, The intruder (The stranger)* 61; *The raven, The tower of London* 62; *Secret invasion, The masque of the red death, The terror* 63; *The tomb of Legeia* 64; *The wild angels* 65; *The trip, The St. Valentine's Day massacre* 67.

110 Cornelius, Henry, Director, b. 1913 in Germany, d. 1958. 1931-33: pupil of Reinhardt and stage producer. 1933: France, then England. 1940-45: shorts. Co-scripted: *It always rains on Sunday.* Films: *Passport to Pimlico* 48; *The galloping major* 51; *Genevieve* 53; *I am a camera* 55; *Next to no time, Law and disorder* (completed by Crichton) 58.

111 Cottafavi, Vittorio, Italian director, b. 1914. Assistant to Blasetti and De Sica. Since 1957: also TV producer. See neo-realism. Scripted: *Il sole sorge ancora.* Main films: *I nostri sogni* 43; *Lo sconosciuto di San Marino* 46; *Traviata '53, In amore si pecca in due* 53; *Una donna libera, Avanzi di galera* 54; *Revolt of the gladiators* 58; *Le legioni di Cleopatra, Messalina* 59; *La vendetta di Ercole* 60; *Ercole alla conquista di Atlantide* 61; *I cento cavalieri (Los cien caballeros)* 64.

112 Cotten, Joseph, American actor, b. 1905. Also stage actor. Main films: *Citizen Kane, Lydia, The magnificent Ambersons, Journey into fear* (also scr.), *Shadow of a doubt, Gaslight, Love letters, Portrait of Jennie, Duel in the sun, The third man, Under Capricorn, Beyond* the forest, The steel trap, Niagara, The killer is loose, The last sunset, Hush, hush, sweet Charlotte, Petulia.

113 Coutard, Raoul, French director of photography, b. 1924. 1951-56: press photographer. See *nouvelle vague*. Main films: *A bout de souffle, Tirez sur le pianiste, Le petit soldat, Lola, Une femme est une femme, Tire au flanc* (62), *Jules et Jim, La poupée, L'amour à vingt ans* (Truffaut ep.), *Vivre sa vie, Als twee druppels water, Les carabiniers, La peau douce, Le mépris, Les plus belles escroqueries du monde* (Godard ep.), *Bande à part, Une femme mariée, Un monsieur de compagnie, La 317ème section, Alphaville, Je vous salue Mafia, Pierrot le Fou, The sailor from Gibraltar, Made in U.S.A., Deux ou trois choses que je sais d'elle, L'horizon, La Chinoise, La mariée était en noir, Week-end, Changing Dublin.*

114 Crawford, Joan, American actress, b. 1904. 1925: stage dancer. Main films: *The boob, Tramp, tramp, tramp, Winners of the wilderness, The unknown, Hollywood Revue of 1929, Possessed, Grand Hotel, Rain* (32), *Today we live, Dancing lady, Chained, Forsaking all others, No more ladies, I live my life, Love on the run, Mannequin, The shining hour, The women, Strange cargo, Susan and God, A woman's face* (41), *Reunion in France, Hollywood canteen, Mildred Pierce, Humoresque, Daisy Kenyon, Flamingo Road, Sudden fear, Torch song, Johnny Guitar, Autumn leaves, The golden virgin, Whatever happened to Baby Jane?, The caretakers* (Borderlines).

115 Crichton, Charles, British director, b. 1910. From 1931: editor.

Main films: *Dead of night* (one episode) 45; *Hue and cry* 46; *Against the wind* 48; *The Lavender Hill Mob* 51; *Hunted* 52; *The Titfield Thunderbolt* 53; *The divided heart* 54; *Law and disorder* (begun by Cornelius) 58; *Battle of the sexes* 59; *He who rides a tiger* 65.

116 Cromwell, John, American director, b. 1888. At first stage actor. Also stage producer. Main films: *Unfaithful* 31; *Anne Vickers* 33; *Of human bondage, The fountain* 34; *Little Lord Fauntleroy* 36; *The prisoner of Zenda* 37; *In name only* 39; *So ends our night* 41; *Since you went away, The enchanted cottage* 45; *Dead reckoning* 47; *Caged* 50; *The racket* 51; *The goddess* 58; *De sista stegen (A matter of morals)* 60.

117 Crosby, Bing, American actor, b. 1904. Also singer. Main films: *King of jazz, The big broadcast, The road to Hollywood, Mississippi, The road to Singapore, Holiday Inn, Going my way, The bells of St. Mary's, The emperor waltz, A Connecticut Yankee in King Arthur's court, Riding high, Here comes the groom, The road to Bali, The country girl, White Christmas, High society.*

118 Cruze, James, American director. 1884-1942. 1900-11: stage, and, 1911-18: film actor. Main films: *Brewster's millions* 21; *One glorious day* 22; *The covered wagon, Hollywood* 23; *Beggar on horseback, The pony express* 25; *The city gone wild, Old ironsides* 27; *The great Gabbo* 30; *If I had a million* (one episode) 32; *Washington merry-go-round* 33; *Gangs of New York* 38.

119 Cukor, George, American director, b. 1899. 1919-29: stage producer. Films: *Grumpy, The virtuous sin* (co. L. Gasnier), *The royal family of Broadway* (co. C. Gardner) 30; *Tarnished lady, Girls about town* 31; *What price Hollywood?, A bill of divorcement, Rockabye, Our betters* 32; *Dinner at eight, Little women* 33; *David Copperfield (The personal history, adventures, experience, and observations of David Copperfield, the younger)* 34; *Sylvia Scarlett* 35; *Romeo and Juliet, Camille* 36; *Holiday (Free to live), Zaza* 38; *The women, Susan and God (The gay Mrs. Trexal)* 39; *The Philadelphia story* 40; *A woman's face, Two-faced woman* 41; *Her cardboard lover, Keeper of the flame* 42; *Resistance and Ohm's law* (army doc). 43; *Gaslight (Murder in Thornton Square), Winged victory* 44; *Desire me, A double life* 47; *Edward my son* (in Engl.) 48; *Adam's rib* 49; *A life of her own, Born yesterday* 50; *The model and the marriage broker, The marrying kind* 51; *Pat and Mike* 52; *The actress, It should happen to you* 53; *A star is born* 54; *Bhowani Junction* 55; *Les girls, Wild is the wind* 57; *Heller in pink tights, Song without end* (begun by C. Vidor) 59; *Let's make love* 60; *The Chapman report* 63; *My fair lady* 65.

120 Curtiz, Michael, Director, b. 1888 in Hungary, d. 1962. Assistant to Stiller and Sjöström in Sweden. 1927: U.S.A. Main films: *God's gift to women* 31; *Mandalay* 34; *The charge of the Light Brigade, The walking dead* 36; *Kid Galahad* 37; *Four daughters, Angels with dirty faces, Four's a crowd, The adventures of Robin Hood* 38; *Captain Blood, Dodge City, The private lives of Elizabeth & Essex, Daughters courageous* 39; *The sea hawk, Santa Fe trail* 40; *The sea wolf* 41; *Casablanca, Yankee doodle*

dandy 42; *Mildred Pierce* 45; *Flamingo Road* 49; *Bright leaf* 50; *Force of arms* 51; *White christmas* 54; *We're no angels* 55; *The Comancheros* 61.

121 Cybulski, Zbigniew, Polish actor, 1927-67. Also stage actor and producer. Co-scripted: *See you tomorrow.* Main films: *A generation, Ashes and diamonds, The cross of valour, Night train, Innocent sorcerers, See you tomorrow, Partings, L'amour à vingt ans* (Wajda episode), *How to be loved, La poupée, Silence, To love, Their everyday life, The Saragossa manuscript, Salto, Jowita, The code.*

D

122 Dahlbeck, Eva, Swedish actress, b. 1920. Also stage actress. Scr. *Woman of darkness.* Main films: *Ride tonight, Eva* (48), *Only a mother, Trots, Waiting women, Barabbas* (53), *A lesson in love, Journey into autumn, Smiles of a summer night, Last pair out, So close to life, De sista stegen (A matter of morals), The counterfeit traitor, Now about these women, Loving couples, Kattorna, Les créatures, People meet and sweet music fills the heart.*

123 Darrieux, Danielle, French actress, b. 1917. At first studied music. Main films: *Le bal, Mayerling, Abus de confiance, Katia, The rage of Paris, Battements de coeur, Premier rendezvous, Ruy Blas, Jean de la lune, Occupetoi d'Amélie, La ronde, Five fingers, Le plaisir, Madame de . . ., Le rouge et le noir, Si Paris nous était conté, Pot Bouille,*

Marie-Octobre, Le crime ne paie pas, Landru, Les demoiselles de Rochefort, Le dimanche de la vie.

124 Dassin, Jules, American director, b. 1911. 1936-40: stage actor and producer. 1950: left U.S.A. because of McCarthy. Acted in some of his own films*. Main shorts: *Arthur Rubinstein, Pablo Casals, The tell-tale heart* 40-41. Films: *Nazi agent, The affairs of Martha* 41; *Reunion in France (Mademoiselle France), Time fortune* 42; *Young ideas, The Canterville ghost* 43; *A letter for Evie* 44; *Two smart people* 46; *Brute force* 47; *The naked city* 48; *Thieves' highway** 49; *Night and the city* 50; *Rififi** (in France) 54; *He who must die* (in Fr. and Greece) 57; *La loi* (in Italy) 58; *Never on Sunday* (in Greece)* 60; *Phaedra* (in Fr. and Greece) 62; *Topkapi* 65; *10.30pm summer* 66; *The great train robbery* 68.

125 Daves, Delmer, American director, b. 1904. 1927: assistant to Cruze. 1927-44: actor and scriptwriter. Scripted: *Singing marine, The go getter, The petrified forest, Love affair, White feather,* and almost all his own films. Also his own producer. Main films: *Destination Tokyo* 43; *Hollywood canteen* 44; *Pride of the marines* 45; *The red house* 46; *Dark passage* 47; *To the victor* 48; *A kiss in the dark, Task force* 49; *Broken arrow* 50; *Bird of paradise* 51; *Return of the Texan* 52; *Treasure of the golden condor, Never let me go, Demetrius and the gladiators* 53; *Drumbeat* 54; *Jubal, The last wagon* 56; *3.10 to Yuma* 57; *Cowboy, Kings go forth, The badlanders* 58; *The hanging tree* 59; *A summer place* 60; *Parrish, Susan Slade* 61; *Rome adventure* 62; *Spencer's*

Mountain, Youngblood Hawke 63; *The Battle of the Villa Fiorita* 64.

126 Davis, Bette, American actress, b. 1908. Since 1926: also stage actress. Main films: *Of human bondage, Bordertown, Fashions of 1934, Dangerous, The petrified forest, Marked woman, Kid Galahad, That certain woman, The sisters, It's love I'm after, Jezebel, Dark victory, Juarez, The private lives of Elizabeth and Essex, The letter, The little foxes, In this our life, Now voyager, Mr. Skeffington, The corn is green, Hollywood canteen, Beyond the forest, All about Eve, The virgin queen, The catered affair, Storm centre, The scapegoat, Pocketful of miracles, Whatever happened to Baby Jane?, La noia, Dead image, Hush, hush, sweet Charlotte, Where love has gone, The nanny The anniversary.*

127 Dean, James, American actor. 1931-55. 1950: TV, then stage actor. Films: *Sailor beware, Fixed bayonets, East of Eden, Rebel without a cause, Giant, The James Dean story* (doc.).

128 Dearden, Basil, British director, b. 1911. At first assistant. Since 1948: Michael Relph has produced and collaborated on most of his films. Main films: *The black sheep of Whitehall* 41; *The goose steps out* 42; *My learned friend* 43 (all three co-dir. W. Hay); *Dead of night* (one episode) 45; *The captive heart* 46; *Frieda* 47; *The blue lamp* 49; *Pool of London* 50; *I believe in you* 51; *Rainbow jacket* 54; *Violent playground* 57; *Sapphire* 59; *League of gentlemen* 60; *Victim* 61; *Life for Ruth (Walk in the shadow)* 62; *The mind benders* 63; *Woman of straw* 64; *Khartoum* 66; *Only when I larf* 67.

28

129 Decaë, Henri, French director of photography, b. 1915. 1941-44: directed shorts. Main films: *Le silence de la mer, Les enfants terribles, Bob le flambeur, S.O.S. Noronha, Ascenseur pour l'échafaud, Les amants, Le beau Serge, Les cousins, Les quatre cents coups, A double tour, Plein soleil, Les bonnes femmes, Quelle joie de vivre, Vie privée, Les sept péchés capitaux* (Godard, Demy, and Vadim ep.), *Léon Morin, prêtre, Les dimanches de Ville d'Avray, Le jour et l'heure, L'aîné des Ferchaux, Dragées au poivre, Les félins, Viva Maria!, Le corniaud, La ronde, Le voleur, The night of the generals, Le samouraï, The comedians, Diaboliquement vôtre.*

130 Decoin, Henri, French director, b. 1896. At first journalist. 1929-32: assistant and scriptwriter. Main films: *Abus de confiance* 37; *Battements de coeur* 39; *Premier rendez-vous* 41; *Les inconnus dans la maison, Le bienfaiteur* 42; *Je suis avec toi, La fille du diable* 43; *Entre onze heures et minuit* 48; *Les amants de Tolède* 53; *Razzia sur la Chnouf* 54; *Charmants garçons* 57; *La chatte* 58.

131 De Havilland, Olivia, American actress. b. 1916. At first stage actress. Sister of Joan Fontaine. Main films: *A midsummer night's dream* (34), *The charge of the Light Brigade, Anthony Adverse, It's love I'm after, Four's a crowd, The adventures of Robin Hood, Gone with the wind, Dodge City, The private lives of Elizabeth and Essex, Santa Fe trail, Raffles, The strawberry blonde, They died with their boots on, In this our life, Princess O'Rourke, To each his own, The dark mirror, The heiress, My cousin Rachel, Not as a stranger, The ambassador's daughter, Lady in a cage.*

132 Delannoy, Jean, French director, b. 1908. At first editor and assistant. Main films: *Paris Deauville* 35; *Macao, l'enfer du jeu* 39; *Pontcarral, colonel d'Empire* 42; *L'éternel retour* 43; *La symphonie pastorale* 46; *Les jeux sont faits* 47; *Chiens perdus sans collier* 55; *Maigret tend un piège* 57; *La Princesse de Clèves* 60; *Vénus impériale* 62; *Les amitiés particulières* 64.

133 De Laurentiis, Dino, Italian producer, b. 1919. 1950: founded "Ponti-De Laurentiis" with Carlo Ponti. They ceased to collaborate in 1957. Main films: *Il bandito, La figlia del capitano, Bitter rice, Europe 51, Le infedeli, Ulisse, Mambo, Dov'è la libertà, War and peace* (55), *L'oro di Napoli, La strada, Le notti di Cabiria, Barrage contre le Pacific, La tempesta, Le streghe, The bible … in the beginning, Matchless, Lo straniero, Barbarella, Un Italiano in America, Danger: Diabolik.*

134 Delerue, Georges, French composer, b. 1925. Also conductor. Also composer for theatre. Main shorts: *La première nuit, Du côté de la côte, Le sourire, Les Marines, Le bureau des mariages, A.* Main films: *Opéra Mouffe, Le bel âge, Classe tous risques, Hiroshima, mon amour* (co. Fusco), *La mort de belle, Les jeux de l'amour, Tirez sur le pianiste, Une aussi longue absence, L'amant de cinq jours, Jules et Jim, Le farceur, Nunca pasa nada, Cartouche, L'aîné des Ferchaux, Le mépris, L'immortelle, La peau douce, The pumpkin eater, Un monsieur de compagnie, Mata Hari,* agent H-21, L'homme de Rio, Les tribulations d'un Chinois en Chine, Viva Maria!, Le roi de coeur, Le vieil homme et l'enfant, Le dimanche de la vie, A man for all seasons.

135 Delluc, Louis, French director. 1890-1924. Also playwright and novelist. One of the founders of film criticism in books such as: Photogénie, Cinéma et Cie., Charlot, Drames du cinéma (1919-23). Scripted: La fête espagnole, Train sans yeux and all his own films. See avant-garde. Films: Le silence 20; Le tonnerre, Fièvre 21; La femme de nulle part 22; L'inondation 24.

136 Delon, Alain, French actor, b. 1936. Also stage actor. 1964: also producer. Main films: Quand la femme s'en mêle, Le chemin des écoliers, Plein soleil, Rocco e i suoi fratelli, Quelle joie de vivre, L'eclisse, The leopard, Mélodie en sous-sol, Les félins, L'insoumis, The yellow Rolls-Royce, Paris brûle-t-il?, Les aventuriers, Histoires extraordinaires (William Wilson ep.), Le samourai, Diaboliquement vôtre.

137 DeMille, Cecil B., American director. 1881-1959. At first stage actor. From 1921: also producer: The buccaneer (58) and most of his own films. Acted: Sunset Boulevard. Main films: Carmen, The cheat 15; Joan the woman 17; Male and female, Don't change your husband 19; The affairs of Anatol 21; The ten commandments 23; The Volga boatmen 26; The king of kings 27; Godless girl 28; Dynamite 29; The squawman 31; The sign of the cross 32; This day and age 33; Four frightened people, Cleopatra 34; The crusades 35; The plainsman 36; The buccaneer 38;

Union Pacific 39; North West Mounted Police 40; Reap the wild wind 42; The story of Dr. Wassell 44; Unconquered 47; Samson and Delilah 49; The greatest show on earth 52; The ten commandments (remake) 56.

138 Demy, Jacques, French director, b. 1931. Assistant to Rouquier. Shorts: La sabotier du Val de Loire 56; Le bel indifférent 57; Musée Grévin 58; La mère et l'enfant, Ars 59; Films: Lola 60; Les sept péchés capitaux (one episode) 61; La baie des anges 62; Les parapluies de Cherbourg 63; Les demoiselles de Rochefort 66.

139 De Santis, Giuseppe, Italian director, b. 1917. 1939: film critic. Scripted in collaboration: Ossessione, Desiderio, Il sole sorge ancora and all his own films. See neo-realism. Main films: Caccia tragica 47; Bitter rice 49; Non c'è pace tra gli ulivi 50; Roma ore II 52; Giorno d'amore 54; Italiani brava gente 64.

140 De Seta, Vittorio, Italian director, b. 1923. Scripted and photographed all his own films. Main shorts: Lu tempu di li pisci spata, Isole di fucco 54; Sulfatara 55; Pasqua in Sicilia, Contadini del mare, Parabolo d'Oro 56; Pescherecci, Pastori di Orgosolo, Un giorno in barbagia 58; I dimenticati 59. Films: Banditi a Orgosolo 61; Un uomo a metà 66.

141 De Sica, Vittorio, Italian director and actor, b. 1902. Also stage actor. Long collaboration with Zavattini. See neo-realism. Acted: Daro un milione, Ma non è una cosa seria, Il signor Max, I nostri sogni, Lo sconosciuto di San Marino, Roma, città libera, Altri tempi, Madame de . . ., Pane, amore e fantasia, Pane, amore e . . ., Il bigamo, A farewell to arms, Io, io, io e . . . gli altri, Un italiano in America, Il generale della Rovere and*. Films as director: Rose scarlatte*, Maddalena zero in condotta* 40; Teresa Venerdi* 41; Un garibaldino al convento* 42; I bambini ci guardano 43; La porta del cielo 44; Sciuscia 46; Bicycle thieves 48; Miracolo in Milano 51; Umberto D 52; Stazione termini 53; L'oro di Napoli* 54; Il tetto 56; Two women 60; Il giudizio universale, Boccaccio '70 (one episode) 61; Condemned of Altona 62; Il boom, Yesterday, today, and tomorrow 63; Marriage Italian Style 64; Un monde nouveau, Caccia alla volpe 65; Le streghe (one ep.), Sept fois femme 66.

142 **Dickinson, Thorold,** British director, b. 1906. At first editor. 1954: director of U.N.O. Film Service. Main films: Spanish A.B.C. (short, shot in Spain) 36; Gaslight 40; Next of kin 42; Men of two worlds (documentary) 46; Queen of spades 48; Secret people 51; Hill 24 doesn't answer 54.

143 **Dieterle, William,** Director, b. 1893 in Germany. 1918: studied acting under Max Reinhardt. Acted: Hintertreppe, Waxworks, Faust. 1930: U.S.A. Main films: Her Majesty love 31; Adorable 33; Fashions of 1934 34; A midsummer night's dream (co-dir. Max Reinhardt) 34; White angel 36; The life of Emile Zola 37; Juarez, The hunchback of Notre Dame 39; Dr. Ehrlich's magic bullet 40; Kismet 44; Love letters 45; Portrait of Jennie 47; Rope of sand 49; Salome 53.

144 **Dietrich, Marlene,** German actress, b. 1902. 1922-29: stage actress under Max Reinhardt. 1930: U.S.A. Main films: The joyless street, The blue angel, Morocco, Dishonored, Blonde Venus, Shanghai Express, The song of songs, The scarlet empress, The devil is a woman, Desire (36), The garden of Allah (36), Knight without armour, Angel, Destry rides again, Seven sinners, The flame of New Orleans, Manpower, The spoilers, Kismet (44), Follow the boys, A foreign affair, Stage fright, Rancho Notorious, No highway, Around the world in 80 days, Witness for the prosecution, Touch of evil, Judgment at Nuremberg.

145 **Disney, Walt,** American animator and producer, 1901-66. At first cartoonist. From 1927: producer. See animation. Main films (as animator and producer): Alice (series of shorts) 24; Oswald (series) 26; Mickey Mouse (series) 28: Silly Symphonies (series) 29; Snow White 37; Pinocchio 40; Fantasia, Dumbo 41; Saludos amigos, Bambi 42; Cinderella 49; Alice in Wonderland 51; Peter Pan 52; The lady and the tramp 55; The sleeping beauty 58; The 101 Dalmatians 61. Main films as producer only: The living desert, The vanishing prairie, White wilderness, The moon spinners, Mary Poppins, The jungle book.

146 **Di Venanzo, Gianni,** Italian director of photography, 1920-66. At first assistant to Martelli. Main films: Achtung banditi!, Cronache di poveri amanti, Amore in città, Le ragazze di San Frediano, Le amiche, Gli sbandati, Suor Letizia, Kean, Il grido, I soliti ignoti, La sfida, I magliari, Les noces vénitiennes, I delfini, La notte, Salvatore Giuliano,

Eve (62), *L'eclisse, Otto e mezzo, I basilischi, Le mani sulla città, Il momento della verità, La ragazza di Bube, Alta infedeltà* (Monicelli ep.), *La donna è una cosa meravigliosa* (one ep.), *La decima vittima, Oggi, domani, dopodomani* (one ep.), *Giulietta degli spiriti, The honey pot.*

147 Dmytryk, Edward, American director, b. 1908. 1930-39: editor. 1949: left U.S.A. because of McCarthy. 1951: recanted, reinstated. Main films: *Golden gloves* 40; *Confessions of Boston Blackie* 41; *Behind the rising sun, Hitler's children, Tender comrade* 43; *Back to Bataan* 45; *Crossfire* 47; *Give us this day* 49; *The sniper* 52; *The Caine mutiny, Broken lance* 54; *The end of the affair, The left hand of God* 55; *Raintree county* 57; *The young lions* 58; *Warlock, The blue angel* 59; *Walk on the wild side* 62; *The carpetbaggers, Where love has gone* 64; *Alvarez Kelly, Mirage* 65; *Shalako* 68.

148 Donat, Robert, British actor. 1905-58. From 1931: also stage actor. Main films: *The private life of Henry VIII, The 39 steps* (36), *The ghost goes West, Knight without armour, The citadel, Goodbye, Mr. Chips, Perfect strangers, The young Mr. Pitt, The Winslow boy, The magic box, The inn of the sixth happiness.*

149 Donen, Stanley, American director, b. 1924. From 1941: dancer, then assistant choreographer (*Anchors aweigh, Take me out to the ball game* etc.). Gene Kelly (q.v.) co-directed some of his films*. Films: *On the town** 49; *Royal wedding (Wedding bells)* 50; *Love is better than ever* 51; *Singin' in the rain*, Fearless Fagan* 52; *Give a girl a break* 53; *Deep in my heart, Seven brides for seven brothers* 54; *It's always fair weather** 55; *Funny face* 56; *Kiss them for me, The pajama game* (co-dir. George Abbott) 57; *Indiscreet* 58; *Damn Yankees (What Lola wants)* (co-dir. Abbott), *Once more with feeling* 59; *Surprise package, The grass is greener* 60; *Charade* 63; *Arabesque* 65; *Two for the road* 66; *Bedazzled* 67.

150 Donner, Clive, British director, b. 1926. At first worked in theatre. 1942-55: editor. Films: *The secret place* 56; *Heart of a child* 58; *Marriage of convenience* 60; *The purple stream, The sinister man* 61; *Some people* 62; *The caretaker (The guest), Nothing but the best* 63; *Scotland Yard triumphs* (one episode) 64; *What's new, pussycat?* 65; *Luv* 66; *Here we go round the mulberry bush* 67.

151 Donskoi, Mark, Russian director, b. 1897. At first writer and musician. Main films: *In the big city* 28; *Song about happiness* 34; *The Gorky trilogy (Childhood of Gorky* 38; *Among people* 39; *My universities* 40); *Brother of a hero* 40; *How the steel was tempered* 42; *The rainbow* 44; *Unconquered* 45; *The village schoolteacher* 47; *Varvara* 48; *Alitet leaves for the hills* 49; *Mother* 56; *At great cost* 57; *Foma Gordeiev* 60; *Hello children!* 62; *Heart of a mother* 65; *Mother's devotion* 66.

152 Douglas, Kirk, American actor, b. 1916. 1941-46: stage actor. Since 1956: also producer. Main films: *The strange love of Martha Ivers, Mourning becomes Electra, Champion, The big carnival, Detective story, The big sky,*

Jean Cocteau
Gary Cooper
Joan Crawford

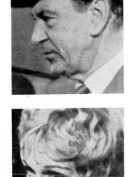

Zbigniew Cybulski
Eva Dahlbeck
Danielle Darrieux

Alain Delon
Jacques Demy
Giuseppe De Santis

Vittorio De Sica
Marlene Dietrich
Mark Donskoi

Friedrich Ermler
Sergei Eisenstein
Alexander Dovzhenko

Federico Fellini
Zoltán Fábri
Robert Enrico

Henry Fonda
Gunnar Fischer
Fernandel

Georges Franju
Carl Foreman
Joan Fontaine

The bad and the beautiful, 20,000 leagues under the sea, The Indian fighter, Man without a star, Ulisse, Lust for life, Gunfight at the O.K. Corral, The devil's disciple, Paths of glory, The Vikings, The last sunset, Spartacus, Strangers when we meet, Town without pity, Lonely are the brave, Two weeks in another town, Seven days in May, In harm's way, Paris brûlet-il?, The heroes of Telemark, The war wagon, The brotherhood.

153 Dovzhenko, Alexander, Russian director. 1894-1956. 1912-22: teacher. Also painter. Scr.: *Vassia, the reformer, The flaming years* (45), *The enchanted Desna* (50), *Poem of the sea* (54), the last three of which were later directed by his wife, Yulia Solntzeva, in 1961, 1964, and 1958 respectively. Films: *Love's berries* 26; *The diplomatic pouch, Zvenigora* 28; *Arsenal* 29; *Earth* 30; *Ivan* 32; *Aerograd* 35; *Shchors* 39; *Liberation* 40; *The fight for our Soviet Ukraine* (co-dir. Solntzeva and Y. Avdeyenko) 43; *Victory in the Ukraine* (co-dir. Solntzeva) 45; *Michurin* 47.

154 Dreyer, Carl, Danish director, b. 1889. 1910: journalist. From 1912: scriptwriter and editor. Main shorts: *Modrehjallpen* 42; *Den Danske Landsbykirke, The seventh age, They caught the ferry* 48; *Thorvaldsen* 49; *Shakespeare Kronborg* 50. Films: *The president* 19; *Pages of Satan's book* 20; *The parson's widow, The marked ones* 21; *Once upon a time* 22; *Mikaël* (in Germany) 24; *Master of the house, Glomsdalsbruden* 25; *La passion de Jeanne d'Arc* (in France) 28; *Vampyr* 31; *Day of wrath* 43; *Tva manniskor* 44; *Ordet* 54; *Gertrud* 64.

155 Dudow, Slatan, German direc-

tor, d. 1963. 1933-45: exiled from Germany. 1946: East Germany. Main films: *Seifenblasen* 29; *Kuhle Wampe* (scr. Bertold Brecht) 32; *Unser täglich Brot* 49; *Familie Benthin* 50; *Frauenschicksale* 52; *Stronger than the night* 54; *The captain of Cologne* 56; *Verwirrung der Liebe* 58; *Christine* 63.

156 Dulac, Germaine, French woman director. 1882-1942. At first drama critic and authoress. 1930-40: director of Pathé newsreels. See *avant garde.* Main films: *Ames de fous* 18; *La cigarette, La fête espagnole* 19; *La souriante Madame Beudet* 23; *Le diable dans la ville* 24; *Ame d'artiste* 25; *La coquille et le clergyman* (scr. Antonin Artaud), *La folie des vaillants* 26; *Antoinette Sabrier, L'invitation au voyage* 27; *Disque 927, Arabesque, Thème et variations* 29 (last four: shorts).

157 Dupont, Ewald A., German director. 1891-1956. 1911: one of first film critics in Germany. 1943: U.S.A. See *expressionism.* Main films: *Baruch* 24; *Variété* 25; *Love me and the world is mine* (in England) 27; *Piccadilly* (in England) 29; *Menschen im Käfig* 30; *Salto mortale* 31; *Forgotten faces* 36; *A night of mystery* 37.

158 Duvivier, Julien, French director, 1896-1967. At first actor. Assistant to L'Herbier and Feuillade. 1940-44: U.S.A. Scripted most of his own films. Main films: *Poil de carotte* 32; *Golgotha, Maria Chapdelaine* 34; *La Bandéra* 35; *La belle équipe, Pépé le Moko, L'homme du jour* 36; *Un carnet de bal* 37; *La fin du jour, La charrette fantôme* 39; *Untel, père et fils* 40; *Lydia* 41; *Tales of Manhattan* 42; *The imposter* 43; *Panique* 46;

Anna Karenina (in England) 48; *Le petit monde de Don Camillo* 51; *Pot-Bouille* 57; *Marie-Octobre* 58; *Diaboliquement vôtre* 67.

159 Dwan, Allan, American director, b. 1885. At first scriptwriter. Has also been producer. Main films: *Robin Hood* 22; *Zaza* 23; *The iron mask* 29; *Wicked* 31; *Trail of the vigilantes* 40; *Brewster's millions* 45; *The sands of Iwo Jima* 49; *Montana Belle* 52; *Silver Lode, Passion* 54; *Escape to Burma, Tennessee's partner, Pearl of the South Pacific* 55; *Slightly scarlet* 56; *The river's edge* 57; *The most dangerous man alive* 61.

E

160 Edwards, Blake, American director, b. 1922. At first writer for radio and TV. Scripted: *Sound off* (also acted), *My sister Eileen, Operation Mad Ball, The notorious landlady.* Also producer with Richard Quine. Films: *Bring your smile along* 55; *He laughed last* 56; *Mister Cory* 57; *This happy feeling, The perfect furlough (Strictly for pleasure)* 58; *Operation Petticoat* 59; *High time* 60; *Breakfast at Tiffany's* 61; *Experiment in terror (The grip of fear)* 62; *Days of wine and roses, The pink panther* 63; *A shot in the dark, The great race* 64; *What did you do in the war, daddy?* 66; *Gunn, The party* 67; *Darling Lili* 68.

161 Eisenstein, Sergei, Russian director, 1898-1948. 1917: cartoonist. 1921: studied under Meyerhold. 1919-

23: set designer, actor, and stage producer. 1924: edited Russian version of *Dr. Mabuse the gambler.* 1929-30: U.S.A. with Alexandrov and Tissé, and 1931: Mexico. 1932: returned to U.S.S.R. Also author and theorist: *Film Form, Film Sense, Notes of a film director.* Films: *Gloumov's diary* (short) 23; *Strike* 24; *Battleship Potemkin* 25; *October* 27; *The general line (Old and new)* 29; *Que viva Mexico!* 31 (abandoned in editing stage; later edited by Sol Lesser into *Thunder over Mexico* 32; and by Marie Seton into *A time in the sun* 39); *Bezhin meadow* (unfinished) 36; *Alexander Nevsky* 38; *Ivan the Terrible I* 45; *Ivan the Terrible II* 46 (released in 58).

162 Eisler, Hanns, German composer, 1898-1963. Studied under Schoenberg. 1939: U.S.A. 1949: East Germany. Main films: *Kuhle Wampe, New earth, Le grand jeu, Komsomol, The 400 millions, El pueblo olvidado, Hangmen also die, None but the lonely heart, Jealousy, The Spanish Main, The woman on the beach, Unser täglich Brot, Herr Puntila und sein Knecht Matti, Nuit et brouillard, Bel ami, Aktion J.*

163 Emmer, Luciano, Italian director, b. 1918. Co-scripted all his own films. Main shorts (all co-dir. by E. Gras up to 1949): *Romanzo di un'epoca, Destino d'amore* 42; *Isole nella laguna, Sulla via di Damasco, Bianchi pascoli, Romantica a Venezia* 48; *Goya* 50; *Leonardo da Vinci* 52; *Picasso* 54. Main films: *Domenica d'agosto* 50; *Parigi è sempre Parigi* 51; *Ragazze di Piazza di Spagna* 52; *Camilla* 54; *Il bigamo* 56; *Il momento più bello, Paradiso terrestre* (documentary, co-dir. R. Enrico) 57; *La ragazza in vetrina* 60.

164 Engel, Morris, American director, b. 1918. At first photographer. Ruth Orkin collaborated on his first two films. Films: *The little fugitive* 53; *Lovers and lollipops* (also dir. of photography) 55; *Weddings and babies* 58.

165 Enrico, Robert, French director, b. 1931. At first editor and assistant. Main shorts: *Thaumetopoea* 60; *Montagnes magiques* 62. Films: *Paradiso terrestre* (documentary, co-dir. L. Emmer) 57; *Au coeur de la vie* (which includes *La rivière du hibou*) 62; *La belle vie* 63; *Les grandes gueules* 65; *Les aventuriers* 66; *Tante Zita* 67; *Ho* 68.

166 Epstein, Jean, French director, 1897-1953. His sister, Marie Epstein, often collaborated on his films. Also author and theorist (*L'esprit du cinéma* etc.). See *avant-garde*. Films: *Pasteur* (co-dir. Benoit-Lévy) 22; *L'auberge rouge, Coeur fidèle, La belle Nivernaise, La montagne infidèle* 23; *Le lion des Mogols, L'affiche* 24; *Le double amour, Les aventures de Robert Macaire* 25; *Mauprat, Six et demi - Onze, La glace à trois faces* 27; *La chute de la maison Usher, Finis terrae* 28; *Sa tête* 29; *Mor' Vran* 30; *L'or des mers, L'homme à l'Hispano* 32; *La châtelaine du Liban* 33; *Les bâtisseurs* 37; *Le tempestaire* 47.

167 Ermler, Friedrich, Russian director, 1898-1967. From 1924: actor. Main films: *Children of storm* 26; *Katka's Reinette apples* 27; *The Parisian cobbler, The house in the snow-drifts* 28; *Fragment of an empire* 29; *Counterplan* (co-dir. Yutkevitch) 32; *Peasants* 35; *A great citizen I and II* 38-39; *She defends her country* 43; *The great turning point* 46; *Unfinished story* 55; *The first day* 58; *Under the trial of history* 64.

168 Etaix, Pierre, French director, b. 1928. At first clown, TV and music hall actor. Gagman on *Mon oncle.* Acted: *Pickpocket,* and all his own films. Scripted all his own films in collab. with J-C. Carrière. Shorts: *Rupture, Heureux anniversaire* 61. Films: *Le soupirant* 62; *Yoyo* 65; *Tant qu'on a la santé* 66.

169 expressionism: movement in art which, from about 1918-1925, strongly influenced such German directors as Lang, Murnau, Leni, Lupu-Pick, Dupont (all q.v.), Wiene, Robison, Grune and von Gerlach, the scriptwriters von Harbou and Mayer (both q.v.), the directors of photography Freund and Wagner (both q.v.), and the set-designers Walter Röhrig (q.v.), Hermann Warm and Walter Reimann. The stage producer, Max Reinhardt, also influenced the movement. Expressionist films were characterised by fantasy and lack of realism in the lighting, costumes and sets, and by symbolic, mime-like acting. Their aim was to capture the truth by means of the subjective intuition of the artist, and not by presenting the external realistic world. In the words of Carl Hauptmann: "The phenomena on the screen are the phenomena of the soul." Films usually grouped under the heading of German expressionism include: *The cabinet of Dr. Caligari* 19, *Genuine* 20 (both R. Wiene), *The Golem, Witchcraft through the ages* (in Denmark), *Scherben, Der müde Tod, Hintertreppe, Vanina* (A. von Gerlach 22), *Dr. Mabuse the gambler, Nosferatu, Warning shadows* (A. Robison 22), *The street* (K. Grune 23), *The Nibelungen, Sylvester, The last laugh, Variété, Wax-*

works, *Zur Chronik von Grieshuus* (A. von Gerlach 25), and *Metropolis*.

F

170 Fábri, Zoltán, Hungarian director, b. 1917. At first painter, then set-designer and stage producer. Main films: *Colony underground* 51 ; *The storm* 52; *Fourteen lives in danger* 54; *Merry-go-round, Professor Hannibal* 56; *Summer clouds* 57; *Anna* 58; *The brute* 60; *The last goal* 61 ; *Darkness in daytime* 63; *Twenty hours* 65; *Late season* 67.

171 Fairbanks, Douglas, (senior) American actor. 1883-1939. At first stage actor. Main films: *The lamb, Intolerance, In and out again, Reaching for the moon, The mark of Zorro, The three musketeers* (21), *Robin Hood* (22), *The thief of Bagdad* (24), *Don Q, son of Zorro, The iron mask* (also scripted), *The taming of the shrew, The private life of Don Juan*.

172 Fejos, Paul, Hungarian director. 1898-1963. Also ethnologist. At first set-designer. 1921: U.S.A. 1931: returned to Europe. Main films: *Pan* 19; *The black captain, The queen of spades* 20; *The last moment* 27; *Lonesome* 28; *Erik the great illusionist, Broadway* 29; *The big house* 30; *Fantômas* (in France) 31; *Marie, légende hongroise* (in France) 32; *Sonnenstrahl* (in Austria) 33; *Menschen im Sturm* (in Hungary) 34; *A handful of rice* (in Siam) 38.

173 Fellini, Federico, Italian director, b. 1920. At first cartoonist. Assistant to Rossellini. Scripted in collaboration: *Roma, città aperta, Paisa, L'ebreo errante, In nome della legge, Senza pietà, Il cammino della speranza* and*. Acted: *L'amore*. See neo-realism. Films: *Luci del varietà* (co-dir. Lattuada) * 50; *Lo sceicco bianco* 52; *I vitelloni, Amore in città* (one episode) 53; *La strada* * 54; *Il bidone* 55; *Le notti di Cabiria* 57; *La dolce vita* 59; *Boccaccio '70* (one episode)* 62; *Otto e mezzo* 63; *Giulietta degli spiriti* 65; *A tre passi dal delirio* (one ep.) 67.

174 Fernandel, French actor, b. 1903. 1921-30: actor in music hall and operetta. Main films: *Le rosier de Madame Husson, Angèle, François Ier, Les rois du sport, Un carnet de bal, Regain, Le Schpountz, Fric-Frac, La fille du puisatier, Nais, Topaze* (51), *Le petit monde de Don Camillo, L'auberge rouge, Mam'zelle Nitouche* (53), *Ali Baba, Around the world in 80 days, Crésus*.

175 Fernandez, Emilio, Mexican director, b. 1904. 1924-33: U.S.A. Acted: *The gaucho, Janitzio, La cucaracha, The reward, The Appaloosa* and *. Main films: *La isla de la pasión* 41; *Maria Candelaria* 43; *La perla, Enamorada* 46; *Rio Escondido* 47; *Maclovia* 48; *La Malquerida* 49; *The torch, Victimas del pecado* 50; *La red* 53; *La tierra del fuego se apaga* 55; *Pueblito* 62; *A loyal soldier of Pancho Villa* * 66.

176 Ferreri, Marco, Italian director, b. 1928. At first journalist. 1955-60: Spain. Scripted in collaboration*. Films: *El pisito* 58; *Los chicos* 59; *El cochecito* 60; *Le italiane e l'amore* (one episode) 61; *Ape regina* * 63; *La donna* scimmia*, Controsesso (one ep.) 64; Oggi, domani, dopodomani, Marcia nuziale 65.

177 Feuillade, Louis, French director. 1873-1925. From 1906: journalist, scriptwriter. Main films: Les films esthétiques (series of 12 films) 09-10; Bébé (26 films) 10-12; La vie telle qu'elle est (30 films, incl. Les vipères, La tare, etc.) 11-13; La vie drôle (4 films) 13-14; Bout-de-Zan (38 films) 13-15; Fantômas (serial in 5 parts) 13-14; Les vampires (serial in 12 parts) 15-16; Judex (serial) 16; La nouvelle mission de Judex (serial) 17; Tih Minh (serial) 18; Barrabas (serial) 19; Les deux gamines (serial) 20; L'orpheline, Parisette (serials) 21; Le fils du flibustier (serial) 22.

178 Feuillère, Edwige, French actress, b. 1907. Since 1930: also stage actress. Main films: Mam'zelle Nitouche, Topaze (32), Golgotha, Lucrèce Borgia, La dame de Malacca, Marthe Richard, J'étais une aventurière, Sans lendemain, De Mayerling à Sarajevo, La duchesse de Langeais, L'honorable Catherine, L'idiot, L'aigle à deux têtes, Souvenirs perdus, Le blé en herbe, En cas de malheur, Quand la femme s'en mêle, Le crime ne paie pas.

179 FEX: (Factory of the eccentric actor) movement founded in Russia in 1921 to counter the theories of Dziga Vertov (q.v.). FEX according to its founders, Kozintsev, Trauberg, Yutkevitch, and Moskvin (qq.v.), was intended to create a new school of acting in the tradition of music hall and circus, in which "the body movements of the actor are considered extremely important and significant as they are in Oriental theatre" (Yutkevitch). The most typical products of this school, which has many similarities with expressionism (q.v.), though probably not influenced by it, include: The adventures of Oktyabrina, The devil's wheel, The cloak, Lace, The new Babylon.

180 Feyder, Jacques, French director. 1888-1948. At first actor, then assistant. 1929-33: U.S.A. Main films: L'Atlantide 21; Crainquebille 23; Visages d'enfants 24; L'image, Gribiche, Carmen 26; Thérèse Raquin, Les nouveaux messieurs 28; The kiss 29; Daybreak 32; Le grand jeu 34; Pension Mimosas 35; La Kermesse héroïque 36; Knight without armour (in England) 37; Les gens du voyage 38; La loi du Nord 39; Une femme disparait 42; Macadam (completed by M. Blistène) 46.

181 Fields W. C., American actor, 1879-1946. From 1897: stage comedian. 1915-21: Ziegfeld Follies. Films: Pool sharks, Janice Meredith, Sally of the sawdust, That Royle girl, It's the old army game, So's your old man, The potters, Running wild, Two flaming youths, Tillie's punctured romance, Fool's for luck, Her Majesty love, Million dollar legs, If I had a million, International house, Tillie and Gus, Alice in Wonderland, Six of a kind, You're telling me, The old-fashioned way, Mrs. Wiggs of the cabbage patch, It's a gift, David Copperfield, Mississippi, The man on the flying trapeze, Poppy, The big broadcast of 1938, You can't cheat an honest man, My little chickadee, The bank dick (The bank detective), Never give a sucker an even break (What a man), Follow the boys, Song of the open road, Sensations of 1945.

182 Figueroa, Gabriel, Mexican director of photography, b. 1907. 1935-36: U.S.A., assistant to Toland. Main films: *María Candelaria, La perla, The fugitive, Enamorada, Río Escondido, Maclovia, The torch, Victimas del pecado, Los olvidados, El, La tierra del fuego se apaga, La cucaracha, Nazarin, Republic of sin, The young one, The exterminating angel, The night of the iguana, Simon del desierto.*

183 Fischer, Gunnar, Swedish director of photography. Long collaboration with Bergman. Main films: *Night in the harbour, Port of call, Private Bom, Thirst, To joy, Summer interlude, Summer with Monika, Waiting women, Smiles of a summer night, The seventh seal, Wild strawberries, So close to life, The face, The devil's eye, Lustgården, 491, Oj oj oj . . ., The black palm trees.*

184 Fisher, Terence, British director, b. 1904. From 1933: editor. Also director of films for TV (*Robin Hood* series). Main films: *The curse of Frankenstein* 57; *The revenge of Frankenstein, Dracula* 58; *The mummy, The hound of the Baskervilles, The stranglers of Bombay* 59; *The brides of Dracula, The two faces of Dr. Jekyll (House of fright)* 60; *The curse of the werewolf* 61; *The phantom of the opera* 62; *The gorgon, The earth dies screaming* 64; *Dracula, prince of darkness* 65; *Island of terror, Frankenstein created woman* 66.

185 Flaherty, Robert, American director of documentaries, 1884-1951. At first miner and explorer. 1930-39: England. Scr. or co-scr. all his own films and *It's all true*. Also director of photography. Films: *Nanook of the North* 20-21; *Moana* 23-25; *The pottery maker* 25; *The twenty four dollar island* 26; *White shadows of the South Seas* (co. W. S. Van Dyke) 27; *Tabu* (co. Murnau) 29-31; *Industrial Britain* 31; *Man of Aran* 32-34; *Elephant boy* (exteriors; interiors Z. Korda) 37; *The land* 39-42; *Louisiana story* 46-48.

186 Fleischer, Richard, American director, b. 1916. 1937-40: stage producer. 1940-45: documentaries (*This is America* series) and montage films (*Flickers flashbacks* series). 1962: Italy. Main films: *So this is New York* 48; *Follow me quietly* 49; *20,000 leagues under the sea* 54; *Violent Saturday* 55; *Bandido, The girl on the red velvet swing* 56; *Between heaven and hell* 57; *The Vikings* 58; *Compulsion* 59; *Crack in the mirror* 60; *The big gamble* 61; *Barabbas* 62; *Fantastic voyage* 66; *Doctor Dolittle* 67; *The Boston strangler* 68.

187 Fleming, Victor, American director. 1883-1949. 1915: cameraman to Griffith. Main films: *Reaching for the moon* 18; *The way of all flesh, Mantrap, Hula* 27; *Red dust* 32; *Bombshell* 33; *Treasure Island, Reckless* 34; *Captains courageous* 37; *Test pilot* 38; *The wizard of Oz, Gone with the wind* 39; *Dr. Jekyll and Mr. Hyde* 41; *Tortilla Flat* 42; *A guy named Joe* 43.

188 Florey, Robert, French director, b. 1900. 1921: U.S.A. 1925: assistant to Sternberg. Scripted: *Frankenstein* (31). Since 1921: also journalist and author. 1950: TV producer. Main films: *The cocoanuts* (co. J. Santley) 29; *La route est belle* (in France) 30; *Le blanc et le noir* (co-dir. M. Allégret) 31; *Murders in the rue Morgue* 32; *Smarty*

34; *Hollywood Boulevard, King of gamblers* 37; *The beast with five fingers* 46; *Monsieur Verdoux* (co-dir. Chaplin) 47; *Vicious years* 50.

189 Flynn, Errol, American actor, b. in Australia, 1909-59. At first boxer, gold prospector. Main films: *Captain Blood, The charge of the Light Brigade, The princess and the pauper, The adventures of Robin Hood, Four's a crowd, The sisters, Dodge City, The private lives of Elizabeth and Essex, Sante Fe trail, They died with their boots on, Desperate journey, Gentleman Jim, Edge of darkness, Objective Burma, The Forsyte Saga (That Forsyte woman), Kim, Il maestro di Don Giovanni, The sun also rises, The roots of heaven.*

190 Fonda, Henry, American actor, b. 1905. Since 1925: also stage actor. Main films: *Way down East, The trail of the Lonesome Pine, You only live once, That certain woman, Jezebel, Young Mr. Lincoln, Drums along the Mohawk, The grapes of wrath, Chad Hanna, The return of Frank James, The lady Eve, Rings on her fingers, Tales of Manhattan, The Oxbow incident, My darling Clementine, The long night, The fugitive, On our merry way, Daisy Kenyon, Fort Apache, Mister Roberts, War and peace* (55), *The wrong man, The tin star, Stage struck, Twelve angry men, Warlock, Advise and consent, How the West was won, The longest day, Spencer's mountain, Sex and the single girl, The best man, How to murder your wife, Fail safe, In harm's way, Battle of the bulge.*

191 Fontaine, Joan, American actress, b. 1917. 1935-37: stage actress. Sister of Olivia De Havilland. Main films: *Quality Street, A damsel in distress, Gunga Din, The women, Rebecca, Suspicion, The constant nymph, Jane Eyre, The affairs of Susan, Ivy, The emperor waltz, Letter from an unknown woman, Born to be bad, Something to live for, Ivanhoe, The bigamist, Serenade, Beyond a reasonable doubt, Island in the sun, Until they sail, Tender is the night.*

192 Ford, Aleksander, Polish director, b. 1908. 1939-44: U.S.S.R. Main films: *The mascot* 30; *The legion of the street* 32; *The awakening, Sabra* 34; *People of the Vistula* (co-dir. J. Zarzyzcki) 37; *Majdanek* (short) 44; *Border street* 48; *The young Chopin* 51; *Five boys from Barska Street* 53; *The eighth day of the week* 57; *Knights of the Teutonic Order* 60; *The first day of freedom* 64; *Phone number 72866.*

193 Ford, John, American director, b. 1895. 1917-24: about 50 short and medium length films. Since 1947: also own producer. Films: *Silver wings* 22; *Cameo Kirby* 23; *The iron horse* 24; *Three bad men* 26; *Four sons* 28; *Men without women, Born reckless, Up the river, The seas beneath* 30; *The brat, Arrowsmith* 31; *Air mail, Flesh* 32; *Pilgrimage, Doctor Bull* 33; *The lost patrol, The world moves on, Judge Priest* 34; *The whole town's talking, The informer, Steamboat round the bend* 35; *The prisoner of Shark Island, Mary of Scotland, The plough and the stars* 36; *Wee Willie Winkie, The hurricane* 37; *Four men and a prayer, Submarine patrol* 38; *Stagecoach, Young Mr. Lincoln, Drums along the Mohawk* 39; *The grapes of wrath, The long voyage home* 40; *Sex hygiene* (army doc.), *How green was my valley* 41; *The battle of Midway* (doc.)

42; *December 7th, We sail at midnight* (docs.) 43; *They were expendable* (doc.) 45; *My darling Clementine* 46; *The fugitive* 47; *Fort Apache, Three godfathers* 48; *She wore a yellow ribbon, Pinky* (completed by Kazan) 49; *When Willie comes marching home, Wagonmaster, Rio Grande* 50; *This is Korea* (doc.) 51; *What price glory, The quiet man* 52; *The sun shines bright, Mogambo* 53; *The long gray line, Mister Roberts* 55; *The searchers* 56; *The wings of eagles, The rising of the moon* 57; *The last hurrah* 58; *Gideon's day* (*Gideon of Scotland Yard*), *Korea* (doc.), *The horse soldiers* 59; *Sergeant Rutledge* 60; *Two rode together, The man who shot Liberty Valance* 61; *How the West was won* (one ep.), *Donovan's Reef* 63; *Cheyenne autumn, Young Cassidy* (completed by Cardiff) 64; *Seven women* 65.

194 Foreman, Carl, American scriptwriter and director, b. 1914. At first journalist, then worked in radio. Left America because of McCarthy. Scripted: *So this is New York, Home of the brave, Champion, The men, High noon, The sleeping tiger, The bridge on the River Kwai, The key, The guns of Navarone, MacKenna's gold.* Film (as director and scriptwriter): *The victors* 62. (Also produced last three.)

195 Forman, Milos, Czechoslovakian director, b. 1932. Scr.: *Youngsters.* Films: *Talent competition, If there were no music* (both shorts; later edited into one film) 63; *Peter and Pavla* 64; *Loves of a blonde* 65; *Fire, fire!* 67.

196 Franju, Georges, French director, b. 1912. At first stage set designer. 1937: with Henri Langlois founded Cinémathèque Française. Main shorts: *Le métro* 34; *Le sang des bêtes* 49; *En passant par la Lorraine* 50; *Hôtel des Invalides, Le grand Méliès* 51; *Mon chien* 55; *Le Théâtre National Populaire* 56; *Notre Dame, cathédrale de Paris* 57; *La première nuit* 58. Films: *La tête contre les murs* 58; *Les yeux sans visage* 59; *Pleins feux sur l'assassin* 61; *Thérèse Desqueyroux* 62; *Judex* 63; *Thomas l'imposteur* 65; *Les rideaux blancs* 66.

197 Frankenheimer, John, American director, b. 1930. At first stage producer and actor. Also TV producer. Films: *The young stranger* 57; *The young savages* 61; *All fall down, Birdman of Alcatraz, The Manchurian candidate* 62; *Seven days in May* 63; *The train* 64; *Seconds* 65; *Grand Prix* 66; *The extraordinary seaman* 67; *The fixer* 68.

198 free cinema: British documentary movement launched by Lindsay Anderson and Karel Reisz (qq.v.), the former editors of the review *Sequence* (1947-51); influenced by the Grierson (q.v.) school of documentaries and the films of Jennings (q.v.), their aims, as laid out in their manifesto of 1956, were to make films "which share an attitude: a belief in freedom, in the importance of the individual, and in the significance of the everyday" (cf. *neo-realism*). Tony Richardson, Walter Lassally, the director of photography (qq.v.), Gavin Lambert, and Lorenza Mazzetti also contributed to the movement. The films of free cinema include: *O dreamland, Momma don't allow, Together, Another sky, Every day except Christmas, We are the Lambeth boys, March to Aldermaston.*

199 Freed, Arthur, American producer, b. 1894. Also song composer. Since 1940: producer for M.G.M. responsible for many musicals. Main films: *Strike up the band, Babes in arms, Babes on Broadway, Lady be good, Ziegfeld girl, For me and my gal, Cabin in the sky, Girl crazy, Meet me in St. Louis, The clock, Yolanda and the thief, Ziegfeld Follies, The Harvey girls, Good news, Easter Parade, The pirate, Summer holiday, The Barkleys of Broadway, Take me out to the ball game, On the town, Annie get your gun, Royal wedding, Show boat, An American in Paris, Crisis, The belle of New York, Singin' in the rain, The band wagon, Brigadoon, It's always fair weather, Kismet* (55), *Invitation to the dance, Silk stockings, Gigi, Bells are ringing.*

200 Fresnay, Pierre, French actor, b. 1897. Since 1914: stage actor and producer. Also theatre director. Main films: *Marius, La dame aux camélias, Fanny, Le roman d'un jeune homme pauvre, The man who knew too much* (34), *Koenigsmark* (36), *Sous les yeux de l'occident, César, Mademoiselle Docteur, La grande illusion, Le puritain, Le duel* (also dir., 39), *La charrette fantôme, La main du diable, L'assassin habite au 21, Le corbeau, Le voyageur sans bagages, Je suis avec toi, La fille du diable, Monsieur Vincent, La valse de Paris.*

201 Freund, Karl, German director of photography, b. 1890. 1908: newsreel cameraman. See *expressionism*. Since 1929: U.S.A. Since 1950: TV. Acted: *Mikaël*. Main films: *Engelein, Venetian nights, Das Brillantenschiff, Es werde Licht, Der Golem* (20), *Satanas, Der Bucklige und die Tänzerin, Der Januskopf, Marizza, genannt die Schmuggler-Madonna, Der brennende Acker* (co. Wagner), *Die Austreibung, Die Finanzen des Grossherzogs, Lukrezia Borgia, Mikaël, The last laugh, Madame wants no children, Tartuffe, Metropolis, Variété, Faust, Berlin, rhythm of a city, A night in London, Dr. Jekyll and Mr. Hyde* (31), *Air mail, Dracula* (31), *Murders in the rue Morgue, The mummy* (also dir., 32), *Back street, Mad love* (also dir., 35), *Camille, Parnell, Conquest, Golden boy, Green hell, Pride and prejudice, Tortilla Flat, A guy named Joe, The seventh cross, The thin man goes home, A letter for Evie, Two smart people, Undercurrent, Key Largo.*

202 Fuller, Samuel, American director, b. 1911. At first crime reporter and detective story writer. Scripted: *Shockproof* and all his own films. Also TV producer. Films: *I shot Jesse James* 48; *The baron of Arizona* 49; *The steel helmet* 50; *Fixed bayonets* 51; *Park Row, Pickup on South Street* 52; *Hell and high water* 53; *House of bamboo* 55; *Run of the arrow* 56; *China Gate, Forty guns* 57; *Verboten!* 58; *The crimson kimono* 59; *Underworld U.S.A.* 60; *Merrill's marauders* 61; *Shock corridor* 63; *The naked kiss* 64; *Twist of the knife* 67.

203 Furie, Sidney, Canadian director, b. 1933. 1957: England. Main films: *Cool sound from hell, A dangerous age* 56; *During one night* 60; *The young ones* 61; *The boys* 62; *The leather boys* 63; *Wonderful life* 64; *The Ipcress file* 65; *The appaloosa (Southwest to Sonora)* 66; *The naked runner* 67.

204 Fusco, Giovanni, Italian composer, b. 1906. Main films: *Traviata,*

Avanzi di galera, N.U., L'amorosa menzogna, Superstizione, La Villa dei Mostri, Cronaca di un amore, La signora senza camelie, I vinti, Le amiche, La signora senza camelie, I vinti, Le amiche, Il grido, Hiroshima, mon amour (co. Delerue), Il rossetto, L'avventura, I delfini, Climats, L'eclisse, Il mare, Deserto rosso, I fuorilegge del matrimonio, Tre notti d'amore (one ep.), La corruzione, La guerre est finie.

G

205 Gabin, Jean, French actor, b. 1904. 1923-30: actor in music hall and operetta. 1941-45: U.S.A. Main films: Maria Chapdelaine, La Bandéra, Golgotha, La belle équipe, Les bas-fonds, Pépé le Moko, La grande illusion, Gueule d'amour, Quai des brumes, La bête humaine, Le jour se léve, Remorques, The imposter, Au delà des grilles, La Marie du port, Le plaisir, Touchez pas au grisbi, L'air de Paris, Le port du désir, Napoléon (55), Razzia sur la Chnouf, French Cancan, La traversée de Paris, Maigret tend un piège, En cas de malheur, Mélodie en sous-sol, Le tonnerre de Dieu.

206 Gable, Clark, American actor. 1901-1960. 1920-30: stage actor. Main films: The merry widow, A free soul, Susan Lennox, her fall and rise, Possessed, Strange interlude, Red dust, Dancing lady, It happened one night, Forsaking all others, After office hours, Call of the wild, Manhattan melodrama, Mutiny on the Bounty (35), Wife versus secretary, San Francisco, Love on the run, Test pilot, Gone with the wind, Strange cargo, Comrade X, Command decision, Across the wide Missouri, Mogambo, The tall men, The king and four queens, Band of angels, Run silent, run deep, The misfits.

207 Gance, Abel, French director, b. 1889. Also poet, playwright, actor. Invented: stereophonic sound, pictograph, polyvision (from which Cinerama was developed). Main films: La folie du Dr. Tube 16; La zone de la mort, Mater dolorosa 17; La dixième symphonie, J'accuse 18; La roue, Au secours 23; Napoléon 27; La fin du monde 30; Mater dolorosa (sound version of above) 32; La dame aux camélias, Napoléon (sound version of the above) 34; Le roman d'un jeune homme pauvre, Lucrèce Borgia 35; Un grand amour de Beethoven, Jérôme Perreau 36; J'accuse (sound version of above) 37; Louise 38; Paradis perdu 39; La Vénus aveugle 41; Le capitaine Fracasse 42; La tour de Nesle 54; Magirama (anthology of his former films) 56; Austerlitz 60; Cyrano et d'Artagnan 63.

208 Garat, Henri, French actor. 1902-59. At first music hall actor. Often partnered by Lilian Harvey*. Main films: Le congrès s'amuse*, Le chemin du paradis*, Un rêve blond*, Adorable, On a volé un homme, Un mauvais garçon, La chaste Suzanne.

209 Garbo, Greta, Swedish actress, b. 1905. Since 1925: U.S.A. Films: Luffar-Petter, The saga of Gösta Berling, The joyless street, The torrent, The temptress, Flesh and the devil, Love, The divine woman, The mysterious lady, A woman of affairs, Wild orchids, The single standard, The kiss, Anna Christie, Romance, Inspiration, Susan Lennox, her fall and rise, Mata-Hari, Grand Hotel, As you desire me, Queen Christina, The painted veil, Anna Karenina (35), Camille, Conquest, Ninotchka, Two faced woman.

210 Gardner, Ava, American actress, b. 1922. Main films: *Young ideas, The killers, One touch of Venus, The bribe, Show boat, Pandora and the Flying Dutchman, The snows of Kilimanjaro, Mogambo, The barefoot contessa, Bhowani Junction, The sun also rises, The naked Maja, On the beach, 55 days at Peking, The night of the iguana, Seven days in May, The Bible . . . in the beginning.*

211 Garfein, Jack, American director, b. 1930 in Czechoslovakia. Since 1947: stage and TV producer. Worked under Piscator. Assistant to Kazan on *Baby doll*, and to Stevens on *Giant*. Films: *The strange one (End as a man)* 56; *Something wild* 61.

212 Garland, Judy, American actress, b. 1923. Main films: *Broadway melody of 1938, The wizard of Oz, Babes in arms, Strike up the band, Ziegfeld girl, Girl crazy, Thousands cheer, The Harvey girls, Babes on Broadway, For me and my gal, Meet me in St. Louis, Ziegfeld Follies, The pirate, Easter parade, A star is born* (54), *Judgment at Nuremberg, I could go on singing, A child is waiting.*

213 Garnett, Tay, American director, b. 1905. From 1926: scriptwriter. Main films: *Her man* 30; *One way passage* 32; *Love is news* 37; *Seven sinners* 40; *Bataan* 43; *Mrs. Parkington* 44; *The postman always rings twice* 46; *Wild harvest* 47; *A Connecticut Yankee in King Arthur's court* 49; *The black knight* 54; *A terrible beauty (The night fighter)* 60.

214 Gassman, Vittorio, Italian actor, b. 1922. Since 1943: also stage actor and producer. Main films: *L'ebreo errante, La figlia del capitano, Bitter rice, Mambo, La donna più bella del mondo, War and peace, Kean* (also co-dir. with F. Rosi, 56) *La tempesta, I soliti ignoti, La grande guerra, Il sorpasso, Il giudizio universale, Barabbas, Frenesia dell' estate, I mostri, L'armata Brancaleone, Sept fois femme, Questi fantasmi.*

215 Gerasimov, Sergei, Russian director, b. 1906. 1925-29: actor and assistant in films of Kozintsev and Trauberg (q.v.), and in *Deserter*. Main films: *Do I love you?* 34; *The bold seven* 36; *Komsomolsk* 38; *Teacher* 39; *Masquerade, Fighting film album* (with others) 41; *Invincible* (co-dir. Kalatozov) 43; *Young guard* 47; *Country doctor* 52; *Nadejda* 55; *Quiet flows the Don* 57; *Song about Koltsov* 60; *Men and beasts* (in E. Germany) 62; *A true story* 63; *The journalist* 67.

216 Germi, Pietro, Italian director, b. 1914. Also acted in some of his own films*. Scripted all his own films in collaboration. See *neo-realism*. Main films: *Il testimone* 46; *Gioventù perduta* 47; *In nome della legge* 49; *Il cammino della speranza* 50; *Il ferroviere** 56; *L'uomo di paglia** 57; *Un maledetto imbroglio** 59; *Divorzia all' italiana* 61; *Sedotta e abbandonata* 63; *Signore e signori* 65; *La bomba* 66; *L'immorale* 67.

217 Gish, Lillian, American actress, b. 1896. Since 1902: also stage actress. Long collaboration with Griffith. Main films: *An unseen enemy, The mothering heart, Judith of Bethulia, Home sweet home, The birth of a nation, Hearts of the world, The great love, Broken blossoms, The greatest question, True heart Susie, Remodelling her husband* (also dir., 20), *Way down East, Orphans of the storm, The white sister, Romola, La Bohème, The scarlet letter, The wind, Duel in the sun, The cobweb, The night of the hunter, Orders to kill, The unforgiven, The comedians.*

218 Godard, Jean-Luc, French director, b. 1930. At first film critic. Acted: *Le signe du lion, Paris nous appartient.* See *nouvelle vague.* Shorts: *Opération béton* 54; *Une femme coquette* 55; *Tous les garçons s'appellent Patrick* 57; *Charlotte et son Jules, Une histoire d'eau* (co-dir. Truffaut) 58. Films: *A bout de souffle, Le petit soldat* 60; *Une femme est une femme, Les sept péchés capitaux* (one episode) 61; *Vivre sa vie, Rogopag* (one episode) 62; *Les carabiniers, Les plus belles escroqueries du monde* (one episode), *Le mépris* 63; *Bande à part, Une femme mariée* 64; *Alphaville, Paris vu par . . .* (one ep.), *Pierrot le Fou, Masculin féminin* 65; *Made in U.S.A., Deux ou trois choses que je sais d'elle* 66; *Vangelo* 70 (one ep.), *Le plus vieux métier du monde* (one ep.), *La Chinoise, Loin du Viêtnam* (in coll.), *Week-end* 67; *Le gai savoir* 68.

219 Gosho, Heinosuke, Japanese director, b. 1902. At first assistant to Shimazu. Main films: *The lonely roughneck, Tricky girl* 27; *The village bride* 28; *Bachelors beware* 30; *The neighbour's wife and mine, Chorus of Tokyo* 31; *The bride talks in her sleep* 33; *Bundle of life, Dancing girl from Izu* 35; *Everything that lives* 36; *New snow* 42; *The girls of Izu* 45; *Dispersing clouds* 51; *Four chimneys* 53; *The valley between life and death, An inn at Osaka* 54; *Growing up* 55; *Elegy of the North, Behold thy son* 57; *Hotarubi, Yoku, Hibari no Takekurabe* 58; *When a woman loves, Ryoju* 60; *As the clouds scatter* 61; *An innocent witch* 65; *Our wonderful years* 66; *Rebellion of Japan* 67.

220 Goulding, Edmund, Director, b. 1891 in London, d. 1959. 1914: U.S.A. From 1921: scriptwriter and actor. Main films: *Love* 27; *Broadway melody, The trespasser* 29; *Grand Hotel* 32; *That certain woman* 37; *Dark victory, We are not alone, The old maid* 39; *Forever and a day* (one ep.) 42; *Claudia, The constant nymph* 43; *The razor's edge* 46; *We're not married* 52.

221 Grant, Cary, Actor, b. 1904 in England. 1925: U.S.A. 1916-32: stage and music hall actor. Main films: *Devil and the deep, Blonde Venus, She done him wrong, I'm no angel, Alice in Wonderland, Sylvia Scarlett, Suzy, Topper, The awful truth, Bringing up baby, Holiday, Gunga Din, Only angels have wings, In name only, His girl Friday, My favourite wife, The Philadelphia story, Penny serenade, Suspicion, The talk of the town, Once upon a honeymoon, Destination Tokyo, Arsenic and old lace, None but the lonely heart, Notorious, The bachelor and the bobbysoxer, I was a male war bride, Crisis, People will talk, Monkey business* (52), *To catch a thief, An affair to remember, The pride and the passion, Kiss them for me, Indiscreet, North by Northwest, That touch of mink, The grass is greener, Charade, Walk, don't run.*

44

222 Grémillon, Jean, French director. 1901-1959. Studied music under Vincent d'Indy. Wrote the music of most of his own films. 1923-25: shorts. 1933-35: Spain. Main films: *Tour au large* 26; *Maldone* 27; *Gardiens de phare* 29; *La petite Lise* 30; *La Dolorosa* (in Spain) 34; *Gueule d'amour*, *L'étrange Monsieur Victor* 37; *Remorques* 41; *Lumière d'été* 42; *Le ciel est à vous* 43; *Le six juin à l'aube* 45; *Pattes blanches* 48; *Les charmes de l'existence* (short, co-dir. P. Kast) 49; *L'étrange Madame X* 50; *Astrologie* (short) 52; *L'amour d'une femme* 53; *La maison aux images* 55; *Haute-Lisse* 56.

223 Gréville, Edmond, French director, 1906-66. Also novelist and playwright. Acted: *Sous les toits de Paris.* 1929-30: assistant to Dupont and Gance. Main films: *Elle est bicidimine* (co-dir. J. Brunius) 27; *Le train des suicidés* 31; *Princesse Tam-Tam* 35; *Secret lives* (in England) 38; *Menaces* 39; *Dorothée cherche l'amour* 45; *Pour une nuit d'amour* 46; *Le diable souffle* 47; *L'envers du paradis* 53; *Le port du désir* 54; *Quand sonnera midi* 57; *L'île au bout du monde* 58; *Les mains d'Orlac* 59; *Beat girl* (in England) 60; *Les menteurs* 61; *L'accident* 62.

224 Grierson, John, British director and producer of documentaries, b. 1898. 1924-27: U.S.A. 1928-33: director of Empire Marketing Board Film Unit. 1933-37: dir. of G.P.O. Film Unit. 1938-48: U.S.A. and Canada (National Film Board). Films (as director): *Drifters* 29; *The fishing banks of Skye* 34. Grierson founded a school of documentarists who believed that material shot not in a studio but from real life could, in the hands of the artist, become a new and essential art form which would be more significant (and in the philosophical sense of the word, more real) than the fictional film. Cf. Dziga Vertov and *cinéma-vérité* (qq.v.). Those who belonged to this movement and whose films he often produced include: Cavalcanti, Watt, Rotha, Wright (qq.v.), **Sir Arthur Elton** (b. 1906): *Shadow on the mountain* 31; *Voice of the world* 32; *Aero-engine* (full length doc.) 34; *Workers and jobs* 35; and **Edgar Anstey** (b. 1907): *Uncharted waters* 32; *Granton trawler* 34; *Housing problems* 35; *March of time* (newsreel) 36-38.

225 Griffith, David Wark, American director. 1875-1948. From 1902: journalist, writer, poet. 1907: actor. Main films: *The adventures of Dollie, For love of gold, After many years* 08; *The drunkard's reformation, The lonely villa, Pippa passes* 09; *The thread of destiny, Ramona* 10; *The Lonedale operator* 11; *Man's genesis, New York hat, Lena and the geese, An unseen enemy, The massacre* 12; *The mothering heart, Judith of Bethulia* 13; *Home sweet home* 14; *The birth of a nation* 15; *Intolerance* 16; *Hearts of the world, The great love* 18; *Broken blossoms, The greatest question, True heart Susie* 19; *Way down East* 20; *Dream Street* 21; *Orphans of the storm, One exciting night* 22; *The white rose* 23; *America, Isn't life wonderful* 24; *Sally of the sawdust, That Royle girl* 25; *Sorrows of Satan* 26; *Drums of love, The battle of the sexes* 28; *Lady of the pavements* 29; *Abraham Lincoln* 30; *The struggle* 31.

226 Guazzoni, Enrico, Italian di-

45

rector. 1876-1949. Studied art. Designed the sets and costumes for all his own films up to 1924. Main films: *Agrippina* 10; *Quo vadis?* 12; *Marcantonio e Cleopatra* 13; *Caius Julius Caesar* 14; *Messalina* 23; *Re burlone* 35.

227 Guinness, Sir Alec, British actor, b. 1914. Since 1934: also stage actor. Main films: *Great expectations, Oliver Twist, Kind hearts and coronets, The Lavender Hill Mob, The man in the white suit, The card (The promoter), Father Brown, To Paris with love, The ladykillers, The swan, The bridge on the River Kwai, The horse's mouth* (also scripted), *The scapegoat, Our man in Havana, Lawrence of Arabia, The fall of the Roman Empire, Dr. Zhivago, A gift from heaven, Hotel Paradiso, The Quiller memorandum, The comedians.*

228 Guitry, Sacha, French director and actor. 1885-1957. 1902-57: also stage actor and producer, playwright, poet, novelist. Scripted all his own films and also acted in*. Main films: *Ceux de chez nous* 14 (remade with commentary 52); *Faisons un rêve, Le roman d'un tricheur** 36; *Les perles de la couronne** 37; *Remontons les Champs-Elysées** 38; *Ils étaient neuf célibataires** 39; *La poison* 51; *La vie d'un honnête homme* 52; *Si Versailles m'était conté** 53; *Napoléon**, *Si Paris nous était conté** 55; *Assassins et voleurs* 56; *Les trois font la paire* 57.

H

229 Haanstra, Bert, Dutch director of documentaries, b. 1916. At first press photographer. 1952-54: worked with Royal Dutch/Shell Film Unit. Main films: *The Muiden circle lives again* 49; *Mirror of Holland* 50; *Medieval Dutch sculpture, Panta rhei* 51; *The dike builders* 52; *The changing earth, The search for oil, The wildcat* 53; *The oilfield* 54; *The rival world, God Shiva* 55; *And there was no more sea, Rembrandt, painter of man* 56; *Glass, Fanfare* (feature film) 58; *The M.P. case* 60; *Delta phase one, Zoo* 62; *Alleman* 64; *The voice of the water* 66.

230 Hamer, Robert, British director. 1911-1963. 1935-43: editor. From 1956: also TV producer. Scripted in collaboration most of his own films and *A jolly bad fellow.* Films: *Dead of night* (one episode), *Pink string and sealing wax* 45; *It always rains on Sunday* 47; *Kind hearts and coronets* 48; *The spider and the fly* 51; *His Excellency* 52; *The long memory* 53; *Father Brown (The detective)* 54; *To Paris with love* 55; *The scapegoat* 58; *School for scoundrels* 60.

231 Hani, Susumu, Japanese director, b. 1930. 1954-60: shorts (*Tokyo '58* 58 etc.). Films: *Bad boys* 61; *A full life* 62; *Children hand in hand* 63; *She and he* 64; *The story of Bwana Toshi* 65; *Bride of the Andes* 66; *The bramble bush* 67.

232 Harbou, Thea von, German scriptwriter. 1888-1954. See *expressionism.* Main films: *Das indische Grabmal* (co. F. Lang), *Das wandernde Bild, Vier um die Frau, Der müde Tod, Der brennende Acker* (co. others), *Die Austreibung, Phantom, Dr. Mabuse the gambler, Die Finanzen des Grossherzogs,*

The Nibelungen, Zur Chronik von Grieshuus, Metropolis, Spione, Frau im Mond, M, The last will of Dr. Mabuse, Elisabeth und der Narr (also dir., 33), Der Herrscher, Jugend.

233 Harlan, Veit, German director. 1899-1964. Studied theatre under Reinhardt. 1915-34: stage and film actor. Nazi. Main films: *Die Kreutzersonate* 36; *Der Herrscher* 37; *Jugend* 38; *Jud Süss* 40; *Der grosse König, Die goldene Stadt* 42; *Immensee* 43; *Opfergang* 44; *Sterne über Colombo* 53; *Das dritte Geschlecht* 57.

234 Harlow, Jean, American actress. 1911-37. Main films: *Bacon grabbers, New York nights, The love parade, Hell's angels, Public enemy, Platinum blonde, Night after night, Red dust, Bombshell, Reckless, Dinner at eight, Wife versus secretary, Suzy, The girl from Missouri, Libeled lady, Saratoga.*

235 Harrison, Rex, British actor, b. 1908. Since 1924: also stage actor. Main films: *Storm in a tea-cup, The citadel, Night train to Munich, Blithe spirit, The ghost and Mrs. Muir, Escape, Unfaithfully yours, The four poster, The reluctant debutante, Midnight lace, Cleopatra* (63), *The yellow Rolls-Royce, My fair lady, The agony and the ecstasy, The honey pot, Dr. Dolittle.*

236 Hart, William, American actor. 1870-1946. 1889-1914: stage actor. Also novelist. Also directed many of his films*. Main films: *The bargain, The passing of Two Gun Hicks, The disciple** (15), *Hell's hinges, The Aryan, The captive god, The sheriff, The primal lure, The dawn maker, The silent man** (17),

Blue Blazes Rawden*, The tiger man* (18), Wild Bill Hickok (also scripted), Tumbleweeds.

237 Has, Wojciech, Polish director, b. 1923. Studied art. Film school. 1948-56: shorts (*The mouth organ* etc). Films: *The noose* 57; *Farewells* 58; *One room* 59; *Partings* 61; *How to be loved, Gold dreams* 62; *The Saragossa manuscript* 64; *The code* 66.

238 Hathaway, Henry, American director, b. 1898. From 1908: actor. 1921: assistant to F. Lloyd. Also produced some of his films. Main films: *Lives of a Bengal Lancer, Peter Ibbetson* 35; *Go West, young man, The trail of the Lonesome Pine* 36; *Souls at sea* 37; *Johnny Apollo* 40; *China girl* 42; *The house on 92nd Street* 45; *13 rue Madeleine* 46; *Kiss of death, Call Northside 777* 47; *The black rose* 50; *Rawhide, 14 hours* 51; *Niagara, White witch doctor* 53; *Prince Valiant* 54; *The racers* 55; *23 paces to Baker Street* 56; *Legend of the lost* 57; *Man hunt* 58; *Woman obsessed* 59; *Seven thieves, North to Alaska* 60; *How the West was won* (three ep.), *Circus world (The magnificent showman)* 63; *The sons of Katie Elder* 65; *Nevada Smith* 66; *Five card Stud* 68.

239 Hawks, Howard, American director, b. 1896. 1912-17: racing pilot. Scr. all his own films, often in coll., and *The thing.* Also producer of many of his own films* and *The thing.* Films: *The road to glory, Fig leaves** 26; *The cradle snatchers, Paid to love** 27; *A girl in every port*, Fazil, The air circus* (co. L. Seiler) 28; *Trent's last case* 29; *The dawn patrol* 30; *The criminal code** 31; *The crowd roars, Scarface, Tiger shark* 32;

*Today we live** 33; *Viva Villa!* (completed by J. Conway), *Twentieth century** 34; *Barbary coast* 35; *Ceiling zero, The road to glory* (remake of above), *Come and get it* (completed by Wyler) 36; *Bringing up baby** 38; *Only angels have wings**, *His girl Friday** 39; *The outlaw* (completed by Hughes) 40; *Sergeant York**, *Ball of fire* 41; *Air force** 43; *To have and have not** 44; *The big sleep** 46; *Red River** , *A song is born* 48; *I was a male war bride (You can't sleep here)* 49; *The big sky**,O. Henry's full house* (one ep.), *Monkey business* 52; *Gentlemen prefer blondes* 53; *Land of the Pharaohs** 55; *Rio Bravo** 58; *Hatari!** 61; *Man's favourite sport?** 63; *Red Line 7000** 65; *El Dorado** 66.

240 Hay, Will, British actor. 1888-1949. Many of his films were directed by M. Varnel*. Main films: *Those were the days, Boys will be boys, Good morning boys** (37), *Convict 99** (38), *Oh Mr. Porter*,! Old bones of the river** (39), *Ask a policeman** (41), *The black sheep of Whitehall, The goose steps out, My learned friend* (also co-dir. last three with Dearden).

241 Hayakawa, Sessue, Japanese actor, b. 1889. Since 1908: U.S.A. 1936-39: France. Main films: *For freedom of Cuba, The ambassador's envoy, The last of the line, The wrath of the gods, The typhoon, The cheat, Yoshiwara, Tempête sur l'Asie, Macao, l'enfer du jeu, Tokyo Joe, House of bamboo, The bridge on the River Kwai, The geisha boy, Green mansions.*

242 Hayworth, Rita, American actress, b. 1918. At first: vaudeville. Main films: *Only angels have wings,* *Susan and God, The strawberry blonde, Blood and sand, Tales of Manhattan, Cover girl, Gilda, The lady from Shanghai, The loves of Carmen, Salome, Fire down below, Pal Joey, Separate tables, They came to Cordura, The story on page one, Circus world (The magnificent showman).*

243 Hecht, Ben, American scriptwriter and director, 1894-1964. From 1911: journalist. From 1925: novelist. Main films as scriptwriter (sometimes co. C. MacArthur*): *Underworld, The great Gabbo, Scarface, Hallelujah I'm a bum, Design for living, Viva Villa!, Twentieth century, Barbary coast, Goldwyn Follies, Gunga Din**, *Wuthering Heights**, *His girl Friday,Nothing sacred, Lydia, Comrade X, Tales of Manhattan, The black swan, China girl, Spellbound**, *Notorious**, *Gilda, Kiss of death, The Paradine case, The miracle of the bells, Love happy, Ulisse, Whirlpool, Monkey business* (52), *The Indian fighter, A farewell to arms* (57), *Legend of the lost, Circus world* (co.). Main films as director and scriptwriter: *Crime without passion* 34; *The scoundrel* 35 (both co-dir. C. MacArthur); *Until I die* 40; *Spectre of the rose* 46; *Actors and sin* 52.

244 Heifitz, Josif, Russian director, b. 1905. Film school. Main films: *Baltic deputy* 37; *Member of the government* 40; *Her name is Sukhe-Bator* 42; *In the name of life* 47 (all co-dir. A. Zarkhi); *The big family* 54; *The Rumiantsev case* 56; *Lady with a little dog* 60; *Horizon* 62; *A day of happiness* 63; *In the town of "S"* 66.

245 Hellinger, Mark, American producer. 1903-47. Also scriptwriter:

Pierre Fresnay
Clark Gable
Abel Gance

Ava Gardner
Vittorio Gassman
Lillian Gish

Cary Grant
Wojciech Has
Robert Hamer

Howard Hawks
Audrey Hepburn
Katharine Hepburn

James Wong Howe
Trevor Howard
Alfred Hitchcock

Gene Kelly
Boris Karloff
Danny Kaye

Alberto Lattuada
Fritz Lang
Burt Lancaster

Gina Lollobrigida
Max Linder
Jerry Lewis

Broadway Bill, Comet over Broadway, The roaring twenties. Main films: It all came true, They drive by night, High sierra, Manpower, Moontide, The killers, Brute force, The naked city.

246 Hepburn, Audrey, American actress, b. 1929 in Belgium. At first stage actress in England. 1952: U.S.A. Main films: Laughter in paradise, The Lavender Hill mob, Roman holiday, Sabrina, War and peace, Funny face, Love in the afternoon, The nun's story, Green mansions, The unforgiven, Breakfast at Tiffany's, The children's hour (The loudest whisper), Charade, My fair lady, Paris when it sizzles, How to steal a million, Two for the road.

247 Hepburn, Katharine, American actress, b. 1909. Since 1928: also stage actress. Main films: A bill of divorcement, Morning glory, Little women, Alice Adams, Sylvia Scarlett, Mary of Scotland, A woman rebels, Quality Street, Stage door, Bringing up baby, Holiday, The Philadelphia story, The keeper of the flame, Woman of the year, Undercurrent, The sea of grass, State of the Union, Adam's rib, The African Queen, Pat and Mike, Summer madness, The rainmaker, Suddenly last summer, Long day's journey into night, Guess who's coming to dinner, The lion in winter.

248 Herrmann, Bernard, American composer, b. 1911. Also orchestral conductor. Main films: Citizen Kane, The magnificent Ambersons, Jane Eyre, The lodger (43), Hangover Square, The ghost and Mrs. Muir, On dangerous ground, Five fingers, The day the earth stood still, The snows of Kilimanjaro, White witch doctor, The Kentuckian, The trouble with Harry, The man who knew too much (56), The wrong man, A hatful of rain, The naked and the dead, Vertigo, North by Northwest, Psycho, Cape Fear, The birds, Tender is the night, Marnie, Fahrenheit 451, La mariée était en noir.

249 Hitchcock, Alfred, British director, b. 1899. At first scr., set-designer, and assistant on: Woman to woman, The white shadow, The passionate adventure, The blackguard, The prude's fall. Also scr. some of his own films†. Also produced many of his own films*. Since 1939: U.S.A. Since 1955: also TV producer. Films: Number thirteen (unfinished)* 22; The pleasure garden 25; The mountain eagle, The lodger† 26; Downhill, Easy virtue, The ring† 27; The farmer's wife†, Champagne 28; Harmony heaven, The manxman, Blackmail† 29; Elstree calling, Juno and the paycock†, Murder 30; The skin game† 31; Rich and strange, Number seventeen 32; Waltzes from Vienna 33; The man who knew too much 34; The thirty-nine steps 35; The secret agent, Sabotage (A woman alone) 36; Young and innocent (A girl was young) 37; The lady vanishes 38; Jamaica Inn 39; Rebecca, Foreign correspondent 40; Mr. and Mrs. Smith, Suspicion 41; Saboteur 42; Shadow of a doubt, Life boat 43; Bon voyage, Aventure Malgache (both shorts) 44; Spellbound 45; Notorious* 46; The Paradine case 47; Rope 48; Under Capricorn 49; Stage fright* 50; Strangers on a train *51; I confess* 52; Dial M for murder*, Rear window* 54; To catch a thief* 55; The trouble with Harry*, The man who knew too much* (remake of above) 56; The wrong man* 57; Vertigo* 58; North by Northwest*

59; *Psycho** 60; *The birds** 61; *Marnie**
64; *Torn curtain** 66.

250 **Holliday, Judy,** American actress, 1923-65. At first music hall and
cabaret dancer. Main films: *Winged
victory, Adam's rib, Born yesterday, The
marrying kind, It should happen to you,
Phffft, The solid gold Cadillac, Full of
life, Bells are ringing.*

251 **Holt, Seth,** British director, b.
1923 (in Palestine). 1942-54: editor.
1959-60: TV producer. Films: *Nowhere
to go* 58; *Taste of fear* 61; *Station Six
Sahara* 62; *The nanny* 65; *Escape route,
People who make no noise are dangerous*
67.

252 **Hope, Bob,** American actor, b.
1903 in England. Since 1927: also stage
and revue actor. Main films: *The big
broadcast of 1938, The cat and the canary, The road to Singapore, The princess
and the pirate, The paleface, Road to
Bali, The private navy of Sgt. O'Farrell.*

253 **Houseman, John,** American
producer, b. 1902 in Rumania. 1925:
U.S.A. Since 1932: also stage producer.
Also TV producer. Acted: *Seven days in
May.* Main films: *Jane Eyre* (associate
prod.), *Letter from an unknown woman,
They live by night, On dangerous ground,
The bad and the beautiful, Julius Caesar,
Executive suite, Moonfleet, The cobweb,
Lust for life, All fall down, Two weeks in
another town.*

254 **Howard, Leslie,** British actor.
1893-1943. 1917-36: stage actor. Main
films: *A free soul, Secrets, Never the
twain shall meet, Smilin' through, Of
human bondage, The scarlet pimpernel,*
The petrified forest, Romeo and Juliet
(36), *It's love I'm after, Pygmalion, Intermezzo, a love story, Gone with the
wind, Pimpernel Smith* (also dir., 41),
*49th Parallel, The first of the few (Spit-
fire)* (also dir., 42).

255 **Howard, Trevor,** British actor,
b. 1916. Since 1933: also stage actor.
Main films: *The way ahead, The way to
the stars, Brief encounter, They made me
a fugitive, Passionate friends, The third
man, Odette, The outcast of the islands,
The heart of the matter, Cockleshell
heroes, Around the world in 80 days,
Manuela, The key* (58), *The roots of
heaven, Sons and lovers, Moment of
danger, Mutiny on the Bounty* (62), *The
lion, The saboteur — code name Morituri, The liquidator, The charge of the
Light Brigade.*

256 **Howe, James Wong,** American
director of photography, b. 1899 in
China. Since 1904: U.S.A. At first
boxer. 1917: assistant. Main films: *The
trail of the Lonesome Pine, Mantrap, The
criminal code, Chandu the magician,
Walking down Broadway, Viva Villa!,
Mark of the vampire, Manhattan melodrama, The thin man, Fire over England,
Under the red robe* (co. Périnal), *The
prisoner of Zenda* (37), *The adventures of
Tom Sawyer, Comet over Broadway, They
made me a criminal, The Oklahoma Kid,
Daughters courageous, Dr. Ehrlich's
magic bullet, The strawberry blonde,
King's Row, Yankee doodle dandy, Hang-
men also die, Air force, The North Star,
Confidential agent, Objective Burma!,
Pursued, Body and soul, The baron of
Arizona, The brave bulls, Come back,
little Sheba, The rose tattoo, Picnic,
Sweet smell of success, The old man and*

the sea, Bell book and candle, Song without end, The story on page one, Hud, The outrage, Seconds, This property is condemned, Hombre.

257 Hubley, John, American animator, b. 1914. At first worked for U.P.A. See *animation.* Main films: *The magic fluke* 45; *Hat hatting, Robin Hoodlum* 46; *Fuddy duddy buddy, Ragtime bear* 49; *Trouble indemnity* 50; *Sloppy jalopy* 51; *Rooty toot toot* 52; *The fourposter* 53; *Adventures of an asterisk* 57; *The tender game, Harlem Wednesday, A date with Dizzy* 58; *Seven lively arts* 59; *Moonbird* 60; *Of stars and men* 61; *The hole* 62; *The hat* 64; *Herb Alpert and the Tijuana Brass Double Feature* 66; *Gulliver's troubles* 67.

258 Hughes, Howard, American producer, b. 1905. Since 1935: also aviator. Producer since 1927. Main films: *Hell's angels* (also dir., 30), *Front page, Scarface, The outlaw* (also dir., 40; started by Hawks), *The racket, Jet pilot, Double dynamite, Macao, Two tickets to Broadway, Montana Belle.*

259 Huston, John, American director, b. 1906. At first boxer, actor. Since 1939: also stage producer. Scripted: *The amazing Dr. Clitterhouse, Juarez, Dr. Ehrlich's magic bullet, High sierra, Sergeant York, The stranger* (co.) and most of his own films. Acted: *The cardinal* and *. Films: *The Maltese falcon* 41; *In this our life* 42; *Across the Pacific, Report from the Aleutians* (army documentary) 43; *The battle of San Pietro* (army doc.) 44; *Let there be light* (army doc.) 45; *Treasure of Sierra Madre* 47; *Key Largo* 48; *We were strangers* 49; *The asphalt jungle* 50;

The red badge of courage, The African Queen 51; *Moulin Rouge* 52; *Beat the devil* 54; *Moby Dick* 55; *Heaven knows Mr. Allison* 56; *The barbarian and the geisha* 57; *The roots of heaven* 58; *The unforgiven* 59; *The misfits* 60; *Freud (The secret passion)* 62; *The list of Adrian Messenger* 63; *Night of the Iguana* 64; *The Bible . . . in the beginning* 66; *Casino Royale* (one ep.), *Reflections in a golden eye, Sinful Davey* 67.

I

260 Ichikawa, Kon, Japanese director, b. 1915. At first animator. Also co-scr. some of his own films*. Main films: *A girl at Dojo Temple* (full length puppet film) 45; *365 nights* 48; *The woman who touched the legs* 52; *Mr. Poo* 53; *The Burmese harp, Punishment room* 56; *The hole, The men of Tohoku* 57; *Conflagration, Goodbye, good day* 58; *The key (Odd obsession)*, Fires on the plain* 59; *Bonchi*, A woman's testament (Code of women)* (one ep.), *Her brother* 60; *The sin, Being two isn't easy* 62; *An actor's revenge, My enemy the sea (Alone on the Pacific)* 63; *Tokyo Olympiad* 65; *Hey! buddy* 66; *Topo Gigio e i sei ladre* (partly animated; in Italy) 67.

261 Imai, Tadashi, Japanese director, b. 1912. Also scriptwriter. Main films: *The suicide troops of the watchtower* 42; *An enemy of the people* 46; *Blue mountains* 47; *Until the day we meet again* 50; *And yet we live* 51; *Muddy waters, The tower of lilies* 53; *Here is a spring* 55; *Shadows in sunlight (or Dark-*

ness at noon) 56; *Men of the rice fields, The story of a pure love* 57; *The adulteress* 58; *Kiku and Isamu, The cliff* 59; *Pan-chopali* 61; *Bushido Zankoku monogatari* 62; *A story from Echigo* 64; *When the cookie crumbles* 67.

262 Ince, Thomas, American director. 1882-1924. From 1899: stage and music hall actor. 1911: directed first Westerns. Main films: *For freedom of Cuba, Custer's last fight* 12; *The ambassador's envoy* 13; *The last of the line, The wrath of the gods, The battle of Gettysburg, The typhoon* 14; *The despoiler* 15; *Civilisation* 16. Ince also produced and closely supervised several hundred films by other directors, among whom were William Hart (q.v.) and Reginald Barker: *Blue Blazes Rawden; The passing of Two Gun Hicks* 13; *The fugitive* 14; *The bargain, The coward* 15; *Hell's hinges, The Aryan, The captive god* 16; *Golden Rule Kate* 17; *Carmen of the Klondike* 18.

263 Ingram, Rex, American director, b. 1892 in Ireland, d. 1950. 1911: U.S.A. 1926: France, where he founded his own studio and continued to make films for U.S.A. Main films: *The great problem* 16; *The four horsemen of the Apocalypse* 21; *The conquering power, The prisoner of Zenda* 22; *Where the pavement ends, Scaramouche* 23; *Mare nostrum, The magician* 26; *The garden of Allah* 27; *The three passions* 29; *Baroud* (also acted) 32.

264 Ivens, Joris, Dutch director of documentaries, b. 1898. 1940-45: U.S.A. Scr. or co-scr. nearly all his films. Films: *The bridge* 28; *Rain, The breakers* 29; *We are building, Zuyder-*

zee 30; *Industrial symphony, Creosote* 31; *Komsomol* (in U.S.S.R.) 32; *Borinage* (in Belg.) 33; *New earth* 34; *Spanish earth* (in Spain) 37; *The 400 millions* (in China) 39; *The power and the land* 40; *Our Russian front* (co. Milestone) 41; *Action stations* (in Canada) 42; *Know your enemy: Japan* (co. Capra) 45; *Indonesia calling* (in Australia) 46; *The first years* 47; *Peace will overcome* 50 (last two in Poland); *Friendship will overcome* (co. I. Pyriev; in U.S.S.R.) 51; *The drive for peace* (in Poland) 52; *The song of the rivers* (in E. Germany) 53; *La Seine a rencontré Paris* (in France) 57; *Letters from China, The war of the 600 million people* 58 (both in China); *Demain à Nanguila* (in Mali), *Carnet de viaje, Pueblo en armas* (last two in Cuba) 60; *A Valparaiso, El circo mas pequeno del mundo* (last two in Peru) 63; *Mistral* (in France: unfinished) 64; *Rotterdam — Europoort, The threatening sky* (in Vietnam) 66; *Loin du Viêtnam* (in coll.) 67.

J

265 Jancsó, Miklós, Hungarian director, b. 1921. Film school. See *new cinema:* Hungary. Main shorts: *In the outskirts of the city* 57; *Immortality* 59; *The wheel of time* 61. Films: *The bells have gone to Rome* 58; *The stars* (one ep.) 60; *Cantata* 63; *My way home* 64; *The round-up* 65; *Internationalists* 67; *Silence and cry* 68.

266 Jannings, Emil, German actor. 1884-1950. From 1914: also stage actor, worked under Reinhardt. 1926-

30: U.S.A. Main films: *Wenn Vier dasselbe tun, Das fidele Gefängnis, The eyes of the mummy, Madame Dubarry, Kohlhiesel's daughters, Deception, The loves of Pharaoh, Vendetta, Othello* (22), *Waxworks, Quo vadis?* (25), *The last laugh, Tartuffe, Variété, Faust, The way of all flesh, The street of sin, The last command, The patriot, The blue angel* (30), *Stürme der Leidenschaft, Der Herrscher.*

267 Jarre, Maurice, French composer, b. 1924. Also composer for theatre. Main films: *Hôtel des Invalides, Toute la mémoire du monde, Le bel indifférent, La tête contre les murs, Les yeux sans visage, Crack in the mirror, Lawrence of Arabia, The longest day, Recours en grâce, The big gamble, Plein feux sur l'assassin, Les oliviers de la justice, Thérèse Desqueyroux, Les dimanches de Ville d'Avray, Mourir à Madrid, Judex, Behold a pale horse, The train, Un roi sans divertissement, Dr. Zhivago, The collector, Grand Prix, The professionals, Paris brûle-t-il?, Night of the generals.*

268 Jasny, Vojtech, Czechoslovakian director, b. 1925. 1953-58: shorts in collaboration with Kachyna. Films: *September nights* 58; *Desire* 59; *I survived my death* 60; *The pilgrimage to the virgin* 61; *One day a cat* 62; *The chimneysweep and the weathercocks* 64; *The pipes* 65.

269 Jennings, Humphrey, British director of documentaries. 1907-50. At first art and literary critic. 1934: joined Grierson (q.v.) on G.P.O. Film Unit. See *free cinema.* Films: *Birth of a robot* (co-dir. L. Lye; see *animation*) 36; *The first days* (co-dir. Watt and P. Jackson),

Spare time, An unrecorded victory, Speaking from America, Her last trip 39; *London can take it* (co-dir. Watt); *Welfare of the workers* 40; *Words for battle, Heart of Britain, Listen to Britain* 41; *The silent village, Fires were started* 43; *The story of Lilli Marlene* 44; *A diary for Timothy, A defeated people* 45; *The Cumberland story* 47; *Dim little island* 49; *Family portrait* 50.

270 Jessua, Alain, French director, b. 1932. Assistant to Becker, Ophüls, Y. Allégret, and Carné. Short: *Léon la Lune* 56. Films: *La vie à l'envers* 64; *Jeu de massacre* 66.

271 Jouvet, Louis, French actor. 1887-1951. 1907-51: also stage actor and producer, and theatre director. 1939-45: Switzerland and South America. Main films: *Topaze* (32), *Knock* (34), *La Kermesse héroïque, Les basfonds, Mister Flow, Mademoiselle Docteur, Un carnet de bal, Drôle de drame, Forfaiture, L'alibi, La Marseillaise, Le drame de Shanghai, Entrée des artistes, Untel père et fils, Hôtel du Nord, La fin du jour, Volpone, La charrette fantôme, Un revenant, Quai des orfèvres, Miquette et sa mère, Entre 11 heures et minuit, Knock* (remake of above 50.)

272 Jurgens, Curt, German actor, b. 1912. Since 1936: also stage actor. Main films: *Zu neuen Ufern, Prämien auf den Tod* (also co-scripted with K. Heuse and directed, 50), *Gangsterpremiere* (also co-scripted with F. Griebitz and directed, 51), *Das Bekenntnis der Ina Kahr, The devil's general, Die Ratten, Les héros son fatigués, Et Dieu créa la femme, Ohne Dich wird es Nacht* (also directed, 56), *Oeil pour oeil, Bitter* victory, Les espions, This happy feeling, Me and the colonel, The inn of the sixth happiness, The blue angel (59), I aim at the stars, The longest day, Lord Jim, Psyche 59, Château en Suède.

K

273 Kachyna, Karel, Czechoslovakian director, b. 1924. Film school. 1953-58: shorts with Jasny. Films: Trials and tribulations 62; Vertigo, Hope 63; The big wall 64; Long live the republic! 65; The car 66; The night of the nun 67.

274 Kalatozov, Mikhail, Russian director, b. 1903. From 1927: editor and cameraman. Main films: Salt for Svanetia 30; A nail in the boot 32; Manhood 39; Valeri Chkalov (or Wings of victory) 41; Invincible (co-dir. Gerasimov) 43; Conspiracy of the doomed 50; True friends 54; The first echelon, The cranes are flying 57; The letter that was not sent 60; Here is Cuba! 63.

275 Kanin, Garson, American director and scriptwriter, b. 1912. Since 1933: also stage actor and producer. Main films as scriptwriter: A double life, Adam's rib, Born yesterday, The marrying kind, Pat and Mike, It should happen to you, The girl can't help it, High Time, The rat race. Main films as director: A man to remember, Next time I marry 38; The great man votes, Bachelor mother 39; My favourite wife, They knew what they wanted 40; Tom, Dick and Harry 41; The true glory (doc., co-dir. C. Reed) 45.

276 Karloff, Boris, Actor, b. 1887 in England. Since 1909: U.S.A. Also TV actor. Main films: The criminal code, Frankenstein, The mummy, The old dark house, Scarface, Night world, The mask of Fu-Manchu, The black cat, The lost patrol, Son of Frankenstein, Black Friday, The walking dead, The body snatcher, Black Sunday, Unconquered, I tre volti della paura, The terror, The comedy of terrors, The raven.

277 Kaufman, Boris, Director of photography, b. in Poland. Brother of Dziga Vertov. 1929-42: France. Since 1942: U.S.A. Main films: La marche des machines, A propos de Nice, Taris, Zéro de conduite, L'Atalante, Journey into medicine, Terribly talented, On the waterfront, Patterns (Patterns of power), Baby doll, Twelve angry men, That kind of woman, The fugitive kind, Splendour in the grass, Long day's journey into night, The world of Henry Orient, The pawnbroker, The group, Bye bye, Braverman.

278 Käutner, Helmut, German director, b. 1908. Since 1931: also stage actor and producer. Main films: Kleider machen Leute 40; Auf Wiedersehen Franziska 41; Wir machen Musik 42; Romanze in Moll 43; In jenen tagen 47; Der Apfel ist ab 48; Die letzte Brücke 54; The devil's general 55; Der Hauptmann von Köpenick, Ein Mädchen aus Flandern 56; The wonderful years 58; The rest is silence 59; Black gravel 61; The redhead 62; Das Haus in Montevideo 64.

279 Kawalerowicz, Jerzy, Polish director, b. 1922. From 1947: assistant, then scriptwriter. Films: The community (co-dir. K. Sumerski) 51; Under the Phrygian Star (pts. I. & II.) 53-54; The shadow 56; The real end of the Great War 57; Night train 59; The devil and the nun 60; Pharaoh 64.

280 Kaye, Danny, American actor, b. 1913. Since 1940: also stage actor and dancer. Main films: The wonder man, The kid from Brooklyn, The secret life of Walter Mitty, A song is born, The inspector general, On the Riviera, Hans Christian Andersen, Knock on wood, White Christmas, The court jester, Merry Andrew, Me and the colonel, Five pennies, The man from the Diners' Club.

281 Kazan, Elia, American director, b. 1909 in Istanbul. 1913: U.S.A. 1933-40: stage and film actor. Since 1940: also stage producer. Films: A tree grows in Brooklyn 44; The sea of grass, Boomerang 46; Gentleman's agreement 47; Pinky (started by Ford) 49; Panic in the streets, A streetcar named Desire 50; Viva Zapata! 51; Man on a tightrope 52; On the waterfront, East of Eden 54; Baby doll, A face in the crowd 56; Wild river, Splendour in the grass 60; America, America (The Anatolian smile) 63; The arrangement 68.

282 Keaton, Buster, American actor and director, 1896-1966. 1900-17: vaudeville actor with his parents. Main films as actor: A reckless Romeo, The saphead, College, Steamboat Bill junior, The cameraman, Spite marriage, Hollywood Revue of 1929, Free and easy, Dough boys, Parlor bedroom and bath, Buster se marie (French version of latter film), Sidewalks of New York, Speak easily, The passionate plumber, What! No beer?, The gold ghost, Le roi

des Champs Elysées, Mooching through Georgia, Pardon my berth marks, She's oil mine, Forever and a day, Sunset Boulevard, Limelight, Around the world in 80 days, It's a mad, mad, mad, mad world, Pajama party, The railrodder, Film, A funny thing happened on the way to the forum. Films as actor and director: One week, The scarecrow, Neighbours 20; The haunted house, Hard luck, The high sign, The goat, The playhouse, The boat, The paleface 21; Cops, The electric house, My wife's relations, The frozen North, The blacksmith, Daydreams 22; The balloonatic, The love nest, The three ages, Our hospitality 23; Sherlock Junior, The navigator 24; Seven chances, Go West 25; Battling butler, The general 26.

283 Kelly, Gene, American actor, dancer, and director, b. 1912. Choreographer of most of his own films. Also worked in TV. Main films as actor: For me and my gal, Cover girl, Ziegfeld Follies, Thousands cheer, Anchors aweigh, The pirate, Take me out to the ball game, An American in Paris, Brigadoon, Les Girls, The three musketeers (48), Inherit the wind, What a way to go!, Les demoiselles de Rochefort and all his own films except*. Films as director: On the town (co-dir. Donen) 49; Singin' in the rain (co-dir. Donen) 51; Invitation to the dance 52; It's always fair weather (co-dir. Donen) 55; The happy road 56; The tunnel of love* 58; Gigot* 62; A guide for the married man* 67; Hello, Dolly!* 68.

284 Kershner, Irvin, American director. Also TV producer. Films: Stake out on Dope Street (also co-scripted) 58; The young captives 59; The hoodlum priest 61; A face in the rain 62; The luck of Ginger Coffey 63; A fine madness 66; The flim-flam man (One born every minute) 67.

285 Khutsiev, Marlen, Russian director, b. 1925. 1955: assistant to Barnet. Films: Spring in Zaretchnaia Street 56; The two Fedors 59; Ilitch's suburb (I am twenty) 63; Rain in July 66.

286 King, Henry, American director, b. 1888. 1909-17: vaudeville, stage and film actor. Main films: $23^1/_2$ hours' leave 19; Tol'able David 21; The white sister 23; Romola 24; Stella Dallas 25; The winning of Barbara Worth 26; The magic flame 27; Hell Harbor 30; The woman in Room 13 32; Carolina, Maria Galante 34; Way down East 35; Lloyds of London 36; Seventh heaven, In old Chicago 37; Alexander's Ragtime Band 38; Jesse James, Stanley and Livingstone 39; Chad Hanna 40; The black swan 42; The song of Bernadette 44; Prince of foxes 49; Twelve o'clock high, The gunfighter 50; I'd climb the highest mountain, David and Bethsheba 51; The snows of Kilimanjaro 57; Beloved infidel 59; Tender is the night 61.

287 Kinoshita, Keisuke, Japanese director, b. 1912. At first still photographer. Assistant to Shimazu. Main films: The living Sugoroku, The blossoming port 43; The girl I loved, A morning with the Osone family 46; Marriage 47; Apostasy 48; Broken drum, The Yotsuya ghost story 49; Carmen comes home 51; Carmen's pure love 52; A Japanese tragedy 53; The garden of women, Twenty four eyes 54; She was like a daisy 55; Clouds at twilight 56; The lighthouse, Danger stalks near (Candle in the wind) 57; Legend of Nayarama, The eternal rainbow 58; Snow flurry, Thus another day, Sekishuncho 59; Spring dreams 60; The River Fuefuki, The bitter spirit 61; New Year's love, Ballad of a workman 62; A legend . . . or was it? 63; The scent of incense 64; Eyes, the sea, and a ball 66.

288 Kinugasa, Teinosuke, Japanese director, b. 1898. 1917-22: actor. Main films: A crazy page 26; Crossways 28; Before dawn 31; Kimpei from Koina, Two stone lanterns 33; The summer battle of the Osaka 37; Lord for a night 46; Actress 47; Gate of hell 53; Naruto hicho 57; Symphony of love, A woman of Osaka, The white heron 58; Joen, Stop the old fox! 59; Uta-andon 60: The little runaway (co. B. Nkandorovitch) 66.

289 Kobayashi, Masaki, Japanese director, b. 1916. Assistant to Kinoshita. Films: I'll buy you, Room with thick walls 56; Black river 57; Ningen no Joken (trilogy) (No greater love 57; Road to eternity 59; A soldier's prayer 60); The inheritance 61; Harakiri 62; Kwaidan 64; Rebellion 67.

290 Komeda, Krzysztof, Polish composer. Main films: Two men and a wardrobe, When angels fall, Le gros et le maigre, Knife in the water, Innocent sorcerers, See you tomorrow, Mammals, Les plus belles escroqueries du monde (Polanski ep.), Walkover, Cul-de-sac, Hunger, Barrier, Le départ, People meet and sweet music fills the heart.

291 Korda, Alexander, Director and producer, b. 1893 in Hungary, d. 1956 in England. 1914-19: dir. films in Hungary. 1927-30: U.S.A. From 1931: England. Main films as producer:

Catherine the Great, The ghost goes West, Things to come, Under the red robe, To be or not to be, The Scarlet Pimpernel, Elephant boy, The drum, Sanders of the river, Knight without armour, Four feathers, The thief of Bagdad, Lydia, The jungle book, Anna Karenina (48), The fallen idol, The third man, Cry the beloved country!, The outcast of the islands, The sound barrier, The man between, Richard III, and most of the films he directed. Main films as director: Madame wants no children (in Germ.) 26; Marius (in France) 31; The girl from Maxim's, The private life of Henry VIII 33; The private life of Don Juan 34; Rembrandt 37; Conquest of the air 40; Lady Hamilton (That Hamilton woman) 41; Perfect strangers 45; An ideal husband 48.

292 Korda, Zoltan, Director, b. 1895 in Hungary, d. 1961 in England. Brother of above. From 1933: England. 1940-48: U.S.A. Main films: Sanders of the river 35; Elephant boy (interiors; exteriors R. Flaherty) 37; The drum 38; Four feathers 39; The thief of Bagdad (co. Powell) 40; The jungle book 42; Sahara 43; The Macomber affair 47; Cry the beloved country! (African fury) 52.

293 Kosma, Joseph, Composer, b. 1905 in Hungary. Since 1933: France. Main films: Le crime de Monsieur Lange, Jenny, La grande illusion, La bête humaine, Les visiteurs du soir, Adieu Léonard, Les enfants du paradis, Une partie de campagne, Les portes de la nuit, Voyage surprise, Juliette ou la clé des songes, Les amants de Vérone, Le sang des bêtes, Calle Mayor, Cela s'appelle l'aurore, La bergère et le ramoneur, Le port du désir, Eléna et les hommes, La chatte, Le déjeuner sur l'herbe, Le huitième jour, Le testament du Docteur Cordelier, La poupée, In the French style.

294 Kozintsev, Grigori, Russian director, b. 1905. 1922: founded FEX (q.v.) with Leonid Trauberg and Yutkevitch. Also stage producer. Main films in collaboration with Trauberg: The adventures of Oktyabrina 24; The devil's wheel, The cloak 26; Bratishka, The club of the big deed 27; The new Babylon 29; Alone 31; The youth of Maxim 35; The return of Maxim 37; The Vyborg Side 39; Incident in a telegraph office (short) 41; Plain people 45 (released in 56). Films by Kozintsev alone: Pirogov 47; Bielinsky 53; Don Quixote 57; Hamlet (pts. I and II) 63-64.

295 Kramer, Stanley, American producer and director, b. 1913. From 1933: editor and scriptwriter. Since 1942: producer (1949-55: for Columbia). Main films as producer: The moon and sixpence, Home of the brave, Champion, The men, High noon, Death of a salesman, The sniper, The wild one, Member of the wedding, The Caine mutiny, A child is waiting. Films as director and producer: Not as a stranger 55; The pride and the passion 57; The defiant ones 58; On the beach 59; Inherit the wind 60; Judgment at Nuremberg 61; It's a mad, mad, mad, mad world 63; Ship of fools 64; Guess who's coming to dinner 67.

296 Krasker, Robert, Australian director of photography, b. 1913. 1926: France. Since 1930: England. Assistant to Périnal. Main films: Henry V, The rising of the moon, Brief encounter, Odd man out, The third man, Cry the beloved country!, Romeo and Juliet (54), Alexander the Great, Senso (begun by Aldo), Trapeze, The criminal, The golden virgin, The quiet American, Billy Budd, Guns of darkness, The fall of the Roman Empire, Romanoff and Juliet, The collector (co.), The heroes of Telemark.

297 Krasna, Norman, American scriptwriter, b. 1909. Main films: Hands across the table, Fury, The king and the chorus-girl (co.), The big city, You and me, Bachelor mother, The devil and Miss Jones, The flame of New Orleans, Mr. and Mrs. Smith, Princess O'Rourke (also directed, 43), White Christmas, The ambassador's daughter (also directed, 56), Indiscreet, My geisha, Let's make love, Sunday in New York.

298 Krauss, Werner, German actor, 1884-1959. 1907-57: also stage actor. Main films: The cabinet of Dr. Caligari, Scherben, Othello, Der brennende Acker, Der Schatz, Lady Hamilton, Waxworks, The joyless street, Tartuffe, Secrets of a soul, Nana, Napoléon auf St. Helena, Jud Süss, Paracelsus.

299 Krejcik, Jiri, Czechoslovakian director, b. 1918. At first scriptwriter. Main films: Conscience 48; Awakening 59; A higher principle 61; Labyrinth of the heart, Midnight mass 62; The boarding house for bachelors 66.

300 Kristl, Vlado, Jugoslavian director, b. 1923. At first actor and painter. Some of his shorts are animated* (see animation: Jugoslavia). Since 1963: W. Germany. See new cinema: W. Germany. Shorts: The theft of jewels* 59; Peau de chagrin* 60; Don Quixote* 61; The general 62; Arme Leute, Madeleine-Madeleine 63; Autorennen, Maulwürfe 64; Prometheus* 65; Das Land des Überflusses* 67. Films: The dam 64; The letter 66.

301 Kubrick, Stanley, American director, b. 1928. At first journalist. Also scr. some of his films*. Also photographed and edited some of his films†. Shorts: Day of the fight, Flying padre 51. Since 1962: England. Films: Fear and desire†* 53; Killer's kiss†* 55; The killing* 56; Paths of glory* 58; Spartacus 60; Lolita 62; Dr. Strangelove, or how I learned to stop worrying and love the bomb* 63; 2001 — a space Odyssey 68.

302 Kuleshov, Lev, Russian director, b. 1899. From 1916: set-designer. 1922: founded an 'experimental laboratory', with Pudovkin and others as pupils. Now teacher at Moscow film school. Main films: Engineer Prite's project 18; On the Red Front 20; The extraordinary adventures of Mr. West in the land of the Bolsheviks 24; The death ray 25; By the law 26; Your acquaintance 27; The great consoler 33.

303 Kuri, Yoji, Japanese animator, b. 1928. Also producer of animated films. Main films: Human zoo (Clap vocalism) 60; Fantasia of stamps, Here and there 61; Locus, Love, The button, The chair 63; Man, woman and dog, Aos, Ring ring boy 64; The window, The man next door, Samurai 65; Little murmur, The eggs 66; Au fou 67.

304 Kurosawa, Akira, Japanese director, b. 1910. Art studies. At first scriptwriter. Films: The legend of Judo

43; *Most beautifully* 44; *Walkers on tigers' tails* 45; *Those who make our tomorrows* (co-dir. K. Yamamoto), *No regrets for my youth* 46; *Wonderful Sunday* 47; *Drunken angel* 48; *The silent duel*, *Stray dog* 49; *Scandal*, *Rashomon* 50; *The idiot* 51; *Living* 52; *Seven Samurai* 54; *I live in fear* 55; *The lower depths*, *The throne of blood* 57; *Hidden fortress* 58; *The bad sleep well* 59; *Yojimbo* 61; *Sanjuro*, *High and low* 62; *Red beard* 64; *Tora, tora, tora* 67.

305 Kutz, Kazimierz, Polish director, b. 1929. Film school. From 1954: assistant to Wajda and Kawalerowicz. Films: *The cross of valour* 59; *No one cries out* 60; *Panic on a train* 61; *Wild horses* 62; *Silence* 63; *Heat* 64; *A girl has disappeared* 66.

306 Kyo, Machiko, Japanese actress, b. 1924. 1936-49: dancer. Main films: *Clothes of deception*, *Rashomon*, *Older brother, younger sister*, *Ugetsu monogatari*, *Gate of hell*, *Street of shame*, *The teahouse of the August Moon*, *Marriageable age*, *Yang Kwei Fei*, *Princess Sen*, *A design for dying*, *The hole*, *Night butterflies*, *A woman of Osaka*, *Goodbye, good day*, *The key*, *Bonchi*, *The face of another*, *The little runaway*.

L

307 Lancaster, Burt, American actor, b. 1913. Up to 1940: circus acrobat. Also produced, with Harold Hecht: *Marty*, *Bachelor party*, and*. Main films: *The killers*, *Brute force*, *Sorry wrong number*, *Criss-cross*, *Rope of sand*, *The crimson pirate**, *Come back little Sheba*, *From here to eternity*, *Apache**, *Vera Cruz**, *The rose tattoo*, *The Kentuckian** (also directed, 55), *Trapeze*, *The rainmaker*, *Gunfight at the O.K. Corral*, *Sweet smell of success**, *The devil's disciple**, *Run silent, run deep**, *Separate tables**, *The unforgiven**, *Elmer Gantry*, *The young savages**, *Judgment at Nuremberg*, *Birdman of Alcatraz**, *The leopard*, *Seven days in May*, *The train*, *A child is waiting*, *The Hallelujah trail*, *The professionals*, *The scalphunters*.

308 Lang, Charles, (jr.) American director of photography, b. 1902. Main films: *A farewell to arms*, *Mississippi*, *Lives of a Bengal Lancer*, *Peter Ibbetson*, *Desire*, *Angel*, *You and me*, *Zaza* (39), *A foreign affair*, *The big carnival* (*Ace in the hole*), *Sudden fear*, *The big heat*, *Sabrina*, *It should happen to you*, *The man from Laramie*, *Wild is the wind*, *Autumn leaves*, *The solid gold Cadillac*, *The rainmaker*, *Gunfight at the O.K. Corral*, *Separate tables*, *One eyed jacks*, *Last train from Gun Hill*, *The magnificent seven*, *How the West was won* (one ep.), *Charade*, *Paris when it sizzles*, *Sex and the single girl*, *How to steal a million*, *The flim-flam man*.

309 Lang, Fritz, Austrian director, b. 1890. 1908: art studies in Vienna, Munich, and Paris. See *expressionism*. 1936-58: U.S.A. Acted: *Le mépris*. Scr.: *Die Hochzeit im Exzentrik Klub*, *Hilde Warren und der Tod*, *Pest in Florenz*, *Die Frau mit den Orchiden*, *Das Indische Grabmal* (21). Films: *Halbblut*, *Der Herr der Liebe*, *Die Spinnen* (two pts.: *Der Goldene See* and *Das Brillantenschiff*) 19; *Das wandernde Bild* 20;

Vier um die Frau, Der müde Tod 21; *Dr. Mabuse, the gambler* 22; *The Nibelungen* (two pts.: *The death of Siegfried,* and *Kriemhild's revenge*) 24; *Metropolis* 26; *Spione, Die Frau im Mond* 28; *M, The last will of Dr. Mabuse* 32; *Liliom* (in France) 34; *Fury* 36; *You only live once* 37; *You and me* 38; *The return of Frank James* 40; *Western Union, Man Hunt, Confirm or deny* (completed by Mayo) 41; *Hangmen also die* 42; *The ministry of fear* 43; *The woman in the window* 44; *Scarlet Street* 45; *Cloak and dagger* 46; *The secret beyond the door* 48; *House by the river, An American guerilla in the Philippines (I shall return)* 50; *Rancho Notorious, Clash by night* 51; *The blue gardenia* 52; *The big heat* 53; *Human desire* 54; *Moonfleet* 55; *While the city sleeps, Beyond a reasonable doubt* 56; *Der Tiger von Eschnapur, Das indische Grabmal* (edited together into *The tigress of Bengal*) 58; *The 1000 eyes of Dr. Mabuse* 60 (last three in W. Germany).

310 Langdon, Harry, American actor. 1884-1944. 1894-1923: vaudeville actor. 1924-26: short comedies for Sennett. Main films: *The strong man, Tramp, tramp, tramp, Long pants, Three's a crowd, The chaser, Heart rouble* (also directed last three 28), *Hallelujah I'm a bum, There goes my heart.*

311 Lassally, Walter, British director of photography, b. 1926 in Berlin. See *free cinema*. Main films: *Thursday's children, Another sky, A girl in black, Every day except Christmas, A matter of dignity, Momma don't allow, Together* (in collaboration), *We are the Lambeth boys, Our last spring, The day shall dawn, Beat girl, Electra, A taste of honey, The loneliness of the long distance runner, Tom Jones, Zorba the Greek, Psyche 59, The day the fish came out, Joanna.*

312 Lattuada, Alberto, Italian director, b. 1914. At first writer. Scripted in collaboration: *Piccolo mondo antico* (also assistant), and*. See *neo-realism*. Main films: *Il bandito* 46; *Senza pietà* 48; *Luci del varietà* (co-dir. Fellini) 50; *Anna* 51; *Il cappotto* 52; *La lupa, Amore in città* (one episode) 53; *Guendalina* 57; *La tempesta** 58; *I dolci inganni, Lettere di una novizia** 60; *L'imprevisto* 61; *La steppa* 62; *Mafioso* 63; *La Mandragola* 65; *L'amante di Gramigna, Matchless** 66; *Don Giovanni in Sicilia* 67; *Fräulein Doktor* 68.

313 Laughton, Charles, British actor. 1899-1962. 1926-62: also stage actor and producer. 1939: U.S.A. Film as director only: *The night of the hunter* 55. Main films: *Piccadilly, The old dark house, If I had a million* (Lubitsch ep.), *The sign of the cross, The private life of Henry VIII, The Barretts of Wimpole Street, Ruggles of Red Gap, Mutiny on the Bounty* (35), *Les misérables* (35), *Rembrandt, I Claudius* (unfinished), *Jamaica Inn, The hunchback of Notre Dame, They knew what they wanted, Tales of Manhattan, This land is mine, The Canterville ghost, The suspect, Arch of triumph, The Paradine case, The man on the Eiffel Tower, The bribe, O.Henry's full house* (Koster episode), *Salome, Young Bess, Hobson's choice, Witness for the prosecution, Spartacus, Advise and consent.*

314 Laurel, Stan, and **Hardy,**

Oliver, American actors. Laurel: b. England, 1890-1965. From 1912: U.S.A. Hardy: 1892-1957. 1910: cinema owner. 1926: Laurel and Hardy started their partnership. Main films: *Putting pants on Philip, The battle of the century, Leave 'em laughing, Two tars, Early to bed, You're darn tootin', Bacon grabbers, Perfect day, Men o'war, Big business, Night owls, The hoose-gow, Helpmates, Pardon us, Their first mistake, The music box, Pack up your troubles, Sons of the desert (Fraternally yours), The devil's brother, The Bohemian girl, Way out West, Swiss Miss, Blockheads, A chump at Oxford.*

315 Leacock, Richard, American director of documentaries, b. 1921 in England. Dir. of photography: *To hear your banjo play, Louisiana story, Mount Vernon, Years of change, New York University.* Supervised: *Susan Starr.* See cinéma-vérité. Robert Drew has collaborated on most of his films since 1960. Main films: *Toby and the tall corn* 55; *F 100* 56; *Yankee no!, Primary* 60; *Eddie Sachs at Indianapolis, Pete and Johnnie, Kenya '61, Football, X 15, New frontier* 61; *David, Nehru* 62; *The chair, Jane, Happy birthday Blackie, Aga Khan, Quint city U.S.A.* 63; *Republicans — the new breed* 64; *Igor Stravinsky, a portrait* 66.

316 Lean, David, British director, b. 1908. From 1928: editor. Noël Coward scripted his first four films. Films: *In which we serve* (co-dir. N. Coward) 42; *This happy breed* 43; *Blithe spirit* 44; *Brief encounter* 45; *Great expectations* 46; *Oliver Twist* 47; *The passionate friends (One woman's story)* 48; *Madeleine* 49; *The sound barrier (Breaking the sound barrier)* 52; *Hobson's choice* 53; *Summer madness (Summertime)* 55; *The bridge on the River Kwai* 57; *Lawrence of Arabia* 62; *Doctor Zhivago* 64.

317 Leenhardt, Roger, French director, b. 1903. From 1935: film critic. Acted: *Une femme mariée.* Main shorts: *Le pain de Barbarie* 34; *Naissance du cinéma* 46; *Victor Hugo* 51; *François Mauriac* 54; *Jean-Jacques* 57; *Daumier* 58; *Paul Valéry* 59; Films: *Les dernières vacances* 47; *Le rendez-vous de minuit* 61.

318 Leigh, Vivien, British actress. 1913-67. Since 1935: also stage actress, Main films: *Fire over England, Storm in a tea-cup, Dark journey, A Yank at Oxford, Gone with the wind, Waterloo Bridge, That Hamilton woman (Lady Hamilton), Caesar and Cleopatra, Anna Karenina* (48), *A streetcar named Desire, The Roman spring of Mrs. Stone, Ship of fools.*

319 Lelouch, Claude, French director, b. 1937. Also producer and dir. of photography of many of his own films. Main shorts: *Le rideau se lève, La jungle de Paris* 57. Films: *Le propre de l'homme* 60; *La femme spectacle, L'amour avec des si* 64; *Une fille et des fusils, Les grands moments* 65; *Un homme et une femme* 66; *Vivre pour vivre, Loin du Viêtnam* (in coll.) 67.

320 Leni, Paul, German director. 1885-1929. Set-designer for Reinhardt's stage productions and for all his own films in Germany. 1927: U.S.A. See expressionism. Films: *Dornröschen* 18; *Prinz Kuckuck* 19; *Fiesko*

61

20; *Hintertreppe* 21; *Waxworks* 24; *The cat and the canary* 27; *The Chinese parrot, The man who laughs* 28; *The last warning* 29.

321 Lenica, Jan, Polish animator, b. 1928. 1958-63: France. Since 1963: W. Germany. At first cartoonist and commercial artist. Films: (in collaboration with Borowczyk) *Once upon a time, Love requited* 57; *Dom* 58; (alone) *Monsieur Tête* (co. H. Gruel) 60; *Janko the musician* 61; *Labyrinth* 62; *Rhinoceros* 63; *A, The flower woman* 65; *Adam 2* 68.

322 Leonard, Robert Z., American director, b. 1889. 1907-15: actor. Main films: *The delicious little devil* 19; *Jazzmania* 23; *Dance madness* 26; *Susan Lennox, her fall and rise* 31; *Strange interlude* 32; *Dancing lady* 33; *After office hours, Escapade* 35; *The great Ziegfeld girl* 36; *Broadway serenade* 39; *Pride and prejudice* 40; *Ziegfeld girl* 41; *Week-end at the Waldorf* 45; *B.F.'s daughter (Polly Fulton)* 48; *The bribe* 49; *The king's thief, La donna più bella del mondo (Beautiful but dangerous;* in Italy) 55.

323 Lerner, Irving, American director, b. 1909. Cameraman: *The land.* Editor. Director of educational documentaries. Films: *A place to live, Muscle beach* (both shorts) 48; *Man crazy* 53; *Murder by contract* 58; *City of fear* 59; *Studs Lonigan* 60; *To be a man* 62; *Cry of battle* 63.

324 LeRoy, Mervyn, American director, b. 1900. 1908-24: stage and vaudeville actor. From 1925: cameraman, scriptwriter, and gagman. Main films: *Little Caesar* 30; *I am a fugitive*

from a chain gang (I am a fugitive) 32; *Gold diggers of 1933* 33; *Anthony Adverse* 36; *They won't forget, The king and the chorus girl* 37; *Waterloo Bridge* 40; *Random harvest* 42; *Madame Curie* 43; *Thirty seconds over Tokyo* 44; *Quo vadis?* 51; *Million dollar mermaid (The one-piece bathing suit)* 53; *Rose Marie* 54; *The bad seed* 56; *Gypsy* 62; *The green berets* (co. J. Wayne) 67.

325 Lester, Richard, American director, b. 1932. At first TV director. Since 1955: England. Short: *The running, jumping, and standing still film* 59. Films: *It's trad dad* 61; *A mouse on the moon* 62; *A hard day's night, The knack . . . and how to get it* 64; *Help!* 65; *A funny thing happened on the way to the forum* 66; *How I won the war, Petulia* 67.

326 Lewin, Albert, American director, b. 1902. At first producer: *Cuban love song, Mutiny on the Bounty* (35), *Zaza* (39), *So ends our night.* Scr. all his own films. Films: *The moon and sixpence* 42; *The picture of Dorian Gray* 45; *The private affairs of Bel Ami* 47; *Pandora and the Flying Dutchman* 51; *Saadia* 54; *The living idol* 57.

327 Lewis, Jerry, American actor and director, b. 1926. Also singer and TV actor. Main films as actor: (with Dean Martin as partner) *My friend Irma, That's my boy, Sailor beware, The stooge, Jumping jacks, The caddy, Scared stiff, You're never too young, Artists and models* (55), *Hollywood or bust, Pardners,* (alone) *The sad sack, Rock-a-bye baby, The geisha boy, Don't give up the ship, Visit to a small planet, Cinderella, It's only money, Who's minding the store?, The disorderly order-*

ly. Films as both director and actor: The bellboy 60; The ladies' man 61; The errand boy 62; The nutty professor 63; The patsy 64; The family jewels 65; Three on a couch 66; The big mouth 67.

328 L'Herbier, Marcel, French director, b. 1890. Also poet and playwright. 1943: founded Institut des Hautes Etudes Cinématographiques (I.D.H.E.C.). From 1953: TV producer. Main films: Phantasmes 17; Rose France 19; Le carnaval des vérités, L'homme du large 20; Eldorado 21; Don Juan et Faust 22; L'inhumaine 23; Feu Mathias Pascal 25; L'argent 27; Forfaiture 37; La nuit fantastique, L'honorable Catherine 42; Les derniers jours de Pompeii 49; Le père de Mademoiselle 53.

329 Linder, Max, French actor and director. 1883-1925. From 1904: stage actor. 1917 and 1921-22: U.S.A. Directed and scripted all his films except Le petit café and Au secours. Main films: Les débuts d'un patineur, Idées d'Apache 07; Max dans la famille, Max et le quinquina, Max lance la mode, Max toréador, Max virtuose, Le duel de Max, Idylle à la ferme, Max et l'inauguration d'une statue, and about 90 other shorts 07-16; Max on a liner, Max comes across 17; Le petit café 19; Seven years' bad luck, Be my wife 21; The three Must-get-theres 22; Au secours 24; Le roi du cirque 25; En compagnie de Max Linder (anthology of his films compiled by his daughter Maud Linder) 63.

330 Lipman, Jerzy, Polish director of photography, b. 1922. 1948-52: film school. Main films: A generation, The shadow, Kanal, The real end of the Great War, The eighth day of the week, Answer to violence, Lotna, Bad luck, Knife in the water, Les plus belles escroqueries du monde (Polanski ep.), Ambulance, Ashes.

331 Litvak, Anatole, Director, b. 1902 in Russia. From 1929: Germany and France. 1937: U.S.A. Main films: L'équipage (in France) 35; Mayerling (in France) 36; The amazing Doctor Clitterhouse, The sisters 38; Confessions of a Nazi spy 39; Nazis strike 42; Divide and conquer 43; The battle of China 44 (last three docs., co. Capra); The long night 47; Sorry wrong number 48; Decision before dawn 51; Anastasia 56; Aimez-vous Brahms? 61; Le couteau dans la plaie (Five miles to midnight) 62; The night of the generals 66.

332 Lizzani, Carlo, Italian director, b. 1922. At first film critic. Assistant to De Santis, Lattuada, Rossellini. Collaborated with Vergano on Il sole sorge ancora. See neo-realism. Main films: Achtung! banditi! 51; Amore in città (one episode), Cronache di poveri amanti 53; Lo svitato 56; La muraglia cinese 58; Il gobbo 60; Il processo di Verona 62; La vita agra, La Celestina 64; Thrilling (one ep.) 65; I sette fratelli, Svegliati e uccidi 66; Vangelo 70 (one ep.), Requiescant 67; Assassinio a Sarajevo 68.

333 Lloyd, Frank, Director, b. 1889 in Scotland, d. 1960. From 1902: actor. From 1910: U.S.A. Main films: Les misérables 18; Oliver Twist 22; Eagle of the sea 26; Children of divorce 27; Hoopla 32; Cavalcade 33; Mutiny on the Bounty 35; Under two flags 36; Wells Fargo 37; The spoilers 42.

334 Lloyd, Harold, American actor, b. 1893. 1915-20: about 175 films for Hal Roach (including *Lonesome Luke* series). Films: *A sailor-made man, Grandma's boy, Doctor Jack, Safety last, Why worry? Girl shy, Hot water, The freshman, For heaven's sake, The kid brother, Speedy, Welcome danger, Feet first, Movie crazy, The cat's paw, The milky way, Professor beware, Mad Wednesday, Harold Lloyd's world of comedy, The funny side of life* (last two compilation films).

335 Lollobrigida, Gina, Italian actress, b. 1927. Main films: *La danse de mort, Achtung! banditi!, Fanfan la tulipe, Altri tempi, Les belles de nuit, La provinciale, Le infedeli, Beat the devil, Pane amore e fantasia, La Romana, Le grand jeu* (54), *La donna più bella del mondo, Trapeze, La loi, Solomon and Sheba, Come September, Vénus impériale, Mare matto, Woman of straw, Il maestro di Don Giovanni, Hotel Paradiso, Le bambole* (Bolognini ep.), *Io, io, io e . . . gli altri, The private navy of Sgt. O'Farrell.*

336 Lombard, Carole, American actress. 1909-42. From 1926: 'bathing beauty' for Sennett. Main films: *Dynamite, White woman, Twentieth century, Bolero, Rumba, Hands across the table, My man Godfrey, The princess comes across, Nothing sacred, True confession, In name only, They knew what they wanted, Mr. and Mrs. Smith, To be or not to be.*

337 Loren, Sophia, Italian actress, b. 1934. 1949: beauty queen. Main films: *Carosello Napoletano, L'oro di Napoli, La donna del fiume, Pane, amore e . . ., The pride and the passion, Legend*

of the lost, Desire under the elms, The key, That kind of woman, The black orchid, Heller in pink tights, The millionairess, Two women, Boccaccio '70, El Cid, The condemned of Altona, Yesterday, today and tomorrow, Marriage Italian style, The fall of the Roman Empire, Lady L, Judith, Arabesque, C'era una volta, A countess from Hong Kong, Questi fantasmi.*

338 Lorentz, Pare, American director of documentaries, b. 1905. 1935: film critic. Produced: *The power and the land, The land.* Films: *The plow that broke the plains* 36; *The river* 37; *The fight for life* 40.

339 Lorre, Peter, Actor, b. 1904 in Hungary, d. 1964. 1922-31: stage actor in Vienna and Berlin. From 1935: U.S.A. Main films: *M* (32), *Du haut en bas, Mad love, Crime and punishment, The man who knew too much* (34), *The secret agent, Think fast Mr. Moto, Thank you Mr. Moto, Mr. Moto takes a chance, The mysterious Mr. Moto, Mr. Moto's last warning, Mr. Moto takes a vacation, Strange cargo, The Maltese falcon, Casablanca, Arsenic and old lace, Three strangers, The mask of Dimitrios, The constant nymph, Hollywood canteen, Rope of sand, Confidential agent, The verdict, The beast with five fingers, Der Verlorene* (also directed; in Germany, 51), *Beat the devil, 20,000 leagues under the sea, The sad sack, Around the world in 80 days, The story of mankind, Silk stockings, Scent of mystery, Tales of terror, The raven, The comedy of terrors, The patsy.*

340 Losey, Joseph, American director, b. 1909. 1930: literary and drama

Sophia Loren
Peter Lorre
Joseph Losey

Shirley MacLaine
Norman McLaren
Anna Magnani

Louis Malle
Fredric March
Chris Marker

Giulietta Masina
James Mason
Marcello Mastroianni

Cecil B. DeMille
Jean-Pierre Melville
Georges Méliès

Robert Mitchum
Vincente Minnelli
Gustaf Molander

Andrzej Munk
Michèle Morgan
Jeanne Moreau

Ermanno Olmi
Laurence Olivier
Paul Newman

critic. Since 1931: also stage producer. 1952: left U.S.A. for England because of McCarthy. Shorts: *Pete Roleum and his cousins* 39; *A child went forth, Youth gets a break* 41; *A gun in his hand* 45; *A man on the beach* 55. Films: *The boy with green hair* 48; *The lawless (The dividing line)* 49; *The prowler, M* 50; *The big night, Stranger on the prowl* 51; *The sleeping tiger* 54; *The intimate stranger* 55; *Time without pity* 56; *The gypsy and the gentleman* 57; *Blind date (Chance meeting)* 59; *The criminal (The concrete jungle)* 60; *The damned (These are the damned)* 61; *Eve* 62; *The servant* 63; *King and country* 64; *Modesty Blaise* 65; *Accident* 66; *Goforth* 67.

341 Loy, Myrna, American actress, b. 1902. At first dancer. Main films: *The ten commandments* (23), *The thief of Bagdad* (24), *So this is Paris* (24), *Ben Hur* (26), *The jazz singer, Arrowsmith, Love me tonight, The mask of Fu Manchu, The prize fighter and the lady, The woman in Room 13, Manhattan melodrama, The barbarian, Broadway Bill, Wife versus secretary, The thin man, The great Ziegfeld, Libeled lady, Parnell, After the thin man, Double wedding, Another thin man, I love you again, Test pilot, Shadow of the thin man, The thin man goes home, The best years of our lives, The bachelor and the bobbysoxer, The red pony, The ambassador's daughter, From the terrace, Midnight lace.*

342 Lubitsch, Ernst, German director, 1892-1947. 1911-18: stage actor under Reinhardt. From 1923: U.S.A. Supervised *Desire* (36). Also acted in some of his own films*. Shorts: *Blinde*

Kuh*, *Auf Eis geführt**, *Zucker und Zimt* 15; *Wo ist mein Schatz?**, *Der Schwarze Moritz**, *Schuhpalast Pinkus**, *Der gemischte Frauenchor** 16; *Ossis Tagebuch, Der Blusenkönig**, *Wenn Vier dasselbe tun**, *Das fidele Gefängnis* 17; *Prinz Sami, Der Rodelcavalier, Der Fall Rosentopf* 18; *Meyer from Berlin**, *My wife the movie star** 19. Films: *The eyes of the mummy, The ballet girl, Carmen* 18; *The Schwab maiden, The oyster princess, Intoxication, Madame Du Barry (Passion), The doll* 19; *Kohlhiesel's daughters, Romeo and Juliet in the snow, One Arabian night (Sumurun), Deception* 20; *The wildcat, Vendetta* 21; *The loves of Pharaoh* 22; *Montmartre, Rosita* 23; *The marriage circle, Three women, Forbidden paradise* 24; *Kiss me again, Lady Windermere's fan* 25; *So this is Paris* 26; *The student prince (In old Heidelberg)* 27; *The patriot, Eternal love* 28; *The love parade* 29; *Paramount on parade* (co.), *Monte Carlo* 30; *The smiling lieutenant* 31; *The man I killed (Broken lullaby), One hour with you, Trouble in paradise, If I had a million* (one episode) 32; *Design for living* 33; *The merry widow* 34; *Angel* 37; *Bluebeard's eighth wife* 38; *Ninotchka* 39; *The shop around the corner* 40; *That uncertain feeling* 41; *To be or not to be* 42; *Heaven can wait* 43; *Cluny Brown* 46; *That lady in ermine* (completed by Preminger) 48.

343 Lugosi, Bela, Actor, b. 1882 in Hungary, d. 1956. From 1901: also stage actor. From 1921: U.S.A. Main films: *Der Januskopf, Dracula* (31), *Murders in the rue Morgue, Chandu the magician, White zombie, The black cat, Mark of the vampire, Son of Frankenstein, Ninotchka, Dracula's daughters, Black Friday, Body snatcher.*

344 **Lumet, Sidney,** American director, b. 1924. At first stage actor (as a child) and producer. 1950: TV producer. Films: *Twelve angry men* 57; *Stage struck* 58; *That kind of woman* 59; *The fugitive kind* 60; *A view from the bridge* 61; *Long day's journey into night* 62; *Fail safe, The pawnbroker* 63; *The hill* 65; *The group, The deadly affair* 66; *Bye, bye, Braverman* 67; *The appointment* 68.

345 **Lumière, Louis,** French director, 1864-1948. In collaboration with his brother, Auguste, he followed up the researches of Marey, Démeny and Edison, and gave the first public demonstration of the 'cinematograph' in 1895. In contrast to Méliès (q.v.) he restricted himself to recording events or filming simple gags. Main films: *La sortie des usines Lumière, Arrivée d'un train en gare de La Ciotat, Le Déjeuner de bébé, Le déjeuner d'un chat, Lancement d'un navire, Chapeau à transformations, L'arroseur arrosé* 1895-97.

346 **Lupino, Ida,** Director and actress, b. 1918 in England. 1930: drama studies. Since 1934: U.S.A. Since 1956: TV producer. Scripted all the films she has directed and *Private Hell 36*. Main films as actress: *Peter Ibbetson, The gay desperado, Artists and models* (37), *The light that failed, They drive by night, High sierra, Forever and a day* (Clair ep.), *The sea wolf, On dangerous ground, Private Hell 36, The big knife, While the city sleeps.* Films as director: *Never fear, Outrage* 50; *Hard, fast, and beautiful* 51; *The bigamist* (also acted) 52; *The hitchhiker* 53; *The trouble with angels* 66.

347 **Lupu-Pick,** German director. 1886-1931. At first stage actor under Reinhardt. Actor: *Waxworks* and*. See *expressionism*. Main films: *Der Dummkopf*, Scherben* 21; *Sylvester* 23; *Napoléon auf St. Helena, A night in London* 29; *Gassenhauer* 31.

M

348 **McCarey, Leo,** American director, b. 1898. 1923-28: worked under Roach (q.v.). Scr. and supervised: *Putting pants on Philip, The battle of the century, Leave 'em laughing, Two tars, Early to bed, You're darn tootin', Bacon grabbers, Perfect day, Men o'war, Big business, Night owls, The hoose-gow.* Also scr. many of his own films. Main films: *The sophomore* 29; *Part time wife* 30; *The kid from Spain* 32; *Duck soup* 33; *Six of a kind, Ruggles of Red Gap, Belle of the '90s* 34; *The milky way* 36; *The awful truth* 37; *Love affair* 39; *Once upon a honeymoon* 42; *Going my way* 44; *The bells of St. Mary's* 45; *Good Sam* 49; *An affair to remember* 57; *Rally round the flag boys* 58; *Satan never sleeps* 62.

349 **Machaty, Gustav,** Czechoslovakian director, 1898-1963. 1920-24: U.S.A., assistant to Stroheim. 1936-45: U.S.A. Scripted most of his own films* and, in collaboration, *The jackboot mutiny.* Main films: *The Kreutzer Sonata* 26; *Erotikon* 29; *From Saturday to Sunday* 31; *Extase* 33; *Nocturno* (in Austria) 34; *Ballerine* (in Italy) 36; *Within the law* 39; *Jealousy* 45.

350 Mackendrick, Alexander, British director, b. 1912. 1938-47: dir. shorts. Scr.: *The blue lamp.* Films: *Whisky galore (Tight little island)* 48; *The man in the white suit* 51; *Mandy (The crash of silence)* 52; *The Maggie (High and dry)* 53; *The ladykillers* 55; *Sweet smell of success* (in U.S.A.) 57; *Sammy going South (A boy ten feet tall)* 62; *A high wind in Jamaica* 65; *Don't make waves* 67.

351 MacLaine, Shirley, American actress, b. 1934. At first stage dancer and singer. Films: *The trouble with Harry, Artists and models* (55), *Around the world in 80 days, Hot spell, The matchmaker, The sheepman, Some came running, Ask any girl, The apartment, Career, Can-Can, Two loves (Spinster), Ocean's eleven, My geisha, Two for the seesaw, Irma la Douce, The children's hour (The loudest whisper), What a way to go, The yellow Rolls-Royce, John Goldfarb, please come home, Gambit, Sept fois femme.*

352 McLaren, Norman, British animator, b. 1914. Art studies. 1936-39: worked with Grierson (q.v.). 1939-41: U.S.A. Since 1941: Canada. 1949-50: China. See *animation.* Films: *Seven till five* (not animated) 33; *Camera makes whoopee, Colour cocktail* 35; *Hell unlimited* 36; *Book bargain, News for the navy, Money a pickle, Love on the wing* 37; *The obedient flame, Allegro, Rumba, Stars and stripes* 39; *Dots, Loops, Boogie doodle, Spook sport* 40; *Mail early for Christmas, V for victory* 41; *Hen hop, Five for four* 42; *Dollar dance* 43; *Alouette* (co. R. Jodoin) *Keep your mouth shut* 44; *C'est l'aviron* 45; *Là-haut sur ces montagnes, A little phantasy on a 19th century painting, Hoppity pop* 46; *Fiddle de dee, La poulette grise* 47; *Begone dull care* 49; *Pen point percussion, Chalk river ballet, Around is around* 50; *Now is the time* 51; *A phantasy, Neighbours, Two bagatelles* 52; *Blinkity blank* 54; *One two three* (unfinished), *Rythmetic* 56; *A chairy tale* 57; *Le merle* 58; *Serenal, Short and suite, Mail early for Christmas, The wonderful world of Jack Paar* (credits) 59; *Lines vertical, Opening speech, Welcome to Canada* (lightboard) 60; *Lines horizontal* 62; *Christmas crackers* (credits) 64; *Canon* 64; *Mosaic* 65.

353 McLeod, Norman Z., American director, 1898-1964. Main films: *Monkey business* 31; *Horse feathers, If I had a million* (one episode) 32; *Alice in Wonderland* 33; *It's a gift* 34; *Topper* 37; *There goes my heart, Merrily we live* 38; *Lady be good* 41; *The Kid from Brooklyn* 46; *The secret life of Walter Mitty* 47; *The paleface* 48.

354 Magnani, Anna, Italian actress, b. 1910. Since 1926: stage actress. Main films: *Cavalleria, Teresa Venerdi, Roma, città aperta, Il bandito, L'onorevole Angelina, Amore, Bellissima, Le carrosse d'or, Siamo donne, The rose tattoo, Suor Letizia, Nella città l'inferno, Wild is the wind, The fugitive kind, Mamma Roma, Herrenpartie.*

355 Malle, Louis, French director, b. 1932. 1950: assistant to Bresson. 1963: TV documentaries. Films: *Le monde du silence* (co-dir. J. Cousteau) 55; *Ascenseur pour l'échafaud* 57; *Les amants* 58; *Zazie dans le métro* 60; *Vie privée* 61; *Le feu follet* 63; *Viva Maria!* 65; *Le voleur* 66; *Histoires extraordinaires (William Wilson ep.)* 67.

356 Mamoulian, Rouben, Director, b. 1896 in Russia. Pupil of Stanislavsky. Since 1923: U.S.A. Since 1922: also stage producer. Films: *Applause* 29; *City streets, Dr. Jekyll and Mr. Hyde* 31; *Love me tonight* 32; *The song of songs, Queen Christina* 33; *We live again* 34; *Becky Sharp* 35; *The gay desperado* 36; *High wide and handsome, Golden boy* 39; *The mark of Zorro, Blood and sand* 40; *Rings on her fingers* 42; *Summer holiday* 48; *Silk stockings* 57.

357 Mankiewicz, Joseph, American director, b. 1909. Also stage producer. Also producer: *The shining hour,* and*. At first scriptwriter: *Skippy, Million dollar legs, If I had a million* (in collab.), *Alice in Wonderland, Manhattan melodrama, Forsaking all others, I live my life, After office hours, Fury*, Love on the run*, Mannequin*, Double wedding*, Three comrades*, Strange cargo*, The Philadelphia story*, The woman of the year*, The keys of the kingdom**, and almost all his own films. Films: *Dragonwyck, The late George Apley* 46; *The ghost and Mrs. Muir, Somewhere in the night* 47; *Escape, A letter to three wives* 48; *House of strangers* 49; *No way out, All about Eve* 50; *People will talk* 51; *Five fingers* 52; *Julius Caesar* 53; *The barefoot contessa** 54; *Guys and dolls* 55; *The quiet American** 57; *Suddenly last summer* 59; *Cleopatra* 60-63; *The honey pot** 66.

358 Mann, Anthony, American director, 1906-67. 1922-30: stage actor. 1938: assistant to P. Sturges. Scr.: *Follow me quietly.* Films: *Dr. Broadway, Moonlight in Havana* 42; *Nobody's darling* 43; *My best gal, Strangers in the night* 44; *The great Flammarion, Two*

o'clock courage, Sing your way home* 45; *Strange impersonation, The bamboo blonde* 46; *Desperate, Railroaded, T-men* 47; *Raw deal* 48; *Reign of terror, Border incident, Side Street* 49; *Devil's doorway, Winchester 73, The furies* 51; *The tall target* 51; *Bend of the river (Where the river bends)* 52; *The naked spur, Thunder Bay* 53; *The Glenn Miller story, The far country* 54; *Strategic air command, The man from Laramie* 55; *The last frontier, Serenade, Men in war* 56; *The tin star, God's little acre* 57; *Man of the West* 58; *Cimarron* 60; *El Cid* 61; *The fall of the Roman Empire* 63; *The heroes of Telemark* 65; *A dandy in aspic* (completed by L. Harvey) 67.

359 Mann, Delbert, American director, b. 1920. 1947-49: stage producer. 1949-55: TV producer. Main films: *Marty* 55; *Bachelor party* 57; *Desire under the elms, Separate tables* 58; *Middle of the night* 59; *That touch of mink* 62; *Quick before it melts* 64.

360 March, Fredric, American actor, b. 1897. Since 1920: also stage actor. Main films: *The wild party* (29), *The royal family of Broadway, Dr. Jekyll and Mr. Hyde* (31), *Smilin' through, The sign of the cross, Design for living, Death takes a holiday, The Barretts of Wimpole Street, We live again, Les misérables, Anna Karenina* (35), *The dark angel, The road to glory, Anthony Adverse, Mary of Scotland, A star is born* (37), *Nothing sacred, The buccaneer* (38), *There goes my heart, Susan and God, So ends our night, I married a witch, The best years of our lives, Death of a salesman, Man on a tightrope, Executive suite, The bridges of Toko Ri, The desperate hours, Alexander the Great, Middle of the night,*

Inherit the wind, The young doctors, The condemned of Altona, Seven days in May, Hombre.

361 Máriássy, Félix, Hungarian director, b. 1919. From 1939: editor, then assistant. Main films: *With full speed* 48; *Mrs. Szabó* 49; *Catherine's marriage* 50; *Relatives* 54; *Springtime in Budapest, A glass of beer* 55; *A legend of the suburbs* 57; *The smugglers* 58; *The sleepless years, Third class love* 59; *Test trip* 62; *Every day Sunday* 63; *Figleaf* 66.

362 Marker, Chris, French director, b. 1921. Also novelist, literary critic and essayist. 1955: assistant to Resnais. Wrote commentary of *A Valparaiso, Volcan interdit.* Shorts: *Les statues meurent aussi* (co-dir. Resnais) 52; *Dimanche à Pékin* 56; *Le mystère de l'atelier 15* (co-dir. Heinrich, Resnais and others) 57; *Les astronautes* (co-dir. W. Borowczyk — see animation) 59. Films: *Olympia 52* 52; *Lettre de Sibérie* 58; *Description d'un combat* 60; *Cuba si!* 61; *Joli mai* 62; *La jetée* 63; *Le mystère Koumiko* 65; *Loin du Viêtnam* (ed. and supervised).

363 Marshall, Herbert, British actor, 1890-1966. 1911-32: stage actor, From 1932: U.S.A. Main films: *Murder, Blonde Venus, Trouble in paradise, I was a spy, Four frightened people, The painted veil, The good fairy, The dark angel, A woman rebels, Forgotten faces, Angel, Foreign correspondent, Zaza* (39), *The letter, The little foxes, The moon and sixpence, The enchanted cottage, The razor's edge, Duel in the sun, Angel face, The virgin queen, Stage struck, The fly, Midnight lace, The list of Adrian Messenger.*

364 Martelli, Otello, Italian director of photography, b. 1903. 1918: assistant. Main films: *Vecchia guardia, Paisa, Caccia tragica, Amore, Bitter rice, Stromboli, Anna, Luci del varietà, Roma ore II, I vitelloni, La strada, La donna del fiume, Il bidone, Barrage contre le Pacific, La loi, La dolce vita, La ragazza in vetrina, Cyrano et d'Artagnan, Il maestro di Vigevano, La mia signora, La donna è una cosa meravigliosa, I tre volti.*

365 Marx Brothers, The, American team of actors. **Chico:** 1891-1961. **Harpo:** 1893-1964. **Groucho:** b. 1895. **Zeppo:** b. 1901. 1914-29: vaudeville, with their mother, Minnie Marx. Films: (all four brothers) *The cocoanuts, Animal crackers, Monkey business, Horse feathers, Duck soup,* (without Zeppo) *A night at the opera, A day at the races, Room service, At the circus, Go West* (40), *The big store, A night in Casablanca, Love happy, The story of mankind;* (Harpo alone) *Too many kisses, Hollywood canteen;* (Groucho alone) *Copacabana, Mr. Music, Double dynamite, A girl in every port* (52), *Will success spoil Rock Hunter?.* Groucho also co-scripted *The king and the chorus girl* with Krasna.

366 Maselli, Francesco, Italian director, b. 1930. 1947-50: assistant to Antonioni. Scripted in collaboration: *Cronaca di un amore, La signora senza camelie.* Main shorts: *Bagnaia* 49; *Festa dei morti in Sicilia* 53; Films: *Amore in città* (one episode) 53; *Gli sbandati* 55; *La donna del giorno* 56; *I delfini* 60; *Le italiane e l'amore* (one episode) 61; *Gli indifferenti* 63; *Fai in fretta ad uccidermi ... ho freddo!* 66.

367 Masina, Giulietta, Italian actress, b. 1921. Since 1941: also stage actress. Main films: *Senza pietà, Luci del varietà, Europa 51, Lo sceicco bianco, La strada, Il bidone, Le notti di Cabiria, Nella città l'inferno, Giulietta degli spiriti, Non stuzzicate la zanzara.*

368 Mason, James, British actor, b. 1909. Since 1931: also stage actor. Main films: *The private life of Henry VIII, Fire over England, Thunder Rock, Fanny by gaslight, Odd man out, Madame Bovary (49), Caught, The reckless moment, Pandora and the Flying Dutchman, Five fingers, The desert rats, The man between, Julius Caesar, Prince Valiant, A star is born (54), 20,000 leagues under the sea, Bigger than life, Island in the sun, North by Northwest, Cry terror, The trials of Oscar Wilde, Lolita, The fall of the Roman Empire, Hero's island, The pumpkin eater, Lord Jim, Les pianos mécaniques, Georgy girl, The deadly affair, The blue Max.*

369 Massingham, Richard, British director of shorts, 1898-1953. At first doctor. 1936: joined Grierson. Main shorts: *Tell me if it hurts 34; And so to work 36; The five-inch bather, We speak to India 42; A knotty problem 43 (remade 51); Cambridge, Some like it rough 44; Down at the local, Coughs and sneezes 45; Pool of contentment 46; Watch your meters 47; What a life 48; Warning to travellers, Another case of poisoning 49; Help yourself, The cure 50; Facts and fancies, Introducing the new worker 51; Brief city, To the rescue 52; The Blakes slept here 53.*

370 Mastroianni, Marcello, Italian actor, b. 1924. From 1947: stage actor under Visconti. Main films: *Domenica d'agosto, Parigi è sempre Parigi, Le ragazze di piazza di Spagna, Cronache di poveri amanti, Il bigamo, Tam Tam Mayumbe, Le notti bianche, Giorni d'amore, Padri e figli, I soliti ignoti, La loi, Racconti d'estate, Il bell'Antonio, La dolce vita, La notte, Vie privée, Divorzio all'italiana, L'assassino, Otto e mezzo, I compagni, Yesterday today and tomorrow, Cronaca familiare, Marriage Italian style, Casanova 70, La decima vittima, Oggi, domani, dopodomani (Ferreri ep.), Io, io, io e ... gli altri, Lo straniero, La vita di Giacomo Puccini.*

371 Maté, Rudolph, Director of photography and director, b. 1898 in Poland, d. 1964. 1925: assistant to Freund. 1935: U.S.A. Since 1947: director. 1960: Italy. Main films as dir. of photography: *La passion de Jeanne d'Arc, Prix de beauté, Vampyr, Le dernier milliardaire, Liliom, Come and get it, Stella Dallas (37), The adventures of Marco Polo, Blockheads, Love affair, Dodsworth, My favourite wife, Foreign correspondent, Seven sinners, Lady Hamilton, The flame of New Orleans, To be or not to be, Sahara, Gilda, Cover girl.* Main films as director: *The dark past 48; The violent men (Rough company), Miracle in the rain 55; Three violent people 57; The 300 Spartans, Seven seas to Calais* (both in Italy) 62.

372 Mattsson, Arne, Swedish director, b. 1919. At first assistant. Main films: *Röttag 46; When love comes to the village 50; One summer of happiness 51; The bread of love, Salka Valka 54; The people of Hemsö, Litet bo 55; The girl in tails 56; The lady in black 58; The phantom carriage, Mannequin in red*

59; *The doll* 62; *The yellow car* 63; *Blåjackor* 64; *Woman of darkness* 66.

373 Mayakovsky, Vladimir, Russian scriptwriter. 1893-1930. Also poet and playwright. 1911: joined Futurist movement. Acted: *The Futurists of Moscow* (13) and*. 1928: France. Main films: *The young lady and the hooligan**, *Shackled by film**, *Creation can't be bought** 18; *At the front* 20; *Three* 26.

374 Mayer, Carl, German scriptwriter. 1894-1944. 1927: U.S.A. 1931: England. See *expressionism*. Main films: *The cabinet of Dr. Caligari*, *Der Bucklige und die Tänzerin*, *Genuine*, *Hintertreppe*, *Der Gang in die Nacht*, *Schloss Vogelöd*, *Der Dummkopf*, *Scherben*, *Vanina*, *Sylvester*, *The last laugh*, *Tartuffe*, *Berlin, rhythm of a city*, *Sunrise*, *Four devils*, *Ariane*.

375 Mayo, Archie, American director, b. 1898. 1917-26: gagman, scripted and directed short comedies. Main films: *Night after night* 32; *Bordertown*, *Go into your dance* 35; *The petrified forest* 36; *It's love I'm after* 37; *The adventures of Marco Polo* 38; *Confirm or deny* (started by Lang) 41; *Moontide* 42; *A night in Casablanca* 46.

376 Meerson, Lazare, Set designer, b. 1900 in Russia, d. 1938. From 1924: France. Collab. with Cavalcanti on sets of *Feu Mathias Pascal.* Main films: *Gribiche*, *Carmen* (26), *La proie du vent*, *Un chapeau de paille d'Italie*, *Les deux timides* (28), *Les nouveaux messieurs*, *L'argent*, *Cagliostro*, *Le million*, *Sous les toits de Paris*, *A nous la liberté*, *Jean de la Lune* (31), *Quatorze juillet*, *Ciboulette*, *Le grand jeu* (34), *Amok*, *Princess Tam-Tam*, *Les beaux jours*, *Pension Mimosas*, *La Kermesse héroïque*, *As you like it*, *The citadel*, *Fire over England*, *Knight without armour*, *Break the news*.

377 Méliès, Georges, French director. 1861-1938. From 1888: conjuror and illusionist. In contrast to Lumière (q.v.) he used the cinema as a means of creating illusion and fantasy. Often acted in his own films. Main films: *Une partie de cartes* 1896; *Bombardement d'une maison* 1897; *Illusions fantasmagoriques*, *Guillaume Tell*, *L'homme de têtes* 1898; *Le Christ marchant sur les eaux*, *L'affaire Dreyfus*, *Cendrillon*, *L'homme-Protée* 1899; *Jeanne d'Arc*, *Rêves de Noël* 1900; *Le petit chaperon rouge*, *Barbe-Bleue* 01; *L'homme à la tête de caoutchouc*, *L'oeuf magique prolifique*, *Le voyage dans la lune*, *Voyages de Gulliver*, *Robinson Crusoe* 02; *Cake-walk infernal*, *Le royaume des fées*, *La damnation de Faust* 03; *Le merveilleux éventail vivant* 04; *Le palais des mille et une nuits* 05; *Jack le ramoneur*, *Les incendiaires*, *Les quatre cents farces du Diable*, *Robert Macaire et Bertrand* 06; *Deux cent mille lieues sous les mers*, *Le tunnel sous la Manche* 07; *La civilisation à travers les âges*, *Le raid New York — Paris en automobile* 08; *Les aventures du baron Munchausen* 11; *A la conquête du Pôle* 12.

378 Melville, Jean-Pierre, French director, b. 1917. Acted: *Orphée*, *A bout de souffle*, *Zazie dans le métro*, and*. Films: *Vingt quatre heures dans la vie d'un clown* (short) 45; *Le silence de la mer* 48; *Les enfants terribles* 49; *Quand tu liras cette lettre* 53; *Bob le flambeur* 56; *Deux hommes dans Manhattan** 59; *Léon Morin, prêtre* 61; *Le* doulos 62; L'aîné des Ferchaux 63; Le deuxième souffle 66; Le samouraï 67; La chienne 68.

379 Menjou, Adolphe, American actor, 1890-1963. At first stage and vaudeville actor. Main films: The three musketeers (21), A woman of Paris, The marriage circle, Forbidden paradise, The grand duchess and the waiter, The sorrows of Satan, The kiss, Morocco, Friends and lovers, Forbidden, A farewell to arms, Gold diggers of 1935, The milky way, A star is born (37), Stage door, Golden boy, Father takes a wife, State of the Union, The tall target, Across the wide Missouri, The sniper, Man on a tightrope, The ambassador's daughter, Paths of glory.

380 Menzies, William Cameron, American director and set designer. 1896-1957. Sets: Rosita, The thief of Bagdad (24), Fig leaves, The tempest, Alice in Wonderland, The adventures of Tom Sawyer, Gone with the wind, Our town, Foreign correspondent, So ends our night, and*. Main films: Chandu the magician (co-dir. M. Varnel) 32; Things to come* (in England) 36; Drums in the Deep South* 51; Invaders from Mars 53.

381 Mercouri, Melina, Greek actress, b. 1932. Since 1952: also stage actress. Films: Stella, He who must die, The gypsy and the gentleman, La loi, Never on Sunday, Il giudizio universale, Phaedra, The victors, Topkapi, Les pianos mécaniques, 10.30 pm summer.

382 Metty, Russell, American director of photography. Main films: Sylvia Scarlett, Bringing up baby, The stranger, We were strangers, Saskatche-wan, Seminole, The world in his arms, Man without a star, Battle hymn, Written on the wind, Mister Corey, Touch of evil, A time to love and a time to die, Imitation of life, Spartacus, The misfits, Captain Newman, The Appaloosa, The war lord.

383 Mifune, Toshiro, Japanese actor, b. 1920 in China. Since 1947: Japan. Main films: To the end of the silver mountains, The drunken angel, The silent duel, The life of O-Haru, Stray dog, Scandal, Rashomon, The idiot, Seven samurai, I live in fear, Throne of blood, The lower depths, The rickshaw man, Hidden fortress, The bad sleep well, Animas Trujano (in Mexico), Yojimbo, Sanjuro, High and low, Samurai pirate, Red Beard, Rise against the sword, Grand Prix, Rebellion.

384 Milestone, Lewis, American director, b. 1895 in Russia. Since 1913: U.S.A. 1923-24: editor. Assistant to King, Ince and Sennett. Since 1933: also stage producer. Also TV producer. Main films: The garden of Eden 28; The betrayal, New York nights 29; All quiet on the Western front 30; Front page 31; Rain 32; Hallelujah I'm a bum (Hallelujah I'm a tramp) 33; Anything goes, The general died at dawn 36; Of mice and men 39; Our Russian front (co-dir. J. Ivens) 41; Edge of darkness, The North Star 43; A walk in the sun 45; The strange love of Martha Ivers 46; Arch of triumph 48; The red pony 49; Halls of Montezuma 51; Kangaroo 53; Pork Chop Hill 59; Ocean's eleven 60; Mutiny on the Bounty 62.

385 Miller, David, American director, b. 1909. From 1930: editor. Main films: *Billy the Kid* 41; *Flying tigers* 42; *Love happy* 50; *Our very own* 51; *Sudden fear* 52; *The opposite sex* 56; *The golden virgin (The story of Esther Costello)* 57; *Midnight lace* 60; *Lonely are the brave* 62; *Captain Newman* 63.

386 Minnelli, Vincente, American director, b. 1913. From 1916: stage actor. At first set and costume designer. Also producer of stage shows and musicals. Films: *Cabin in the sky* 42; *I dood it* 43; *Meet me in St. Louis, The clock* 44; *Ziegfeld Follies* 45; *Yolanda and the thief, Undercurrent* 46; *The pirate* 47; *Madame Bovary* 49; *Father of the bride, An American in Paris* 50; *Father's little dividend* 51; *The story of three loves* (one episode), *The bad and the beautiful* 52; *The band wagon, The long long trailer* 53; *Brigadoon* 54; *The cobweb, Kismet* 55; *Lust for life, Tea and sympathy* 56; *Designing woman* 57; *Gigi, The reluctant debutante* 58; *Some came running* 59; *Home from the hill, Bells are ringing* 60; *The four horsemen of the Apocalypse* 61; *Two weeks in another town* 62; *The courtship of Eddie's father* 63; *Goodbye Charlie* 64; *The sandpiper* 65.

387 Mitchum, Robert, American actor, b. 1917. From 1925: revue actor. Main films: *Bataan, Thirty seconds over Tokyo, The story of G. I. Joe, Pursued, Crossfire, Undercurrent, Out of the past, Desire me, The big steal, Macao, The racket, The lusty men, Angel face, River of no return, Track of the cat, Man with the gun (The trouble shooter), Foreign intrigue, The night of the hunter, Not as a stranger, Bandido, Fire down below, Heaven knows Mr. Allison, The enemy below, The hunters, The angry hills, The wonderful country, Home from the hill, The sundowners, The grass is greener, Cape Fear, The longest day, Two for the seesaw, The list of Adrian Messenger, Man in the middle, What a way to go, Mister Moses, El Dorado, Villa rides.*

388 Mitra, Subrata, Indian director of photography. Main films: *Pather Panchali, Aparajito, The philosopher's stone, The music room, The world of Apu, The goddess* (60), *Kanchenjungha, Abhijan, Mahanagar, The householder, Charulata, Shakespeare Wallah, Nayak.*

389 Mizoguchi, Kenji, Japanese director. 1898-1956. Painter and actor up to 1923. Main films: *Foggy harbour* 23; *Song of the mountain pass, Turkeys in a row* 24; *Street sketches* 25; *A paper doll's whisper of spring, Passion of a woman teacher* 26; *Tokyo march, Hometown, Metropolitan symphony* 29; *And yet they go on, The dawn of the founding of Manchukuo and Mongolia* 31; *Timely mediator, Gion festival, White threads of the cascades* 32; *Sisters of the Gion, The gorge between love and hate, Osaka elegy* 36; *Ah! my hometown* 37; *The story of the last chrysanthemums* 39; *Woman of Osaka* 40; *The life of an artist* 41; *The loyal 49 ronin of the Genroku era* 42; *Three generations of Danjuro* 44; *Utamaro and his five women, Women's victory* 46; *The love of actress Sumaku* 47; *Women of the night* 48; *Sketch of Madame Yuki* 50; *The life of O-Haru* 52; *Ugetsu monogatari, Gion music* 53; *Sansho dayu, Chikamatsu monogatari, Shin heike monogatari* 54; *Yang Kwei Fei* 55; *Street of shame, An Osaka story* (completed by Yoshimura) 56.

390 Molander, Gustaf, Swedish director, b. 1888. 1913: stage actor.

Scripted: *Terje Vigen, Wanted — a film actress, Thomas Graals best child, The song of the blood-red flower, Herr Arne's treasure.* Main films: *The pirates of Lake Mälar* 23; *Ingmarsvet, Till Österland* 25; *Sin* 28; *One night* 31; *Swedenhielms* 35; *Intermezzo* 36; *A woman's face* 38; *Ride tonight* 42; *The word, A fire is burning* 43; *The emperor of Portugal* 44; *Woman without a face* 47; *Eva* 48; *Frånskild* 50; *Trots* 52; *Enhörningen* 54; *Stimulantia* (one ep.) 66.

391 Monicelli, Mario, Italian director, b. 1915. 1935: assistant. Scripted in collab.: *In nome della legge, Bitter rice,* and most of his own films. Main films: *Totò cerca casa* 49; *Totò e i re di Roma, Guardie e ladri* 51; *Totò e le donne, Le infedeli* 52 (all co-dir. S. Steno); *Proibito* 54; *Totò e Carolina* 55; *Padri e figli* 57; *I soliti ignoti* 58; *Le grande guerra* 59; *Risate di gioia* 60; *Boccaccio '70* (one episode) 62; *I compagni* 63; *Alta infedeltà* (one episode), *Casanova 70* 64; *L'armata Brancaleone* 65; *Le streghe* (one ep.), *Le fata* (one ep.) 66; *La ragazza con la pistola* 67.

392 Monroe, Marilyn, American actress. 1926-1962. At first model. Main films: *Ladies of the chorus, Love happy, The asphalt jungle, All about Eve, As young as you feel, Love nest, Let's make it legal, O. Henry's full house* (Koster ep.), *Clash by night, Don't bother to knock, We're not married, Monkey business* (52), *Niagara, Gentlemen prefer blondes, How to marry a millionaire, River of no return, There's no business like show business, The seven year itch, Bus stop, The prince and the showgirl, Some like it hot, Let's make love, The misfits.*

393 Moorehead, Agnes, American actress, b. 1906. Since 1929: also stage actress. Main films: *Citizen Kane, The magnificent Ambersons, Journey into fear, The seventh cross, Jane Eyre, Since you went away, Mrs. Parkington, Summer holiday, Dark passage, Caged, 14 hours, Show boat, Magnificent obsession, The left hand of God, The swan, The true story of Jesse James, The opposite sex, Jeanne Eagels, The story of mankind, Raintree county, La tempesta, The bat, How the West was won, Who's minding the store?, Hush, hush, sweet Charlotte.*

394 Moreau, Jeanne, French actress, b. 1928. Since 1948: also stage actress. Main films: *Ascenseur pour l'échafaud, Le dos au mur, Les amants, Les liaisons dangereuses, Five branded women, Moderato cantabile, Le dialogue des Carmélites, La notte, Jules et Jim, La baie des anges, Eve, The trial, The victors, Le feu follet, Le journal d'une femme de chambre, The yellow Rolls-Royce, Mata Hari, agent H-21, Viva Maria!, Chimes at midnight, Mademoiselle, The sailor from Gibraltar, Le plus vieux métier du monde* (de Broca ep.), *La mariée était en noir, The great Catherine.*

395 Morgan, Michèle, French actress, b. 1920. 1940-46: U.S.A. Main films: *Gribouille, Orage, Quai des brumes, Remorques, La loi du Nord, Untel, père et fils, La symphonie pastorale, The fallen idol, Fabiola, Le château de verre, L'étrange Madame X, Les orgueilleux, Les sept péchés capitaux* (52), *Napoléon, Oasis, Les grandes manoeuvres, Marguerite de la nuit, Si Paris nous était conté, Le miroir à deux faces, Racconti d'estate, Le crime ne paie pas, Landru, Benjamin.*

74

396 Moskvin, Andrei, Russian director of photography, b. 1901. Long collaboration with Kozintsev and Trauberg. See *FEX*. Main films: *Katka's Reinette apples, The devil's wheel, The cloak, Bratishka, The club of the big deed, The new Babylon, Alone, The youth of Maxim, The return of Maxim, The Vyborg side, Ivan the Terrible* (interiors only), *Pirogov, Bielinsky, Stories about Lenin, Don Quixote* (co. A. Dudko, 57), *Lady with a little dog.*

397 Mozhukin, Ivan, Russian actor. 1889-1939. From 1909: stage actor. From 1927: U.S.A. (where he was known as Mosjoukine). 1928-30: Germany. Main films: *The queen of spades* (16), *Satan triumphant, Andrei Kozhukhov, Father Sergius, The queen's secret, Kean, Le brasier ardent* (also directed and scripted, 23), *Le lion des Mogols* (also scripted), *Feu Mathias Pascal, Casanova, La mille et deuxième nuit.*

398 Munk, Andrzej, Polish director 1921-61. Film school. Also stage and TV producer. Main shorts: *The word of a railwayman* 53; *One Sunday morning* 55; *A walk in the old town* 58. Films: *The stars must shine* (co-dir. W. Lesiewicz) 54; *Men of the Blue Cross* 55; *Man on the track* 56; *Eroica* 57; *Bad luck* 60; *Passenger* 61 (uncompleted; edited and presented by W. Lesiewicz 63).

399 Murnau, Friedrich W., German director. 1889-1931. Worked under Reinhardt. Also stage producer. See *expressionism*. From 1927: U.S.A. Films: *Der Knabe in Blau, Satanas* 19; *Der Bucklige und die Tänzerin, Der Januskopf, Abend . . . Nacht . . . Morgen, Der Gang in die Nacht, Sehnsucht* 20;

Marizza, genannt die Schmuggler-Madonna, Schloss Vogelöd 21; *Nosferatu, Der brennende Acker, Phantom* 22; *Die Austreibung, Die Finanzen des Grossherzogs* 23; *The last laugh* 24; *Tartuffe* 25; *Faust* 26; *Sunrise* 27; *Four devils* 28; *Our daily bread (City girl), Tabu* (co-dir. Flaherty) 29.

N

400 Naruse, Mikio, Japanese director, b. 1905. 1926: assistant. Main films: *Mr. and Mrs. Swordplay, Pure love* 29; *Fickleness gets on the train* 31; *Wife! be like a rose!, The girl in the rumour* 35; *Repast* 51; *Mother, Lightning* 52; *Husband and wife, The wife, Older brother, younger sister* 53; *Sounds from the mountains, Late chrysanthemums* 54; *Floating clouds* 55; *Flowing* 56; *Untamed woman* 57; *Anzukko, The summer clouds* 58; *A whistle in my heart* 59; *Daughters, wives and a mother, When a woman ascends the stairs, The approach of autumn* 60; *The lovelorn geisha, The other woman* 61; *Lonely lane* 63; *Yearning* 64; *The thin line* 65; *Hit and run* 66.

401 Negri, Pola, Actress, b. 1897 in Poland. 1916-22: Germany. 1923-36: U.S.A. 1936-39: Germany. Since 1940: U.S.A. Main films: *The Polish dancer, The eyes of the mummy, Carmen, Madame Du Barry, One Arabian night, The wildcat, Vendetta* (21), *Montmartre, Bella donna, Forbidden paradise, A woman of the world, Hotel Imperial, Woman on trial, Mazurka, Hi diddle diddle, The moon spinners.*

402 Nemec, Jan, Czechoslovakian director, b. 1936. Also scr. all his own shorts and co-scr. all his own features. Shorts: *The loaf of bread* 59; *The memory of our day* 63; *Mother and son* (in Holland) 67. Films: *Diamonds of the night, Little pearls from the bottom (The liars* ep.) 65; *A report on the party and the guests* 66; *The martyrs of love* 67.

403 neo-realism: movement in Italy from about 1943 to 1952, which reacted against the artificiality of the pre-war & Fascist cinema. Although its adherents were diverse and never really formed a school, most of them shared a generally left-wing attitude, and relied on natural decor, unprofessional actors, and a simple direct style of direction. In the words of their spokesman, Zavattini (q.v.), the purest example of neo-realism possible would be a film of 90 consecutive minutes in the life of a worker. The films that may be grouped under the heading of neo-realism include: *Ossessione, La terra trema* (Visconti); *Roma, città aperta, Paisa, Europa 51* (Rossellini); *La porta del cielo, Sciuscia, Bicycle thieves, Miracolo in Milano, Umberto D* (De Sica); *Sotto il sole di Roma, È primavera, Due soldi di speranza* (Castellani); *Il testimone* (Germi); *Il bandito, Senza pietà* (Lattuada); *Domenica d'agosto* (Emmer); *Vivere in pace, Anni difficili* (Zampa); *Caccia tragica, Bitter rice* (De Santis); *Un giorno nella vita* (Blasetti); *Il sole sorge ancora* (Vergano). The scriptwriters Cecchi d'Amico and Amidei (qqv.) as well as Zavattini and the director of photography, Aldo (q.v.), also played an important part in the movement.

404 new cinema: term sometimes given to more or less homogeneous groups of young film-makers which have emerged in various countries over the last few years. Their films are characterised by a freshness of approach and a desire to break away from tradition. The countries in which this phenomenon has been most noticeable include **France** (see *nouvelle vague);* **Brazil: Carlos Diegues** (b. 1940): *Ganga zumba* 65; *The big city* 66; **Ruy Guerra** (b. 1931): *The unscrupulous ones* 62; *The guns* 66; **Leon Hirszman** (b. 1937): *The death* 65; *The boy from the plantation* 66; **Glauber Rocha** (b. 1939): *The brute* 61; *The black god and the white devil* 63; *Earth in revolt* 67; **Nelson Pereira Dos Santos:** *Rio, 40 degrees* 55; *A northern suburb of Rio* 57; *Mandacaru vermelho* 61; *Barren lives* 63; *El justicero* 67; **Roberto Santos** (b. 1928): *The great moment* 64; *The time and hour of Augusto Matraga* 66; **Paolo Saraceni** (b. 1933): *Porto das Caixas* 61; *The challenge* 65.

405 new cinema (cont.) **Czechoslovakia: Milos Forman** (q.v.); **Jan Nemec** (q.v.); **Evald Schorm** (q.v.); **Vera Chytilová** (b. 1929): *The top* 61; *Bag of fleas* 62; *Another way of life* 63; *Little pearls from the bottom (At the world cafeteria* ep.) 65; *Daisies* 66; **Jaromil Jires** (b. 1935): *The first cry* 63; *Little pearls from the bottom (Romance* ep.) 65; *The joke* 67; **Pavel Juracek** (b. 1935): Scr.: *Baron Munchausen, The end of August at the Hotel Ozone, Daisies.* Films: *Josef Kilian* (co. J. Schmidt) 63; *Every young man* 66; **Antonín Mása** (b. 1936): Scr.: *Everyday courage.* Films: *Wandering* 64; *Hotel* *for foreigners* 67; **Jiri Menzel** (b. 1938) Acted: *The top, Everyday courage, The return of the prodigal son, Hotel for foreigners.* Films: *Little pearls from the bottom (The death of Mr. Balthazar* ep.) 65; *Special priority trains* 66; **Ivan Passer** (b. 1933): Scr.: *Talent competition, Peter and Pavla, Loves of a blonde, Fire, fire!* Films: *Little pearls from the bottom (Insipid afternoon* ep.) 65; *Intimate lighting* 66; **Jan Schmidt** (b. 1934): *Josef Kilian* (co. P. Juracek) 63; *The end of August at the Hotel Ozone* 65; **Stefan Uher** (b. 1930): *Catching the sun in a net* 62; *The organ* 64; *The miraculous virgin* 66.

406 new cinema (cont.) **Germany: Vlado Kristl** (q.v.); **Alexander Kluge** (b. 1932): Main shorts: *Brutalität in Stein* 60; *Porträt einer Bewährung* 65. Film: *Yesterday girl* 66; **Hansjürgen Pohland** (b. 1934): *Tobby* 61; *Katz und Maus* 66; *Dieser Mann und Deutschland* 67; *Tamara* 68; **Edgar Reitz** (b. 1932): Dir. of photography: *Yesterday girl.* Main shorts: *Yukatan* 60; *Geschwindigkeit* 63. Film: *Mahlzeiten* 67; *Fussnoten* 68; **Peter Schamoni** (b. 1934): Acted: *The letter.* Film: *Schönzeit für Füchse* 66; **Ulrich Schamoni** (b. 1939): Acted: *The letter.* Shorts: *Hollywood in Jugoslavia* 65; *Lockenköpfchen* 67. Films: *Es* 66; *Alle Jahre wieder* 67; **Volker Schlöndorff** (b. 1939): *Young Törless* 66; *A degree of murder* 67; **Jean-Marie Straub** (b. 1933): *Nicht versöhnt* 65; *Cronaca di Anna Magdalena Bach* (in Italy) 67.

407 new cinema (cont.) **Hungary: Miklós Jancsó** (q.v.): **István Szabó**

(q.v.); **István Gaál** (b. 1933): *Current* 64; *The green years* 65; *Baptism* 67; **Ferenc Kardos** (b. 1937): Short: *Letters to Julia* 64. Films: *Grimace* (co. J. Rózsa) 65; *Holidays* 67; **Ferenc Kosa** (b. 1937): Short: *Light* 62. Film: *Ten thousand days* 65; **András Kovács** (b. 1925): *Summer rain* 60; *On the roofs of Budapest* 61; *Difficult people* 64; *Cold days* 66; *Walls* 68.

408 new cinema (cont.) **Jugoslavia: Dusan Makavejev** (b. 1932): *Man is not a bird* 65; *Love dossier* 66; **Zivojin Pavlovic** (b. 1933): *The homecoming* 64; *The enemy* 65; *The rats awake* 66; **Aleksandar Petrovic** (b. 1929): *The days* 63; *Three* 65; *I met some happy gypsies too* 66; **Dusan Vukotic** (b. 1927): At first animator (see *animation*). Films: *The seventh continent* 66; *Black spot on the conscience* 67.

409 new cinema (cont.) **Spain: Jaime Camino** (b. 1936): *Los felices 60* 63; *El español y el amor* (one ep.) 66; **Mario Camus** (b. 1935): *Los farsantes, Young Sanchez* 63; *La visita que no toco el timbre* 65; *Con el viento solano* 66; **Julio Diamante** (b. 1930): *Cuando estallo la paz* 62; *Tiempo de amor* 64; *El arte de vivir* 65; **Jorge Grau** (b. 1930): *El espontaneo* 63; *Acteon* 64; **Miguel Picazo** (b. 1927): *La tia Tula* 63; *Oscuros sueños de Agosto* 67; **Francisco Regueiro** (b. 1934): *El buen amor* 62; *Amador* 64; *Si volvemos a vernos* 67; **Carlos Saura** (b. 1932): *Los golfos* 60; *Llanto por un bandido* 64; *La caza* 65; *Peppermint frappé* 66; **Manuel Summers** (b. 1935): *Del rosa al amarillo* 63; *La nina de luto* 64; *El juego de la oca* 65; *Juguetes rotos* 66.

410 **new cinema** (cont.) **U.S.A.:** **John Cassavetes** (q.v.); **Morris Engel** (q.v.); **Edward Bland:** *The cry of jazz* 58; **Shirley Clarke:** *Skyscraper* (co. W. van Dyke) 58; *The connection* 60; *The cool world* 63; *Portrait of Jason* 67; **Robert Frank** and **Alfred Leslie:** *Pull my daisy* 59; *The sin of Jesus* 61; **John Korty** (also dir. of photography on own films): *The language of faces* 61; *Breaking the habit, The crazy quilt* 65; *Funnyman* 67; **Carl Lerner:** *Black like me* 64; **Ben Maddow:** Scr.: *The asphalt jungle, Intruder in the dust, Spinster.* Short: *The stairs* 51. Film: *The savage eye* (co. Meyers and Strick) 59; **Adolfas Mekas:** *Hallelujah the hills* 63; *The brig* (co. J. Mekas) 64; **Jonas Mekas:** *Guns of the trees* 62; *The brig* (co. A. Mekas) 64; **Sidney Meyers:** *The quiet one* 48; *The savage eye* (co. Maddow and Strick) 59; **Frank Perry:** *David and Lisa* 62; *Ladybug, Ladybug* 63; **Michael Roemer:** *Nothing but a man* 65; **Lionel Rogosin:** *On the Bowery* 54; *Come back Africa* 58; *Good times, wonderful times* 64; **Leslie Stevens:** *Private property* 60; *The land we love* 62; *Hero's island* 63; **Joseph Strick:** *The savage eye* (co. Maddow and Meyers) 59; *The balcony* 63; *Ulysses* 67; new cinema also includes the large group of avant-garde and experimental filmmakers at present active in the U.S.A., the most important of whom include: **Stan Brakhage** (q.v.); **Kenneth Anger:** *Fireworks, The inauguration of the pleasure dome* 58; *Scorpio rising* 61; *Kustom Kar Kommandos* 66; **Curtis Harrington:** *Night tide* 61; *Games* 67; **Gregory Markopoulos:** *Swain* 50; *Galaxie, Serenity* 60-63; *The Illiac passion* 67; **Ron Rice:** *The queen of Sheba meets the atom man, The flower thief;* **Jack Smith:** *Flaming creatures, Normal love* 63-65; **Andy Warhol:** *Kiss, Sleep, Haircut, Eat, Naomi and Rufus kiss* 64; *Harlot* 65; *The Chelsea girls* 66; *Bike boy* 67.

411 **new cinema** (cont.) **U.S.S.R.:** **Marlen Khutsiev** (q.v.); **Mikhail Bogin** (b. 1936): *Two in love* 65; *Zosya* 66; **Georgy Danelia** (b. 1930): *Seryozha* (co. I. Talankin) 60; *The road to the landing-stage* 62; *Walk around Moscow* 64; *Thirty three* 65; **Andrei Mikhalkov-Konchalovsky** (b. 1937): Co. scr.: *The steamroller and the violin, Andrei Rublyov.* Acted: *I am twenty.* Films: *The first teacher* 65; *The year of the quiet sun* 66; **Sergei Paradjanov** (b. 1924): *The first fellow* 58; *Ukrainian rhapsody* 61; *Shadows of forgotten ancestors* 65; **Igor Talankin** (b. 1927): *Seryozha* (co. G. Danelia) 60; *Introduction* 62; *Day-stars* 65; *Tchaikovsky* 67; **Andrei Tarkovsky** (b. 1932): Acted: *I am twenty.* Films: *The steamroller and the violin* 60; *Ivan's childhood* 62; *Andrei Rublyov* 66.

412 **Newman, Paul,** American actor, b. 1924. Since 1952: also stage actor. Main films: *Somebody up there likes me, Until they sail, The left-handed gun, The long hot summer, Cat on a hot tin roof, Rally round the flag boys, From the terrace, Exodus, Sweet bird of youth, Paris Blues, The hustler, What a way to go, The prize, Hud, Lady L, The outrage, Torn curtain, Hombre, The moving target, Cool hand Luke.*

413 **Niblo, Fred,** American director. 1874-1948. 1894-1916: stage and vaudeville actor. Main films: *The mark* of Zorro 20; *The three musketeers* 21; *Blood and sand* 22; *The red lily* 23; *Ben Hur, The temptress* 26; *Two lovers, The mysterious lady* 28.

414 Nichols, Dudley, American scriptwriter. 1895-1960. At first journalist. Main films: *Men without women, Born reckless, Seas beneath, Pilgrimage, The lost patrol, Judge Priest, Steamboat round the bend, The informer, The crusades, Mary of Scotland, The plough and the stars, The hurricane, Bringing up baby, Carefree, Stagecoach, The long voyage home, Man hunt, Swamp water, This land is mine, Air force, For whom the bells tolls, It happened tomorrow, And then there were none, Scarlet Street, The bells of St. Mary's, Mourning becomes Electra* (also directed, 47), *The fugitive, Pinky, Rawhide, Return of the Texan, The big sky, Prince Valiant, The tin star, Heller in pink tights.*

415 Nielsen, Asta, Danish actress, b. 1883. 1900-39: also stage actress. From 1911: Germany. Main films: *Afgrunden, Engelein, Die Suffragette, Das Liebes A-B-C, Intoxication, Hamlet, Reigen, Vanina, Der Erdgeist, Absturz, Hedda Gabler, The joyless street, Dirnentragödie, Unmögliche Liebe.*

416 Niven, David, British actor, b. 1909. Also novelist. Main films: *Dodsworth, The prisoner of Zenda* (37), *Bluebeard's eighth wife* (38), *Wuthering Heights, Raffles, Bachelor mother, The first of the few, The way ahead, A matter of life and death, The elusive Pimpernel, A kiss in the dark, The moon is blue, The king's thief, Carrington V.C., Around the world in 80 days, The little hut, Bonjour tristesse, Separate tables, Ask any girl, Please don't eat the daisies, The guns of Navarone, Guns of darkness, 55 days at Peking, The pink panther, Lady L, Casino Royale, The eye of the devil, The extraordinary seaman.*

417 nouvelle vague: term invented by the press to describe a group of young directors who broke into French films from 1958-61. The nucleus, centred on the review Les Cahiers du Cinéma, include: **François Truffaut** (q.v.); **Claude Chabrol** (q.v.); **Jean-Luc Godard** (q.v.); **Jacques Rivette** (b. 1928): *Paris nous appartient* 58-60; *La religieuse* 65; *L'amour fou* 67; **Eric Rohmer** (b. 1920): *Le signe du lion* 59; *Paris vu par . . .* (one ep.) 65; *La collectionneuse* 66; **Jacques Doniol-Valcroze** (b. 1920): *L'eau à la bouche* 59; *La dénonciation* 62; *Le viol* 67; and the director of photography, **Coutard** (q.v.); a love of the American cinema, a rebellion against conventionality and an emphasis on style are features of their films. The term has also been used loosely to include certain films of other French directors who started to work in features during the same period: **Jean-Gabriel Albicocco** (b. 1936): *La fille aux yeux d'or* 61; **Armand Gatti** (b. 1924): *L'enclos* 61; **Marcel Hanoun** (b. 1929): *Une simple histoire* 58; *Le huitième jour* 59; **Pierre Kast** (b. 1920): *Le bel âge* 59; *La mortesaison des amours* 60; **Jean-Pierre Mocky** (b. 1929): *Les dragueurs* 59; *Un couple* 60; **Edouard Molinaro** (b. 1928): *Une fille pour l'été* 59; *La mort belle* 60; **Jacques Rozier** (b. 1926): Shorts: *Rentrée des classes* 55; *Blue jeans* 58; *Dans le vent* 63. Film: *Adieu Philippine* 62.

418 Novarro, Ramon, American actor, b. 1899 in Mexico. Since 1917: U.S.A. Since 1918: also stage actor. Main films: *The four horsemen of the Apocalypse* (21), *A small town idol, The prisoner of Zenda* (22), *Where the pavement ends, The red lily, Scaramouche, Ben Hur* (26), *The student prince, Daybreak, Mata Hari, The barbarian, Laughing boy, We were strangers, The big steal, Crisis, Heller in pink tights.*

419 Nykvist, Sven, Swedish director of photography, b. 1922. Main films: *Barabbas* (53), *Sawdust and tinsel* (interiors only), *Karin Månsdotter, Salka Valka, The girl in tails, The lady in black, The virgin spring, The judge, Through a glass darkly, Winter light, The silence, Now about these women, To love, Loving couples, The vine bridge* (also dir. 65), *Persona, The hour of the wolf, The shame.*

O

420 Odets, Clifford, American scriptwriter. 1906-1963. 1923-37: stage actor, and playwright *(The big knife).* Main films: *The general died at dawn, Golden boy, None but the lonely heart* (also directed, 44), *Deadline at dawn, Humoresque, The country girl, Sweet smell of success, The story on page one* (also directed, 60).

421 Olivier, Sir Laurence, British actor and director, b. 1907. Since 1921: also stage actor and producer. Main films as actor: *As you like it, Fire over England, Wuthering Heights, Rebecca,* *Pride and prejudice, Lady Hamilton, 49th Parallel, The demi-paradise, Carrie, The beggars' opera, The devil's disciple, Spartacus, The entertainer, Term of trial, Othello* (66), *Bunny Lake is missing, Khartoum,* and all his own films. Films as director: *Henry V* 45; *Hamlet* 48; *Richard III* 55; *The prince and the showgirl* 57.

422 Olmi, Ermanno, Italian director, b. 1931. At first stage producer. Also TV producer. Scripted all his own films. Main shorts: *La pattuglia di passo S. Giacomo, Manon: finestra 2, Tre fili fino a Milano, Venezia città moderna, Il pensionato* 53-59. Films: *Il tempo si è fermato* 59; *Il posto* 61; *I fidanzati* 62; *E venne un uomo* 64; *Beata gioventù* 67.

423 Ophüls, Max, German director. 1902-57. 1919: actor, then stage producer up to 1932. 1933-41: France. 1941-50: U.S.A. 1950-57: France. Films: *Dann schon lieber Lebertran* 30; *Die lachenden Erben, Die verliebte Firma* 31; *Die verkaufte Braut, Liebelei* 32; *Une histoire d'amour, On a volé un homme* 33; *La signora di tutti* (in Italy) 34; *Divine* 35; *Valse brillante, Ave Maria* (both shorts), *Komoedie om Geld* (in Holland), *La tendre ennemie* 36; *Yoshiwara* 37; *Werther* 38; *Sans lendemain* 39; *De Mayerling à Sarajevo* 40; *Vendetta* (completed by M. G. Ferrer) 46; *The exile* 47; *Letter from an unknown woman, Caught* 48; *The reckless moment* 49; *La ronde* 50; *Le plaisir* 51; *Madame de . . .* 53; *Lola Montès* 55.

424 Oswald, Richard, Austrian director, b. 1880. Main films: *Es werde Licht* 18; *Reigen* 21; *Lady Hamilton, Lukrezia Borgia* 22; *Cagliostro* 29; *Al-*

Max Ophüls
Yasujiro Ozu
Pier Paolo Pasolini

Gregory Peck
Anthony Perkins
Gérard Philipe

Vsevolod Pudovkin
Anthony Quinn
Raimu

László Ranódy
Jean Renoir
Alain Resnais

Mikhail Romm
Edward G. Robinson
Ralph Richardson

Tatiana Samoilova
Roberto Rossellini
Francesco Rosi

Simone Signoret
Dmitri Shostakovitch
Peter Sellers

Mario Soldati
Alf Sjöberg
Victor Sjöström

raune 30; *Unheimlige Geschichten* 32; *Tempête sur l'Asie* 39; *The captain of Koepenick* 41.

425 Ozep, Fedor, Director, b. 1895 in Russia, d. 1948. Scripted: *Aelita,* and*. 1929: Germany. 1932: France. 1940: U.S.A. Main films: *Siemla v plenu** 28; *A living corpse** 29; *The crime of Dmitri Karamazov** 31; *Amok* 34; *Tarakanova* (co-dir. Soldati) 37; *Gibraltar* 38.

426 Ozu, Yasujiro, Japanese director, 1903-63. At first scriptwriter. Main films: *Pumpkin* 28; *Life of an office worker, The revengeful spirit of Eros* 30; *Young miss* 31; *I was born but . . .* 32; *Passing fancy* 33; *A story of floating weeds* 34; *The only son* 36; *The Toda brothers* 41; *There is a father* 42; *The record of a tenement gentleman, A hen in the wind* 48; *Late spring* 49; *The Munakata sisters* 50; *Early summer* 51; *The flavour of green tea and rice* 52; *Tokyo story* 53; *Early spring* 56; *Tokyo twilight* 57; *Equinox flower* 58; *Good morning, Floating weeds* 59; *Late autumn* 61; *Early autumn, An autumn afternoon* 62.

P

427 Pabst, Georg W., German director, 1885-1967. From 1910: stage actor, then producer. 1933: France. Since 1940: Germany and Austria. Films: *Der Schatz* 23; *Gräfin Donelli* 24; *The joyless street* 25; *Secrets of a soul, Man spielt nicht mit der Liebe* 26; *The love of Jeanne Ney* 27; *Pandora's box, Abwege* 28; *Diary of a lost girl, The white*

hell *of Piz Palü* (co-dir. A. Fanck) 29; *Westfront 1918, Skandal um Eva* 30; *The threepenny opera, Kameradschaft* 31; *L'Atlantide* 32; *Don Quixote* 33; *A modern hero* (in U.S.A.), *Du haut en bas* 34; *Mademoiselle Docteur* 37; *Le drame de Shanghai, Jeunes filles en détresse* (remake of L. Sagan's *Mädchen in Uniform* 31) 39; *Komödianten* 41; *Paracelsus* 43; *Der Fall Molander* 45; *Der Prozess* 48; *Geheimnisvolle Tiefe* 49; *La voce del silenzio* (in Italy) 52; *Cose da pazzi* (in Italy) 53; *Ten days to die, Das Bekenntnis der Ina Kahr* 54; *The jackboot mutiny* 55; *Rosen für Bettina, Durch die Wälder, durch die Auen* 56.

428 Pagnol, Marcel, French director, b. 1895. 1922: journalist. Since 1923: also playwright. Scripted: *Marius, Fanny* (32), *Topaze, Tartarin de Tarascon, Le rosier de Madame Husson,* and all his own films. Main films: *César, Un direct au coeur* 33; *Angèle, Joffroi* 34; *Cigalon* 35; *Merleusse* 36; *Regain* 37; *Le Schpountz* 38; *La femme du boulanger* 39; *La fille du puisatier* 40; *Naïs* 45; *La belle meunière* 48; *Topaze* 51; *Manon des sources* 53; *Lettres de mon moulin* 54.

429 Painlevé, Jean, French director of shorts, b. 1902. Made many scientific documentaries. Main shorts: *La pieuvre* 28; *Les oursins* 29; *Le Bernard-l'Hermite* 30; *L'hippocampe* 34; *La quatrième dimension, Barbe-Bleue* (co-dir. R. Bertrand) 37; *Le vampire* 45; *Assassins d'eau douce* 47.

430 Parrish, Robert, American director, b. 1916. At first actor: *City lights, The iron mask, All quiet on the Western front, The informer.* 1939: assistant to G. Stevens. 1939-51: editor. Main films: *The mob, Cry danger* 51; *The purple plain* 53; *Lucy Gallant* 56; *Fire down below* 57; *Saddle the wind* 58; *The wonderful country* 59; *In the French style* 63; *Up from the beach* 65; *Casino Royale* (one ep.), *The bobo* 67; *Duffy* 68.

431 Pasolini, Pier Paolo, Italian director and scriptwriter, b. 1922. Also novelist and poet. Scripted in collaboration: *Le notti di Cabiria, La donna del fiume, La notte brava, Giovani mariti, Il bell'Antonio, La giornata balorda, Morte di un amico, La ragazza in vetrina, La commare secca,* and all his own films. Acted: *Requiescant.* Films: *Accattone* 61; *Mamma Roma, Rogopag* (one episode) 62; *Comizi d'amore* 63; *Il vangelo secondo Matteo* 64; *Uccellacci e uccellini* 66; *Vangelo 70* (one ep.), *Edipo Re* 67.

432 Pastrone, Giovanni, Italian director. 1882-1959. Also known as Piero Fosco. Main films: *Cabiria* 14; *Maciste, Il fuoco* 15; *Maciste alpino, Tigre reale* 16; *Maciste atleta* 18; *Hedda Gabler* 19.

433 Peck, Gregory, American actor, b. 1916. 1938-44: stage actor. Main films: *The keys of the kingdom, Spellbound, Duel in the sun, The Macomber affair, The Paradine case, Gentleman's agreement, Yellow sky, Twelve o'clock high, The gunfighter, Captain Horatio Hornblower, David and Bathsheba, The world in his arms, The purple plain, The snows of Kilimanjaro, Roman holiday, Moby Dick, Designing woman, The big country, Pork Chop Hill, Beloved infidel, On the beach, Cape Fear, The guns of Navarone, How the West* was won, *To kill a mockingbird, Captain Newman, Behold a pale horse, Arabesque, Mirage, MacKenna's gold.*

434 Peckinpah, Sam, American director, b. 1926. Son of Red Indian chief. Since 1950: also TV director (*Jeff, The losers* series). 1956: assistant to Siegel. Films: *The deadly companions, Ride the high country (Guns in the afternoon)* 61; *Major Dundee* 64.

435 Penn, Arthur, American director, b. 1922. Since 1953: also TV producer. Since 1957: also stage producer. Films: *The left-handed gun* 58; *The miracle worker* 61; *Mickey One* 65; *The chase* 66; *Bonnie and Clyde* 67.

436 Périnal, Georges, French director of photography, 1897-1965. 1933: England. From 1957: U.S.A. Main films *La tour* (co.), *Les nouveaux messieurs, Le sang d'un poète, Sous les toits de Paris, Le million, A nous la liberté, Le quatorze juillet, The girl from Maxim's, The private life of Henry VIII, Catherine the Great, The private life of Don Juan, Maria Chapdelaine, Sanders of the river, Things to come, Rembrandt, Under the red robe* (co. Howe), *The drum, Four feathers, The thief of Bagdad* (40), *The life and death of Colonel Blimp, The first of the few, Nicholas Nickleby, Perfect strangers, The fallen idol, A king in New York, Saint Joan, Bonjour tristesse, Once more with feeling, The day they robbed the bank of England, The four horsemen of the Apocalypse* (61).

437 Perkins, Anthony, American actor, b. 1932. Main films: *The actress, Friendly persuasion, Fear strikes out, The tin star, Barrage contre le Pacific, Desire* under the elms, The matchmaker, Green mansions, On the beach, Psycho, Phaedra, The trial, Une ravissante idiote, Paris brûle-t-il?, Le scandale.

438 Perret, Léonce, French director and actor. 1880-1935. 1908: actor under Feuillade. 1917-22: U.S.A. Main films: (as dir. and actor) Léonce veut se marier, L. en voyage, Le coeur de L., L. aux bains de mer, and many others in the 'Léonce' series 10-12; (as dir. only) The million dollar dollies 18; Koenigsmark 24; Madame Sans-gêne 25; La femme nue 27; Sapho 33.

439 Petri, Elio, Italian director, b. 1929. Scripted in collaboration: Il gobbo and all his own films. Films: I sette contadini (short) 49; L'assassino 61; I giorni contati 62; Il maestro di Vigevano 63; Alta infedeltà (one ep.) 64; La decima vittima 65; A ciascuno il suo 66.

440 Philipe, Gérard, French actor, 1922-59. 1942-59: also stage actor. Main films: Les petites du quai aux Fleurs, Le diable au corps, L'idiot, La chartreuse de Parme, Une si jolie petite plage, La beauté du diable, La ronde, Juliette ou la clé des songes, Souvenirs perdus, Fanfan la tulipe, Les sept péchés capitaux (52), Les belles de nuit, Les orgueilleux, Si Versailles m'était conté, Knave of hearts, Le rouge et le noir, Les grandes manoeuvres, La meilleure part, Si Paris nous était conté, Les aventures de Till l'Espiègle (also dir., 56), Montparnasse 19, Pot-Bouille, Le joueur, La fièvre monte à El Pao, Les liaisons dangereuses.

441 Pickford, Mary, Canadian actress, b. 1893. 1898-1909: stage actress.

Since 1923: also producer. Main films: The lonely villa, Pippa passes, The thread of destiny, Ramona, New York hat, Lena and the geese, A good little devil, Tess of the storm country, Cinderella, Rags, A poor little rich girl, A little princess, Rebecca of Sunnybrook Farm, M'Liss, Stella Maris, Daddy Long Legs, Little Lord Fauntleroy, Rosita, Little Annie Rooney, Sparrows, The taming of the shrew (19), Coquette, Kiki, Secrets.

442 Pitts, ZaSu (Liza Susan), American actress, 1898-1963. From 1942: mainly stage actress. Main films: A little princess, Better times, The other half, Poor relations, Rebecca of Sunnybrook Farm, Greed, The wedding march, The honeymoon, Monte Carlo, The man I killed, Dames, Mrs. Wiggs of the cabbage patch, Ruggles of Red Gap, Nurse Edith Cavell, It's a mad, mad, mad, mad world.

443 Poitier, Sidney, American actor, b. 1924. At first stage actor. Main films: No way out, Cry the beloved country!, Red Ball Express, The blackboard jungle, Goodbye my lady, Something of value, Edge of the city (A man is ten feet tall), Band of angels, The defiant ones, Porgy and Bess, A raisin in the sun, Paris Blues, Lilies of the field, The long ships, Duel at Diablo, The greatest story ever told, Guess who's coming to dinner, In the heat of the night, For love of Ivy.

444 Polanski, Roman, Polish director, b. 1933. From 1940: art and film school. Assistant to Munk. Acted: A generation, See you tomorrow, The innocent sorcerers, Lotna, Bad Luck, Samson, and*. Also co-scripted La fille d'en face. Main shorts: A toothy smile 57; Two men and a wardrobe* 58; When angels fall 59; Le gros et le maigre* (in France) 60; Mammals 62; Films: Knife in the water 61; Les plus belles escroqueries du monde (one episode; in France) 63; Repulsion 65; Cul-de-sac 66; The fearless vampire killers 67; Rosemary's baby 68.

445 Pommer, Erich, German producer, 1889-1966. 1915: founded Decla, which later merged with UFA. Since 1934: U.S.A. Main films: The cabinet of Dr. Caligari, Das Indische Grabmal (20), Die Spinnen, Dr. Mabuse the gambler, The Nibelungen, The last laugh, Variété, Metropolis, The blue angel, Liliom, Fire over England, Jamaica Inn, Dance girl dance, They knew what they wanted, Kinder, Mütter, und ein General.

446 Powell, Dick, American actor and director, 1904-63. At first stage actor. Main films as actor: 42nd Street, Gold diggers of 1933, Footlight parade, Wonder Bar, Twenty million sweethearts, Dames, Gold diggers of 1935, Stage struck (36), A midsummer night's dream (34), Hollywood Hotel, Gold diggers of 1937, Singing marine, Varsity show, Christmas in July, Model wife, It happened tomorrow, Johnny O'clock, Cry danger, Tall target, The bad and the beautiful, Susan slept here. Main films as director only: Split second 52; The conqueror 55; The enemy below 57; The hunters 58.

447 Powell, Michael, British director, b. 1905. Also stage producer. Emeric Pressburger co-produced, co-scr., and co-dir. many of his films*. Main films: The edge of the world 37; The spy in black 39; Contraband, The thief of Bagdad (co. Z. Korda) 40; 49th Parallel 41; One of our aircraft is missing (also co-prod. and co-scr. with Pressburger) 42; The life and death of Colonel Blimp*, The volunteer* 43; A Canterbury tale* 44; I know where I'm going* 45; A matter of life and death (Stairway to heaven)* 46; Black narcissus* 47; The red shoes*, The small back room (Hour of glory)* 48; Gone to earth (The wild heart)*, The elusive Pimpernel* 50; Tales of Hoffmann* 51; Oh, Rosalinda!* 55; Battle of the River Plate (Pursuit of the Graf Spee)*, Ill met by moonlight (Night ambush)* 56; Honeymoon 58; Peeping Tom 59; The Queen's guards 60; Bluebeard's castle 64; They're a weird mob 66.

448 Powell, William, American actor, b. 1892. 1912-23: stage actor. Main films: Romola, The last command, The four feathers (29), The canary murder case, The Greene murder case, Paramount on parade, One-way passage, Men in white, The thin man, Manhattan melodrama, Fashions of 1934, Reckless, Escapade, The great Ziegfeld, Libeled lady, After the thin man, My man Godfrey, Double wedding, Another thin man, I love you again, Shadow of the thin man, The thin man goes home, Ziegfeld Follies, Song of the thin man, Mr. Peabody and the mermaid, How to marry a millionaire, Mister Roberts.

449 Preminger, Otto, American director, b. 1906 in Austria. Since 1926: also stage producer. Since 1936: U.S.A. Acted: Margin for error, Stalag 17. Also producer of most of his own films. Main films: Die grosse Liebe 31; Margin for error 43; Laura 44; A royal scandal (Czarina), Fallen angel 45; Forever Amber, Daisy Kenyon 47; That lady in ermine (begun by Lubitsch)

48; *The fan, Whirlpool* 49; *Where the sidewalk ends* 50; *The thirteenth letter* 51; *Angel face* 52; *The moon is blue* 53; *River of no return* 54; *Carmen Jones, The court-martial of Billy Mitchell (One man mutiny)* 55; *The man with the golden arm* 56; *Saint Joan, Bonjour tristesse* 57; *Porgy and Bess* 58; *Anatomy of a murder* 59; *Exodus* 60; *Advise and consent* 62; *The cardinal* 63; *In harm's way* 64; *Bunny Lake is missing* 65; *Hurry sundown* 66.

450 Prévert, Jacques, French scriptwriter, b. 1900. Also poet. Some of his films directed by his brother Pierre Prévert*. Main films: *L'affaire est dans le sac** (32), *Le crime de Monsieur Lange, Une partie de campagne, Jenny, Drôle de drame, Quai des brumes, Le jour se lève, Les visiteurs du soir, Adieu Léonard** (43), *Lumière d'été, Les enfants du paradis, Voyage surprise** (46), *Les portes de la nuit, Les amants de Vérone, Souvenirs perdus* (in collab.), *Bim le petit âne, La bergère et le ramoneur.*

451 Prokofiev, Sergei, Russian composer, 1891-1953. Main films: *Lieutenant Kizhe (The Tsar wants to sleep), Alexander Nevsky, Kotovsky, Lermontov, Ivan the Terrible I and II, Romeo and Juliet.*

452 Protazanov, Yakov, Russian director, 1881-1945. 1920-23: France. Main films: *The queen of spades, Satan triumphant* 16; *Andrei Kozhukhov* 17; *Father Sergius* 18; *The queen's secret* 19; *Le sens de la mort* (in France) 22; *Aelita* 24; *His call (Broken chains)* 25; *The three million case* 26; *The forty first* 27; *Ranks and people* 29; *Holiday of St. Jorgen* 30; *Tommy* 31; *Without dowry*

37; *Salavat Yulayev* 41; *Nasreddin in Bukhara* 43.

453 Ptushko, Alexander, Russian director, b. 1900. 1927-32: dir. puppet films. Trick effects: *Aerograd.* Main films: *A new Gulliver* (full length puppet film) 35; *The golden key* 39; *The stone flower* 46; *Three encounters* (co-dir. Yutkevitch and Pudovkin) 48; *Sadko* 53; *Ilya Muromets* 56; *Sampo* 59; *Crimson sails* 61; *Tale of lost time* 64; *The tale of the Tsar Saltan* 66.

454 Pudovkin, Vsevolod, Russian director, 1893-1953. 1922: joined Kuleshov's 'experimental laboratory'. Scripted: *The death ray, Locksmith and chancellor, The extraordinary adventures of Mr. West in the land of the Bolsheviks.* Acted: *The new Babylon,* and*. Also theorist and author: 'Film technique', 'Film acting'. Films: *Hunger, hunger, hunger* (co-dir. Gardin) 21; *Chess fever* 25; *Mechanics of the brain, Mother** 26; *The end of St. Petersburg** 27; *Storm over Asia* 28; *A simple case* 32; *Deserter* 33; *Victory* 38; *Minin and Pozharsky* 39; *Twenty years of cinema* (co-dir. E. Shub) 40; *Fighting film album* (in collab.) 41; *In the name of the fatherland* (co-dir. D. Vasiliev) 43; *Admiral Nakhimov* 46; *Three encounters* (co-dir. Yutkevitch and Ptushko) 48; *Joukovsky* 50; *The return of Vasili Bortnikov* 53.

Q

455 Quine, Richard, American director, b. 1920. At first actor: *Counsellor at law, Jane Eyre, Babes on Broadway,*

For me and my gal, Words and music, Command decision. Scripted: *Bring your smile along, He laughed last.* Main films: *Purple heart diary* 51; *Sound off* 52; *Pushover, So this is Paris* 54; *My sister Eileen* 55; *The solid gold Cadillac* 56; *Full of life, Operation Mad Ball* 57; *Bell, book and candle* 58; *It happened to Jane* 59; *Strangers when we meet, The world of Suzie Wong* 60; *The notorious landlady* 61; *Paris when it sizzles* 63; *Sex and the single girl, How to murder your wife* 64; *Synanon (Get off my back)* 65; *Hotel* 66; *Oh dad, poor dad* 67.

456 **Quinn, Anthony,** American actor, b. 1915, in Mexico. Since 1936: U.S.A. Main films: *The buccaneer* (38), *The plainsman, Union Pacific, They died with their boots on, Manpower, Blood and sand, The Oxbow incident, Buffalo Bill, Back to Bataan, The brave bulls, Viva Zapata!, Ulisse, La strada, The magnificent matador, Lust for life, The wild party, The river's edge, Wild is the wind, The black orchid, The buccaneer* (remake of above; also dir., 58), *Hot spell, The last train from Gun Hill, Warlock, The savage innocents, Heller in pink tights, The guns of Navarone, Barabbas, Lawrence of Arabia, Requiem for a heavyweight (Blood money), Behold a pale horse, The visit, Zorba the Greek, A high wind in Jamaica, The happening.*

R

457 **Rademakers, Fons,** Dutch director, b. 1921. 1943-53: also stage actor and producer. 1956: assistant to de Sica on *Il tetto.* Films: *Doctor in the village* 58; *Makkers staakt uw wild geraas* 60; *The knife* 61; *Als twee druppels water* 63; *The dance of the heron* 65.

458 **Raft, George,** American actor, b. 1895. Main films: *Scarface, Palmy days, Night after night, If I had a million, The Bowery, Bolero, Rumba, Souls at sea, You and me, Each dawn I die, They drive by night, Manpower, Follow the boys, Black widow, Around the world in 80 days, Some like it hot, Ocean's eleven, The ladies man, The patsy, Casino Royale.*

459 **Raimu,** French actor, 1883-1946. 1900-46: also stage actor. Main films: *Mam'zelle Nitouche, Marius, La petite chocolatière, Le blanc et le noir, Fanny* (32), *Les gaîtés de l'escadron, Tartarin de Tarascon, Faisons un rêve, César, Le secret de Polichinelle, Vous n'avez rien à déclarer?, Les rois du sport, Les perles de la couronne, La chaste Suzanne, Un carnet de bal, Gribouille, L'étrange Monsieur Victor, Dernière jeunesse, La femme du boulanger, Le duel, Les nouveaux riches, Untel, père et fils, La fille du puisatier, Parade en sept nuits, L'Arlésienne, Les inconnus dans la maison, Le bienfaiteur, Le colonel Chabert, Les gueux du paradis, L'homme au chapeau rond.*

460 **Rains, Claude,** British actor, 1889-1967. Since 1900: also stage actor. Since 1933: U.S.A. Main films: *The invisible man, Crime without passion, Hands across the table, Anthony Adverse, The prince and the pauper, They won't forget, The adventures of Robin Hood, Four daughters, They made me a criminal, Juarez, Daughters courageous, Mr. Smith goes to Washington, King's Row,*

The sea hawk, Moontide, Now voyager, Casablanca, Forever and a day, Mrs. Skeffington, Caesar and Cleopatra, Notorious, The passionate friends, Rope of sand, The man who watched trains go by (Paris Express), Lawrence of Arabia, The greatest story ever told.

461 Raizman, Yuli, Russian director, b. 1903. 1927: assistant to Protazanov. Main films: *Katorga* 28; *The earth thirsts* 30; *Flyers* 35; *The last night* 37; *Virgin soil upturned* 40; *Mashenka* 42; *Moscow sky* 44; *Berlin* (co-dir. Y. Svilona) 45; *Rainis* 49; *The cavalier of the golden star* 52; *The communist* 58; *If this be love* 62; *Time of trial and hope* 67.

462 Ranódy, László, Hungarian director, b. 1919. Studied acting. At first assistant. Main films: *Love travelling on a coach* 53; *Discord* 55; *Danse macabre* 57; *For whom the larks sing* 59; *Be good forever* 60; *Skylark* 63; *The golden kite* 66.

463 Ray, Nicholas, American director, b. 1911. At first radio producer. Assistant on Houseman's stage productions. Co-scr. *Circus world.* Films: *They live by night* 47; *A woman's secret, Knock on any door* 48; *In a lonely place* 49; *Born to be bad, On dangerous ground* 50; *Flying leathernecks* 51; *The lusty men* 52; *Johnny Guitar* 53; *Run for cover* 54; *Rebel without a cause, Hot blood* 55; *Bigger than life, The true story of Jesse James (The James brothers)* 56; *Bitter victory* 57; *Wind across the everglades, Party girl* 58; *The savage innocents* 60; *King of kings* 61; *55 days at Peking* (also acted) 62.

464 Ray, Satyajit, Indian director, b. 1922. From 1942: commercial artist. Also composed music of *Shakespeare Wallah,* and*. Films: *Pather Panchali* 52-55; *Aparajito* 56; *The philosopher's stone* 57; *The music room, The world of Apu* 58; *The goddess* 60; *Two daughters, Rabindranath Tagore* (documentary) 61; *Kanchenjungha*, Abhijan** 62; *Mahanagar** 63; *Charulata* 64; *Kapurush* 65; *Nayak* 66.

465 Redgrave, Sir Michael, British actor, b. 1908. Since 1926: also stage actor. Main films: *The secret agent, The lady vanishes, The stars look down, Kipps, Thunder Rock, The way to the stars, Dead of night, The captive heart, The secret beyond the door, Mourning becomes Electra, The Browning version, The importance of being earnest, Oh, Rosalinda!, The dam busters, Confidential report (or Mr. Arkadin), 1984, Time without pity, The happy road, The quiet American, Law and disorder, Shake hands with the devil, The innocents, The loneliness of the long distance runner, Young Cassidy, The hill, The heroes of Telemark.*

466 Reed, Sir Carol, British director, b. 1906. 1924-33: stage actor and producer. Then assistant. Films: *Midshipman Easy* 34; *Laburnum Grove, Talk of the devil* (also scripted) 36; *Bank holiday, Who's your lady friend?* 37; *Penny paradise, Climbing high* 38; *A girl must live, The stars look down* 39; *Night train to Munich, The girl in the news* 40; *Kipps, The young Mr. Pitt* 41; *The way ahead* 44; *The true glory* (doc., co-dir. Kanin) 45; *Odd man out (Gang war)* 47; *The fallen idol* 48; *The third man* 49; *The outcast of the islands* 51; *The man be-*

tween 53; *A kid for two farthings* 55; *Trapeze* 56; *The key* 58; *Our man in Havana* 60; *The running man* 63; *The agony and the ecstasy* 64; *Oliver!* 67.

467 Reiniger, Lotte, German woman director of animated films, b. 1899. Invented silhouette animation. 1936-39 and since 1950: England. Also worked in TV. See *animation.* Main films: *The adventures of Prince Achmed* 26; *The adventures of Dr. Dolittle* (series of shorts) 27-28; *Carmen* 33; *Papageno* 35; *The frog prince* 50; *The gallant little tailor, Jack and the beanstalk* 55.

468 Reisz, Karel, British director, b. 1926 in Czechoslovakia. Came to England at an early age. At first film critic and author. See *free cinema.* Shorts: *Momma don't allow* (co-dir. T. Richardson) 55; *We are the Lambeth boys* 58. Films: *Saturday night and Sunday morning* 60; *Night must fall* 64; *Morgan, a suitable case for treatment* 65; *Isadora* 67.

469 Renoir, Claude, French director of photography, b. 1914. Assistant to Kaufman. Main films: *Toni, Une partie de campagne, Monsieur Vincent, Rendez-vous de juillet, Knock* (50), *The river, Le carrosse d'or, Le mystère Picasso, Eléna et les hommes, Les sorcières de Salem, Une vie, Les tricheurs, Et mourir de plaisir, Symphonie pour un massacre, L'insoumis, L'enfer, La curée, Barbarella.*

470 Renoir, Jean, French director, b. 1894. Son of painter Auguste Renoir. 1940-49: U.S.A. Also playwright and stage producer. Acted: *Le petit chaperon rouge, La p'tite Lili, La règle du jeu.* 1960: also TV producer. Films: *La*

fille de l'eau 24; *Nana* 26; *Charleston, Marquita* 27; *La petite marchande d'allumettes* 28; *Tire-au-flanc, Le tournoi, Le bled* 29; *On purge bébé, La chienne* 31; *La nuit du carrefour, Boudu sauvé des eaux* 32; *Chotard et Cie., Madame Bovary* 33; *Toni, Le crime de Monsieur Lange* 35; *La vie est à nous, Les basfonds, Une partie de campagne* 36; *La grande illusion, La Marseillaise* 37; *La bête humaine* 38; *La règle du jeu* 39; *La Tosca* (in Italy, unfinished) 40; *Swamp water* 41; *This land is mine* 43; *Salute to France* 44; *The Southerner, Diary of a chambermaid* 46; *The woman on the beach* 47; *The river* (in India) 50; *Le carrosse d'or* (in Italy) 52; *French Cancan* 54; *Eléna et les hommes* 56; *Le déjeuner sur l'herbe* 59; *Le testament du Dr. Cordelier* 60; *Le caporal épinglé* 61.

471 Resnais, Alain, French director, b. 1922. At first stage actor. Editor: *Paris 1900, Aux frontières de l'homme* (also assistant), *La pointe courte.* Shorts: *Van Gogh* 48; *Guernica, Gauguin, L'alcool tue* 50; *Les statues meurent aussi* (co-dir. Marker) 52; *Nuit et brouillard* 55; *Toute la mémoire du monde* 56; *Le mystère de l'atelier 15* (co-dir. Heinrich and Marker) 57; *Le chant du styrène* 58. Films: *Hiroshima, mon amour* 59; *L'année dernière à Marienbad* 61; *Muriel, ou le temps d'un retour* 63; *La guerre est finie* 65; *Loin du Viêtnam* (in coll.) 67; *Je t'aime, je t'aime* 68.

472 Révész, György, Hungarian director, b. 1927. Main films: *Two times two is sometimes five* 54; *Gala dinner* 55; *At midnight* 57; *What a night* 58; *Danger on the Danube* 61; *Land of angels,*

Hail days 63; Well, young man? 64; Every beginning is hard 66; One love in three nights 67.

473 Richardson, Sir Ralph, British actor, b. 1902. Since 1920: also stage actor. Main films: *Things to come, The man who could work miracles, The citadel, South Riding, Four feathers, The lion has wings, On the night of the fire, The volunteer, School for secrets, Anna Karenina* (48), *The fallen idol, The heiress, The outcast of the islands, Home at seven* (also dir., 52), *The sound barrier, Richard III, Our man in Havana, Exodus, Long day's journey into night, Woman of straw, Dr. Zhivago, Khartoum.*

474 Richardson, Tony, British director, b. 1928. Since 1949: also TV and stage producer. See *free cinema.* Films: *Momma don't allow* (short, co-dir. Reisz) 55; *Look back in anger* 59; *Sanctuary* (in U.S.A.), *The entertainer* 60; *A taste of honey* 62; *The loneliness of the long distance runner* 62; *Tom Jones* 63; *The loved one* 64; *Mademoiselle* (in France) 65; *The sailor from Gibraltar* 66; *Red white and zero* (one ep.), *The charge of the Light Brigade* 67.

475 Richter, Hans, German director of animated films, b. 1888. Also painter. 1916: joined Dada movement. Collaborated with Viking Eggeling. See *avant-garde* and *animation.* Since 1940: U.S.A. Main films: *Rhythm 21, 23,* and *25* 21-25; *Filmstudie* 26; *Inflation, Vormittagsspuk, Rennsymphonie* 28; *Alles dreht sich, alles bewegt sich* 29; *Metall* 31-33; *The lies of Baron Munchausen* 39; *Dreams that money can buy* 47; *Thirty years of experiment* (anthology of own films, and those of Egge-

ling and Ruttmann) 51; *Passionate pastime* 56; *Dadascope* 57.

476 Riefenstahl, Leni, German woman director, b. 1902. 1923-26: dancer. Acted in the 'mountain' films of Dr. A. Fanck: *Der heilige Berg* 26; *Der grosse Sprung* 27; *The white hell of Piz Palü* (co-dir. Pabst) 29; *Stürme über dem Mont Blanc* 30; and also in some of her own films*. Scripted all her own films. Nazi. Shorts: *The blue light** 32; *Sieg des Glaubens* 33; *Tag des Freiheits* 35. Films: *Triumph of the will* 34; *Olympic Games 1936* 36; *Tiefland** 34-45 (released in 54).

477 Ritt, Martin, American director, b. 1920. Also TV and stage producer. Films: *Edge of the city (A man is ten feet tall)* 56; *No down payment, The long hot summer* 57; *The sound and the fury* 58; *The black orchid* 59; *Five branded women* 60; *Paris Blues* 61; *Adventures of a young man* 62; *Hud* 63; *The outrage* 64; *The spy who came in from the cold* 65; *Hombre* 66; *The brotherhood* 67.

478 Roach, Hal, American producer, b. 1892. At first actor. 1914-22: produced about 175 shorts with Harold Lloyd (including *Lonesome Luke* series). Main films: *Putting pants on Philip, The battle of the century, Leave 'em laughing, Two tars, Early to bed, You're darn tootin', Bacon grabbers, Perfect day, Men o'war, Big business, Night owls, The hoose-gow, Helpmates, Pardon us, Their first mistake, The music box, Pack up your troubles, Sons of the desert, The devil's brother, The Bohemian girl, Topper, Way out West, Merrily we live, Swiss Miss, Blockheads, There goes my heart, One million B.C.* (also dir. 40), *A chump at Oxford, Of mice and men.*

479 **Robinson, Edward G.,** American actor, b. 1893 in Rumania. 1903: U.S.A. Since 1915: also stage actor. Main films: *A lady to love, Little Caesar, Tiger shark, The little giant, The whole town's talking, Barbary Coast, Bullets or ballots, Kid Galahad, A slight case of murder, The amazing Dr. Clitterhouse, Confessions of a Nazi spy, Tales of Manhattan, The sea wolf, Manpower, The woman in the window, Double indemnity, Scarlet street, The stranger, The red house, Our vines have tender grapes, All my sons, House of strangers, Actors and sin, The big leaguer, The violent men, Black Tuesday, Tight spot, The ten commandments* (56), *A hole in the head, Seven thieves, My geisha, Two weeks in another town, Sammy going South, The prize, Cheyenne autumn, The outrage, The Cincinnati Kid, La blonde de Pékin.*

480 **Rogers, Ginger,** American actress, b. 1911. Since 1929: also stage actress, singer and dancer. Main films: *42nd Street, Gold diggers of 1933, Twenty million sweethearts, Flying down to Rio, The gay divorcee, Roberta, Top hat, Follow the fleet, Swing time, Shall we dance, Stage door, Carefree, Vivacious lady, Kitty Foyle, Bachelor mother, The story of Vernon and Irene Castle, Tom, Dick, and Harry, The major and the minor, Tender comrade, Once upon a honeymoon, Tales of Manhattan, Weekend at the Waldorf, The Barkleys of Broadway, We're not married, Monkey business* (52), *Forever female, Tight spot, Black widow.*

481 **Röhrig, Walter,** German setdesigner. Also painter. See *expressionism.* Main films: *The cabinet of Dr. Caligari* (co. Warm and Reimann), *Der müde Tod* (co. Warm), *Schloss Vogelöd* (co. Warm), *The last laugh, Tartuffe, Four devils* (co.), *Zur Chronik von Grieshuus, Faust, Le congrès s'amuse, Flüchtlinge.*

482 **Romm, Mikhaïl,** Russian director, b. 1901. 1930-32: scriptwriter. Assistant on *Men and jobs.* Main films: *Boule de suif* 34; *The thirteen, Lenin in October* 37; *Lenin in 1918* 39; *Dream* 43; *Girl no. 217* 44; *The Russian question* 48; *Admiral Ushakov* 53; *Nine days of one year* 62; *Ordinary Fascism* 64; *Lost letters* (short), *A night of thought* 66.

483 **Rooney, Mickey,** American actor, b. 1921. From 1926: also stage and vaudeville actor. 1927-34: acted in many comic shorts in *Mickey* series (known as 'Mickey McGuire'). Main films: *Manhattan melodrama, Hide out, A midsummer night's dream* (34), *Ah! wilderness!, Little Lord Fauntleroy, Captains courageous, Love finds Andy Hardy, Boys' town, The adventures of Huckleberry Finn, Andy Hardy gets spring fever, Babes in arms, Andy Hardy meets debutante, Strike up the band, Andy Hardy's private secretary, Babes on Broadway, Andy Hardy's double life, Girl crazy, Thousands cheer, Ziegfeld Follies, Summer holiday, Sound off, The bridges of Toko-Ri, Operation Mad Ball, Baby Face Nelson, Andy Hardy comes home, Breakfast at Tiffany's, Requiem for a heavyweight, It's a mad, mad, mad, mad world, The extraordinary seaman.*

484 **Rosay, Françoise,** French actress, b. 1891. Since 1908: also stage actress. 1929-31: U.S.A. (where she acted in many French versions of American films incl. *Buster se marie*).

Main films: *Crainquebille, Gribiche, Les deux timides* (28), *Le rosier de Madame Husson, Le grand jeu* (34), *Pension Mimosas, La Kermesse héroïque, Jenny, Drôle de drame, Un carnet de bal, Les gens du voyage, Une femme disparaît, Macadam, Le mystère Barton, The thirteenth letter, L'auberge rouge* (51), *Les sept péchés capitaux* (52), *Me and the colonel, Le joueur, The sound and the fury.*

485 **Rosi, Francesco,** Italian director, b. 1922. From 1946: stage producer. Assistant to Visconti on *La terra trema.* Co-scr.: *Domenica d'Agosto, Processo alla città, Parigi è sempre Parigi, Bellissima, I vinti, Carosello Napoletano, Proibito, Il sorpasso,* and*. Films: *Camicie rosse* (begun by Alessandrini) 52; *Kean* (co-dir. Gassman) 56; *La sfida** 58; *I magliari** 59; *Salvatore Giuliano** 62; *Le mani sulla città** 63; *Il momento della verità** 64; *C'era una volta** 66.

486 **Rossellini, Roberto,** Italian director, b. 1906. At first technician and editor. Scripted in collab.: *Medico condotto,* and all his own films. See *neo-realism.* Main shorts: *Fantasia sottomarina* 36; *Il ruscello di ripasottile* 40. Films: *La nave bianca* 41; *Un pilota ritorna, L'uomo della croce* 42; *Desiderio* (co-dir. M. Pagliero) 43; *Roma, città aperta* 45; *Paisa* 46; *Amore* 47; *Germania, anno zero, La macchina ammazzacattivi* 48; *Stromboli, Francesco Giulare di Dio,* 49; *Les sept péchés capitaux* (one episode), *Europa* 51 52; *Dov'è la libertà?, Siamo donne* (one episode), *Voyage to Italy* 53; *Amori di mezzo secolo* (one episode), *Giovanna d'Arco al*

rogo 54; *Angst* 55; *India* 58; *Il generale della Rovere* 59; *Era notte a Roma, Viva l'Italia!* 60; *Vanina Vanini* 61; *Anima nera, Rogopag* (one episode) 62; *L'eta del ferro* (doc.) 63; *La prise du pouvoir par Louis XIV* 65.

487 **Rossen, Robert,** American director, 1908-1966. From 1937: scriptwriter: *A walk in the sun, Marked woman, They won't forget, The roaring twenties, The sea wolf, Edge of darkness, The strange love of Martha Ivers,* and almost all his own films. Since 1949: also producer of most of his films. Films: *Johnny O'clock, Body and soul* 47; *All the king's men* 49; *The brave bulls* 51; *Mambo* 54; *Alexander the Great* 55; *Island in the sun* 57; *They came to Cordura* 59; *The hustler* 61; *Lilith* 63.

488 **Rossi, Franco,** Italian director, b. 1919. At first assistant to Camerini and Castellani. Also worked in radio. Main films: *Il seduttore* 54; *Amici per la pelle* 55; *Calypso* 58; *Morte di un amico* 60; *Odissea nuda* 61; *Smog* 62; *Alta infedeltà* (one ep.) 63; *Tre notti d'amore* (one ep.), *Controsesso* (one ep.), *Le bambole* (one ep.) 64; *Una rosa per tutti* 65; *Le streghe* (one ep.), *Non faccio la guerra, faccio l'amore* 66.

489 **Rota, Nino,** Italian composer, b. 1911. Main films: *Le miserie del signor Travet, Vivere in pace, E primavera, I vitelloni, La strada, Il bidone, Amici per la pelle, War and peace, Le notti bianche, Le notti di Cabiria, La grande guerra, La dolce vita, Plein soleil, Rocco e i suoi fratelli, Il brigante, Boccaccio '70, Isola di Arturo, Otto e mezzo, The leopard, Mafioso, Mare matto, Il maestro di Vigevano, Giulietta degli spiriti.*

490 Rotha, Paul, British director, b. 1907. 1931-33: worked with Grierson (q.v.). Also producer and film historian. Scripted many of his films*, most of which are documentaries. Main films: *Contact** 32; *Shipyard**, *The face of Britain** 33; *The fourth estate* 40; *World of plenty** 43; *Land of promise* 46; *The world is rich* 48; *No resting place* (feature) 51; *World without end** (co-dir. Wright) 53; *Cat and mouse* (feature) 57; *The life of Adolf Hitler, The silent raid* (feature) 62.

491 Rotunno, Giuseppe, Italian director of photography. Cameraman: *Senso.* Main films: *Pane, amore e ..., Le notti bianche, The naked Maja, Policarpo ufficiale di scrittura, La grande guerra, Five branded women, On the beach, Rocco e i suoi fratelli, Boccaccio '70* (Visconti episode), *The leopard, Cronaca familiare, I compagni, Yesterday, today and tomorrow, The Bible ... in the beginning, Le streghe, Edipo Re.*

492 Rouch, Jean, Fench director of documentaries, b. 1917. Also ethnographer. Since 1946: dir. many ethnographical shorts. See *cinéma-vérité*. Main shorts: *Initiation à la danse des possédés* 48; *Les gens du Nil* 51; *Les maîtres-fous, Mammy water* 56. Films: *Les fils de l'eau* 55; *Moi un noir* 58; *La pyramide humaine* 60; *Chronique d'un été* (co-dir. E. Morin) 61; *La punition* 62; *Rose et Landry, Monsieur Albert Prophète* (co. J. Ravel) 63; *Paris vu par ...* (one ep.), *La chasse au lion à l'arc* 65; *La goumbe des jeunes noceurs* 66; *Jaguar* 67.

493 Rouquier, Georges, French director of documentaries, b. 1909.

At first typographer. Scripted all his own films. Films: *Vendanges* 29; *Le tonnelier* 42; *Le charron, La part de l'enfant* 43; *Farrébique* 46; *Pasteur* 47; *Le chaudronnier* 49; *Le sel de la terre* 50; *Sang et lumière* (feature) 53; *Lourdes* 54; *Arthur Honegger* 55; *La bête noire, S.O.S. Noronha* (feature) 56.

494 Ruttmann, Walter, German director, 1887-1941. Also abstract painter. 1927: worked with Piscator. Most of his films are documentaries. See *avant-garde*. Main films: *Opus I, II, II, IV* 23-25; *Berlin, rhythm of a city* 27; *Melodie der Welt* 29; *Week-end* 30; *In der Nacht, Feind im Blut* 31; *Acciaio* (in Italy; scripted by Pirandello) 33; *Metall des Himmels* 35; *Mannesmann* 37; *Deutsche Panzer* 40.

S

495 Samoilova, Tatiana, Russian actress, b. 1934. Also stage actress. Films: *The Mexican, The cranes are flying, The letter that was not sent, Vingt mille lieues sur la terre, Alba Regia, Italiani brava gente, Anna Karenina* (67).

496 Samsonov, Samson, Russian director, b. 1921. Films: *The grasshopper* 55; *Behind the shop window* 56; *Born in flames* 57; *Man of the century* 60; *An optimistic tragedy* 63; *Three sisters* 64.

497 Sanders, Denis, American director. His brother, Terry Sanders, collaborates on and produces all his films. Films: *Time out of war* (short) 54; *Crime and punishment* 62 58; *War hunt* 61; *Shock treatment* 63.

498 Sanders, George, British actor, b. 1906. At first stage actor. Since 1936: U.S.A. Main films: *Lloyds of London, Love is news, Four men and a prayer, Confessions of a Nazi spy, Green hell, The house of the seven gables, Rebecca, Foreign correspondent, Man hunt* (41), *The black swan, Rage in heaven, Her cardboard lover, The moon and sixpence, Tales of Manhattan, The lodger* (43), *Hangover Square, The picture of Dorian Gray, The ghost and Mrs. Muir, Lured, Forever Amber, The private affairs of Bel Ami, The fan, Samson and Delilah, The light touch, Voyage to Italy, Ivanhoe, Moonfleet, While the city sleeps, That kind of woman, Solomon and Sheba, A shot in the dark, The Quiller memorandum.*

499 Schlesinger, John, British director, b. 1926. At first actor. 1956-59: dir. shorts for TV. Shorts: *The innocent eye* 58; *Terminus* 60. Films: *A kind of loving* 62; *Billy Liar* 63; *Darling* 65; *Far from the madding crowd* 67.

500 Schoedsack, Ernest B., American director, b. 1893. From 1914: newsreel cameraman. Merian C. Cooper collaborated on some of his films*. Main films: *Grass** 26; *Chang** 27; *The four feathers** 29; *Rango* 31; *The most dangerous game (The hounds of Zaroff)* 32; *King Kong*, Son of Kong, Blind adventure* 33; *Dr. Cyclops* 40; *Mighty Joe Young** 49.

501 Schorm, Evald, Czechoslovakian director, b. 1931. See *new cinema.*

Acted: *A report on the party and the guests, Hotel for foreigners.* Shorts: *Why* 63; *Psalm, The legacy* 65. Films: *Everyday courage* 64; *Little pearls from the bottom (The house of joy* ep.) 65; *The return of the prodigal son* 66; *Five girls to cope with, The end of the priest* 67.

502 Schüfftan, Eugen, German director of photography, b. 1893. 1940: U.S.A. Since 1950: France. Main films: *Dann schon lieber Lebertran, People on Sunday, L'Atlantide* (32), *Du haut en bas, La tendre ennemie, Komoedie om Geld, Yoshiwara, Werther, Drôle de drame, Mademoiselle Docteur, Le drame de Shanghai, Quai des brumes, It happened tomorrow, Sans lendemain, Le rideau cramoisi, La p . . . respectueuse, Ulisse, Mina de Vanghel, La première nuit, La tête contre les murs, Les yeux sans visage, The hustler, Lilith, Phone number 728.*

503 Sellers, Peter, British actor, b. 1925. At first radio comedian. Main films: *The ladykillers, Up the creek, The naked truth (Your past is showing), tom thumb, The mouse that roared, The battle of the sexes, I'm all right Jack, Carleton Browne of the F.O., Two way stretch, The millionairess, Mr. Topaze (I like money)* (also dir., 62), *Only two can play, Dock brief (Trial and error), Waltz of the toreadors, Lolita, The wrong arm of the law, The pink panther, Dr. Strangelove, The world of Henry Orient, What's new pussycat?, A shot in the dark, Caccia alla volpe, Sept fois femme, Casino Royale, The bobo, The party.*

504 Selznick, David O., American producer, 1902-65. 1932: producer at R.K.O. 1933: M.G.M. 1936: founded

Selznick International Pictures. Main films: *White shadows of the South Seas, What price Hollywood, A bill of divorcement, Our betters, Bird of paradise, Dinner at eight, Dancing lady, Viva Villa!, Little women, King Kong, David Copperfield, Anna Karenina* (35), *Little Lord Fauntleroy, The garden of Allah, A star is born* (37), *Nothing sacred, The prisoner of Zenda, Gone with the wind, Rebecca, Jane Eyre, Claudia, The keys of the kingdom, Since you went away, The spiral staircase, Spellbound, Duel in the sun, The Paradine case, The third man, Gone to earth, Stazione termini, A farewell to arms.*

505 Sennett, Mack, American producer, 1880-1960. 1908-12: acted: *The lonely villa* etc. 1912: founded Keystone. 1915: Triangle Keystone. 1923: worked for Pathé. Often scripted own productions. Main films: *Tillie's punctured romance* (also dir., 14), *A submarine pirate, Mickey, Yankee doodle in Berlin, A small town idol, Molly O', Suzanna, The extra girl, The shriek of Araby,* and many hundreds more. Some of them were compiled into: *Anything for laughs* 62. Among the comedians who worked for Sennett were: Chaplin, Gloria Swanson, Keaton, Langdon, W. C. Fields, Carole Lombard (qq.v.), **Mabel Normand** (1894-1930): *Tillie's punctured romance, Mickey, Suzanna, The extra girl* etc.; **Ben Turpin** (1874-1940): *His new job, The champion, Carmen* etc. (all with Chaplin), *Yankee doodle in Berlin, Uncle Tom without a cabin. The shriek of Araby, Down on the farm, The raspberry romance* etc.; **Louise Fazenda** (1895-1962): *The judge, Down on the farm, House of terror, Cuban love song, Rain or shine, Alice in*

Wonderland etc.; **Larry Semon** (1890-1928): (dir. all own films) *Stars and stripes* 19; *The sawmill* 21; *The wizard of Oz* 25 etc.; **Roscoe (Fatty) Arbuckle** (1881-1933): films with Normand and Keaton, *Fatty's reckless fling, Miss Fatty's seaside lover* (also dir. both, 15), *Brewster's millions* etc.; **Sydney Chaplin** (1885-1965), brother of Charles): *A dog's life, Shoulder arms, The king* (also dir., 21), *Pay day* etc.; **Chester Conklin** (b. 1888): *Dough and dynamite, Fool's for luck, Two flaming youths, Tillie's punctured romance, Greed, The haunted house, The house of horror, Hallelujah I'm a bum, Modern times, The great dictator, The beautiful blonde from Bashful Bend.*

506 Servais, Jean, French actor, b. 1910. Since 1931: also stage actor and producer. Main films: *Mater dolorosa* (32), *Les misérables* (33), *Angèle, Amok, Quartier sans soleil, La danse de mort, Une si jolie petite plage, Mina de Vanghel, Le château de verre, Le plaisir, Rue de l'Estrapade, Rififi, Les héros sont fatigués, Celui qui doit mourir (He who must die), Quand la femme s'en mêle, Republic of sin, Les menteurs, Thomas l'imposteur.*

507 Shimazu, Yasujiro, Japanese director, b. 1897. Main films: *Market of human flesh* 23; *Sunday* 24; *A village teacher, Stinker* 25; *ABC lifeline* 31; *First steps ashore* 32; *Maiden in the storm* 33; *The woman that night, Our neighbour Miss Yae* 34; *O-Koto and Sasuke* 35; *A brother and his younger sister* 39; *The daily battle* 44.

508 Shindo, Kaneto, Japanese director, b. 1912. At first assistant to

Yoshimura and Mizoguchi. Also script-writer. Main films: *Story of a beloved wife* 51; *A woman's life, Children of Hiroshima* 52; *Epitome, The avalanche* 53; *Gutter* 54; *Ginko the geisha* 55; *The wolves* 56; *The fishing boat, On this earth* 57; *The lucky dragon no. 5, Kanashimiwa onnadakeni* 58; *The bride from Japan* 59; *The island* 60; *The man* 62; *Mother* 64; *Onibaba* 65; *Dynamite doctor, The lost sex* 66; *The origins of sex (Libido)* 67.

509 Shostakovitch, Dimitri, Russian composer, b. 1906. 1924: cinema pianist. Main films: *The new Babylon, Alone, Golden mountains, Counterplan, Three songs of Lenin, The youth of Maxim, The girl-friends, The return of Maxim, Volochayevsk days, A great citizen, The man with a gun, The Vyborg side, Our Russian front, Zoya, Plain people, Pirogov, Michurin, Young guard, Meeting on the Elbe, The fall of Berlin, The unforgettable year 1919, Bielinsky, The first echelon, The gadfly, Hamlet* (64), *War and peace* (64-67), *The song of the rivers, Katerina Izmailova.*

510 Sidney, George, American director, b. 1916. At first actor. From 1932: directed shorts. Main films: *Free and easy* 41; *Thousands cheer* 43; *Bathing beauty* 44; *Anchors aweigh* 45; *The Harvey girls* 46; *The three musketeers* 48; *Annie get your gun* 50; *Show boat* 51; *Scaramouche* 52; *Young Bess, Kiss me Kate* 53; *Jupiter's darling* 55; *The Eddy Duchin story* 56; *Jeanne Eagels, Pal Joey* 57; *Who was that lady?, Pepe* 60; *Bye bye birdie* 62; *A ticklish affair, Viva Las Vegas (Love in Las Vegas)* 63; *Half a sixpence* 67.

511 Siegel, Donald, American director, b. 1912. From 1933: editor. Since 1963: also TV producer. Main films: *The verdict* 46; *Night unto night, The big steal* 49; *The duel at Silver Creek* 52; *China venture* 53; *Riot in Cell Block 11, Private Hell 36* 54; *An Annapolis story, The blue and the gold* 55; *Invasion of the body snatchers, Crime in the streets* 56; *Baby Face Nelson* 57; *Spanish affair, The lineup* 58; *The hound dog man* 59; *Edge of eternity, Flaming star* 60; *Hell is for heroes* 62; *The killers* 64; *The hanged man* 65; *Madigan* 68.

512 Signoret, Simone, French actress, b. 1921. Also stage actress. Main films: *Les démons de l'aube, Macadam, Dédée d'Anvers, Against the wind, Manèges, La ronde, Casque d'or, Thérèse Raquin, Les diaboliques, La mort en ce jardin, Les sorcières de Salem, Room at the top, Le jour et l'heure, Term of trial, Dragées au poivre, Ship of fools, Compartiment tueurs, The deadly affair, Games.*

513 Simon, Michel, French actor, b. 1895 in Geneva. From 1911: boxer and music hall acrobat. Since 1920: also stage actor. Main films: *Feu Mathias Pascal, La passion de Jeanne d'Arc, Tire au flanc* (29), *Jean de la Lune* (31), *On purge bébé, La chienne, Boudu sauvé des eaux, Du haut en bas, L'Atalante, Sous les yeux de l'Occident, Drôle de drame, Les disparus de St. Agil, Quai des brumes, Les nouveaux riches, La fin du jour, Fric-Frac, La Tosca, Boule de suif* (45), *Panique, Fabiola, La beauté du diable, La poison, La vie d'un honnête homme, Saadia, Les trois font la paire, Austerlitz, Cyrano et d'Artagnan, The train, Le vieil homme et l'enfant.*

514 Sinatra, Frank, American actor, b. 1917. At first journalist, then radio singer. Main films: *Anchors aweigh, Double dynamite, Take me out to the ball game, On the town, From here to eternity, The tender trap, Guys and dolls, The man with the golden arm, Not as a stranger, Johnny Concho, High society, Around the world in 80 days, The pride and the passion, Pal Joey, The young lions, Kings go forth, Some came running, A hole in the head, Can-Can, Sergeants three, The Manchurian candidate, Four for Texas, None but the brave* (also prod. and dir., 64), *The naked runner, Tony Rome.*

515 Singer, Alexander, American director, b. 1932. Also stage producer. Assistant to Kubrick. Films: *A cold wind in August* 61; *Psyche '59* 63; *Love has many faces* 65.

516 Siodmak, Robert, American director, b. 1900. 1901-33: Germany. 1933: France. 1940: U.S.A. 1953: returned to Europe. Main films: *People on Sunday* 29; *Stürme der Leidenschaft* 32; *Mister Flow* 36; *Mollenard* 38; *Pièges* 39; *Phantom lady, The suspect* 44; *The spiral staircase, The dark mirror, The killers (A man afraid)* 46; *Cry of the city* 48; *Criss cross* 49; *The crimson pirate* 52; *Le grand jeu* 54; *Die Ratten* (in Germany) 57; *Katia* 59; *L'affaire Nina B* (in France) 61; *Escape from East Berlin* 62; *Custer of the west* 67.

517 Sirk, Douglas, Director, b. 1900 in Denmark. At first actor, journalist, stage producer. About 1937: U.S.A. 1960: Germany. Main films: *Zu neuen Ufern* 35; *Summer storm* 44; *A scandal in Paris* 46; *Lured* 47; *Sleep my love* 48; *Shockproof* 49; *Thunder on the hill* 51; *The magnificent obsession, Sign of the pagan* 54; *Written on the wind, Battle hymn* 57; *Tarnished angels, A time to love and a time to die* 58; *Imitation of life* 59.

518 Sjöberg, Alf, Swedish director, b. 1903. 1925: stage actor. Since 1925: also stage producer. Scr. most of his own films. Films: *The strongest one* (co. A. Lindblom) 29; *They staked their lives, Blossom time* 40; *Home from Babylon* 41; *The road to heaven* 42; *The royal hunt, Frenzy* 44; *The journey* 45; *Iris* 46; *Only a mother* 49; *Miss Julie* 51; *Barabbas* 53; *Karin Månsdotter* 54; *Wild birds* 55; *The last pair out* 56; *The judge* 60; *The island* 64.

519 Sjöström, Victor, Swedish director and actor, 1879-1960. Also known as Victor Seastrom. At first stage actor. 1923-31: U.S.A. Main films as actor: *The vampire, Wanted — a film actress, Thomas Graal's best child, The word, The emperor of Portugal, To joy, Wild strawberries,* and*. Main films as director: *Ingeborg Holm* 13; *Dödskyssen*, Terje Vigen** 16; *The girl from the marsh croft, The outlaw and his wife** 17; *The sons of Ingmar** 18; *Karin, daughter of Ingmar*, The secret of the monastery, His lordship's will* 19; *Mästerman*, The phantom carriage** 20; *Vem dömer?* 21; *Det omrigade huset*, Eld ombord** 22; *He who gets slapped* 24; *The tower of lies* 25; *The scarlet letter* 26; *The divine woman, The wind* 28; *A lady to love* 30; *Markurells i Wadköping* 31; *Under the red robe* (in England) 36.

520 Skolimowski, Jerzy, Polish director, b. 1938. Also poet, playwright

Charles Spaak
Barbara Stanwyck
Mauritz Stiller

Arne Sucksdorff
Gloria Swanson
Hiroshi Teshigahara

Ingrid Thulin
Totò
Jiri Trnka

François Truffaut
Luchino Visconti
Monica Vitti

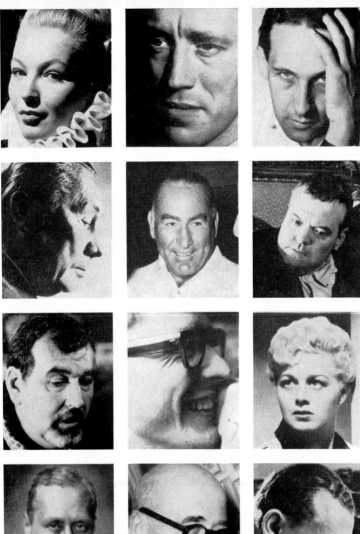

Andrzej Wajda
Max von Sydow
Marina Vlady

Orson Welles
Hal Wallis
Paul Wegener

Shelley Winters
Bo Widerberg
Bernhard Wicki

Karel Zeman
Cesare Zavattini
Gergei Yutkevitch

and boxer. Film school. Co-scr.: *The innocent sorcerers, Knife in the water,* and all his own films. Also acted in some of his own films* and *The innocent sorcerers.* Short: *Boxing* 63. Films: *Identification marks: none** 64; *Walkover** 65; *Barrier* 66; *Le départ* (in Belg.), *Hands up!** 67.

521 Smoktunovsky, Innokenty, Russian actor, b. 1924. Also stage actor. Main films: *The murder in Dante Street, Soldiers, The night visitor, The first day, The letter that was not sent, Nine days of one year, Hamlet* (63-64), *The first visit, On the same planet, Watch your car!, Anna Karenina* (67).

522 Soldati, Mario, Italian director, b. 1906. Also novelist. Scripted (usually in collab.): *Gli uomini, che mascalzoni!, Ma non è una cosa seria, Il signor Max, Una romantica avventura.* Dir. of second unit: *War and peace* (55). Main films: *Tarakanova* (co-dir. F. Ozep) 37; *Piccolo mondo antico* 40; *Malombra* 42; *Le miserie del signor Travet* 45; *La provinciale* 53; *La donna del fiume* 55; *Policarpo ufficiale di scrittura* 59.

523 Spaak, Charles, Belgian scriptwriter, b. 1903. Worked in France since 1928. Main films: *Les nouveaux messieurs, La petite Lise, Le grand jeu* (34), *Pension Mimosas, La Kermesse héroïque, La Bandéra, La belle équipe, Les bas-fonds, La grande illusion, Gueule d'amour, L'étrange Monsieur Victor, La fin du jour, Untel, père et fils, Le ciel est à vous, Panique, L'idiot, Justice est faite, Nous sommes tous des assassins, Avant le déluge, Thérèse Raquin, Charmants garçons, Cartouche, Le caporal épinglé.*

524 Stanwyck, Barbara, American actress, b. 1907. Since 1925: also stage actress and dancer. Since 1958: own TV show. Main films: *Ladies of leisure, The miracle woman, The bitter tea of General Yen, Forbidden, Annie Oakley, The plough and the stars, His brother's wife, Stella Dallas* (37), *Union Pacific, Golden boy, The lady Eve, Ball of fire, Meet John Doe, Double indemnity, The great man's lady, Lady of burlesque, B. F.'s daughter, Sorry wrong number, The strange love of Martha Ivers, The furies, Clash by night, Jeopardy, Blowing wild, Executive suite, Escape to Burma, The violent men, Crime of passion, Forty guns, Walk on the wild side.*

525 Staudte, Wolfgang, German director, b. 1906. Studied theatre under Reinhardt and Piscator. Assistant to Käutner. Acted: *Jud Süss.* 1945: E. Germany. 1955: W. Germany. Scripted all his own films. Main films: *The murderers are amongst us* 46; *Rotation* 49; *The underdog* 51; *Die Geschichte vom kleinen Muck* 53; *Ciske — ein Kind braucht Liebe* 55; *Roses for the prosecutor* 59; *Kirmes* 60; *The threepenny opera* (remake) 62; *Herrenpartie* (in Jugosl.), *The lamb* 64; *Ganovenehre* 66; *Die Klasse* 67.

526 Steiger, Rod, American actor, b. 1925. Also stage actor. Main films: *Teresa, On the waterfront, The big knife, Oklahoma!, The court martial of Billy Mitchell, Jubal, The harder they fall, Run of the arrow, Cry terror, Al Capone, Seven thieves, The mark, Reprieve, The longest day, Le mani sulla città, E venne un uomo, The loved one, Dr. Zhivago, The pawnbroker, In the heat of the night, Assassinio a Sarajevo.*

527 **Sternberg, Josef von,** American director, b. 1894 in Austria. Since 1914: U.S.A. From 1918: editor (also edited all his own films). Scripted: *The street of sin.* Films: *The salvation hunters* 25; *The exquisite sinner, The sea gull, The masked bride* (completed by C. Cabanne) 26; *Underworld* 27; *The last command, The dragnet, The docks of New York* 28; *The case of Lena Smith, Thunderbolt* 29; *The blue angel* (in Germany), *Morocco* 30; *Dishonored, An American tragedy* 31; *Shanghai Express, Blonde Venus* 32; *The scarlet empress* 34; *The devil is a woman* 35; *The king steps out, Crime and punishment* 36; *I Claudius* (unfinished) 37; *Sergeant Madden* 39; *The Shanghai gesture* 41; *The town* 44; *Jet pilot, Macao* 51; *The saga of Anatahan* 53.

528 **Stevens, George,** American director, b. 1904. From 1921: gagman for Roach, cameraman, and dir. of some Laurel and Hardy shorts. Main films: *Alice Adams, Annie Oakley* 35; *Swing time* 36; *Quality Street, A damsel in distress* 37; *Vivacious lady* 38; *Gunga Din* 39; *Penny serenade* 41; *The woman of the year* 42; *The talk of the town, The more the merrier* 43; *A place in the sun, Something to live for* 51; *Shane* 53; *Giant* 56; *The diary of Anne Frank* 58; *The greatest story ever told* 64.

529 **Stewart, James,** American actor, b. 1908. 1932-37: stage actor. Main films: *Seventh heaven, Vivacious lady, You can't take it with you, It's a wonderful world, Jesse James, Destry rides again, Mr. Smith goes to Washington, The shop around the corner, The Philadelphia story, It's a wonderful life, Rope, Ziegfeld girl, Call Northside 777, On our merry way, Winchester 73, Broken arrow, Bend of the river, The greatest show on earth, No highway, The naked spur, Thunder Bay, The Glenn Miller story, The far country, Rear window, Strategic air command, The man from Laramie, The man who knew too much* (54), *The spirit of St. Louis, Vertigo, Bell, book and candle, Anatomy of a murder, Two rode together, How the West was won, The man who shot Liberty Valance, The flight of the phoenix.*

530 **Stiller, Mauritz,** Swedish director, 1883-1928. 1900-12: stage actor and producer. From 1925: U.S.A. Main films: *The black masks, The vampire* 12; *The frontier people, The modern suffragettes* 13; *Artists in love, Storm bird* 14; *Madame de Thèbes, Ports, His wife's past* 15; *Love and journalism* 16; *Alexander the Great, Wanted — a film actress (Thomas Graal's best film)* 17; *Thomas Graal's best child, The song of the blood-red flower* 18; *Herr Arne's treasure, Chains* 19; *Erotikon, Johan* 20; *The emigrants* 21; *Gunnar Hede's saga (The judgement)* 22; *The blizzard* 23; *The saga of Gösta Berling* 24; *Hotel Imperial, Woman on trial* 27; *The street of sin* 28.

531 **Strand, Paul,** American director of documentaries, b. 1890. Scr. all his own films and *The wave.* Also dir. of photography: *The wave, The plow that broke the plains* (co. L. Hurwitz and R. Steiner) and*. Films: *Mannahatta* (co. C. Sheeler) 21; *The heart of Spain** (co. Hurwitz) 37; *Native land** 42.

532 **Stroheim, Erich von,** Director and actor, b. 1885 in Austria, d. 1957.

At first soldier. 1909: U.S.A. 1914: music hall actor, assistant to Griffith. From 1936: France. 1939-45: U.S.A. Scripted: *The devil doll*, and all his own films. Main films as actor: *Hearts of the world, The great Gabbo, The lost squadron, As you desire me, La grande illusion, L'alibi, L'affaire Lafarge, Marthe Richard, Les pirates du rail, Gibraltar, Les disparus de Saint-Agil, Derrière la facade, Pièges, Macao, l'enfer du jeu, Menaces, So ends our night, Five graves to Cairo, The North Star, The great Flammarion, La danse de mort* (also scripted), *Sunset Boulevard, L'envers du paradis, Napoléon* (55), and*. Films as director: *Blind husbands** 18; *The devil's passkey* 20; *Foolish wives** 22; *Merry-go-round* 23; *Greed* 24; *The merry widow* 25; *The wedding march**, *The honeymoon* 27; *Queen Kelly* 28; *Walking down Broadway (Hello sister)* 33.

533 Sturges, John, American director. 1932-42: editor and producer. 1942-45: Army documentaries. Main films: *The capture* 50; *Jeopardy, Escape from Fort Bravo* 53; *Bad day at Black Rock* 54; *Backlash* 55; *Gunfight at the O.K. Corral* 57; *The old man and the sea, The law and Jake Wade* 58; *Last train from Gun Hill, Never so few* 59; *The magnificent seven* 60; *By love possessed, Sergeant's three* 61; *A girl named Tamiko* 62; *The great escape* 63; *The Satan bug* 64; *The Hallelujah trail* 65; *Hour of the gun, Ice Station Zebra* 67.

534 Sturges, Preston, American director, 1898-1959. From 1928: playwright. From 1933: scriptwriter: *The power and the glory, We live again, The good fairy,* and*. Films: *The great McGinty**, *Christmas in July* 40; *The lady Eve, Sullivan's travels* 41; *The Palm Beach story* 42; *The miracle of Morgan's creek, The great moment, Hail the conquering hero** 44; *Mad Wednesday* 46; *Unfaithfully yours** 48; *The beautiful blonde from Bashful Bend** 49; *Les carnets du Major Thompson** (in France) 55.

535 Sucksdorff, Arne, Swedish director of documentaries, b. 1917. Dir. of photog. and scriptwriter of all his own films, some of which are full-length*. Films: *The West Wind* 42; *A summer's tale* 43; *The gull* 44; *Dawn, Shadows on the snow* 45; *Rhythm of a city, Den drömda dalen* 47; *A divided world, The open road* 48; *Strandhugg* 50; *Indian village, The wind and the river* 51; *The great adventure** 53; *A jungle saga** 57; *The boy in the tree ***60; *My home is Copacabana** 64.

536 Swanson, Gloria, American actress, b. 1898. 1916-18: 'bathing beauty' for Sennett. Since 1920: also stage actress. Main films: *Don't change your husband, Male and female, The affairs of Anatol, Beyond the rocks, Madame Sans-gêne* (25), *The loves of Sunya, Sadie Thompson, Queen Kelly, The trespasser, Father takes a wife, Sunset Boulevard, Mio figlio Nerone.*

537 Sydow, Max Von, Swedish actor, b. 1929. Also stage actor since 1951. Main films: *Only a mother, Miss Julie, The seventh seal, Wild strawberries, So close to life, The face, The virgin spring, Through a glass darkly, Winter light, The mistress, The greatest story ever told, The reward, The Quiller memorandum, Hawaii, Here is your life, The hour of the wolf, The black palm trees, The shame.*

538 Szabó, István, Hungarian director, b. 1938. 1956-61: film school. See *new cinema.* Shorts: *Concert, Variations upon a theme* 61; *You* 63. Films: *The age of daydreaming* 64; *Father* 66.

T

539 Tasaka, Tomotaka, Japanese director. Main films: *Behold this mother* 30; *Spring and a girl* 32; *A pebble by the wayside* 38; *Five scouts, Mud and soldiers, Airplane drone* 39; *You and I* 41; *Mother-and-child grass* 42; *Navy* 43; *The maid's kid* 55; *The baby carriage* 57; *The stream of youth* 59; *Run Genta! run!* 61; *A carpenter and children* 62; *Koto — the lake of tears* 66.

540 Tashlin, Frank, American director, b. 1913. 1930-44: cartoonist and animator (with Disney). From 1945: scriptwriter: *The paleface, One touch of Venus, Love happy,* and*. Main films: *Marry me again* 53; *Susan slept here* 54; *Artists and models** 55; *The lieutenant wore skirts, Hollywood or bust, The girl can't help it* 56; *Will success spoil Rock Hunter? (Oh for a man!)** 57; *Rock-a-bye-baby, The geisha boy** 58; *Say one for me* 59; *Cinderfella* 60; *Bachelor flat* 62; *It's only money, The man from the Diners' Club, Who's minding the store?* 63; *The disorderly orderly* 65; *The glass bottom boat* 66; *The private navy of Sgt. O'Farrell* 67.

541 Tati, Jacques, French director and actor, b. 1908. At first rugby player and music hall actor. Acted only: *Sylvie et le fantôme, Le diable au corps.* Scripted and acted: *On demande une brute, Gai dimanche, Soigne ton gauche,* and all his own films. Films: *Oscar, champion de tennis* 32; *Retour à la terre* 45; *L'école des facteurs* 46 (all shorts); *Jour de fête* 47; *Les vacances de Monsieur Hulot* 52; *Mon oncle* 58; *Playtime* 64-67.

542 Taylor, Elizabeth, American actress, b. 1932 in England. Since 1939: U.S.A. Main films: *Jane Eyre, A place in the sun, Ivanhoe, Father of the bride, Beau Brummel, The last time I saw Paris, Giant, Raintree county, Cat on a hot tin roof, Suddenly last summer, Cleopatra* (63), *The V.I.P.s, The sandpiper, Who's afraid of Virginia Woolf?, The taming of the shrew* (66), *Reflections in a golden eye, Goforth.*

543 Teshigahara, Hiroshi, Japanese director, b. 1927. At first painter. Shorts: *Hokusai* 56; *José Torres* 59. Films: *Pitfall* 60; *Woman of the dunes* 63; *The face of another* 66; *Bakuso* 67.

544 Thulin, Ingrid, Swedish actress, b. 1929. Since 1950: also stage actress. Also director of short films. Main films: *When love comes to the village, Foreign intrigue, Wild strawberries, So close to life, The face, The judge, The four horsemen of the Apocalypse, Agostino, Winter light, The silence, Sekstet, Return from the ashes, Night games, La guerre est finie, The hour of the wolf, The bathers.*

545 Tiomkin, Dimitri, American composer, b. 1899. Main films: *Alice in Wonderland, Lost horizon, You can't take it with you, Mr. Smith goes to Washington, Meet John Doe, The Westerner,*

Prelude to war, Tunisian victory, Two down — one to go, Shadow of a doubt, Duel in the sun, It's a wonderful life, Red River, Champion, Strangers on a train, High noon, The thing, Drums in the Deep South, Take the high ground, The high and the mighty, The big sky, I confess, Dial M for murder, Friendly persuasion, Giant, Gunfight at the O.K. Corral, The old man and the sea, Rio Bravo, Land of the Pharaohs, Last train from Gun ,Hill, The unforgiven, The guns of Navarone, The fall of the Roman Empire, Circus world, The war wagon.

546 Tissé, Edward, Russian director of photography, 1897-1961. 1929-32: U.S.A. and Mexico with Eisenstein. Main films: Hunger . . . hunger . . . hunger, Strike, Battleship Potemkin, October, The general line, Frauennot-Frauenglück (also dir. 30; in Switz.), Romance sentimentale, Que viva Mexico! Aerograd, Bezhin meadow, Alexander Nevsky, Ivan the Terrible I and II (exteriors only), In the mountains of Yugoslavia, Meeting on the Elbe, Glinka, Bessmertnyi garnizon.

547 Toland, Gregg, American director of photography, 1904-48. 1920: assistant. Developed technique of deep-focus photography. Main films: We live again, The wedding night, These three, Come and get it!, Dead end, The road to glory, History is made at night, Goldwyn Follies, Wuthering heights, The grapes of wrath, The Westerner, The long voyage home, Citizen Kane, Ball of fire, The little foxes, The outlaw, The best years of our lives, A song is born.

548 Tone, Franchot, American actor, b. 1906. Since 1927: also stage actor. Main films: Today we live, Dancing lady, The world moves on, The stranger's return, Reckless, The lives of a Bengal Lancer, Mutiny on the Bounty (35), Love on the run, They gave him a gun, The king steps out, Quality Street, Fast and furious, Trail of the Vigilantes, Five graves to Cairo, Phantom lady, Here comes the groom, The man on the Eiffel Tower, Advise and consent, In harm's way, Mickey One.

549 Torre Nilsson, Leopoldo, Argentinian director, b. 1924. 1939-49: assistant to his father, Leopoldo Torres Rios. Scripted all his own films (since 1958, in collab. with B. Guido). Main films: El muro (short) 47; Days of hatred 54; Graciela 56; The house of the angel 57; The kidnapper 58; The fall, The party is over 59; A tough guy of 1900, The hand in the trap 60; Summer skin 61; Seventy times seven, Four women for one hero (Homage at siesta time) 62; The roof garden (The terrace) 63; The eavesdropper 64; Monday's child 66.

550 Totò, Italian actor, 1898-1967. Since 1917: also stage actor and clown. Main films: Animali pazzi, San Giovanni decollato, Totò cerca casa, Totò e i re di Roma, Guardie e ladri, Totò e le donne, Dov'è la libertà?, Una di quelle, L'oro di Napoli, Totò e Carolina, Racconti romani, Totò nella luna, I soliti ignoti, Risate di gioia, La Mandragola, Le belle famiglie, Uccellacci e uccellini.

551 Tourneur, Jacques, American director, b. 1904 in France. Since 1913: U.S.A. Son of below. 1927-34: France. Main films: Cat people 42; I walked with a zombie 43; Out of the past (Build my gallows high) 47; Way of a gaucho 52;

Appointment in Honduras 53; Wichita 55; Great day in the morning, Nightfall 56; Night of the demon (Curse of the demon) 57; Timbuktu, Frontier rangers 59; The comedy of terrors 64.

552 Tourneur, Maurice, French director, 1878-1961. 1914-27: U.S.A. Main films: Mother, The wishing ring, The man of the hour 14; Trilby, The ivory snuff box 15; The pride of the clan, A poor little rich girl, Barbary sheep 17; Sporting life, Prunella, The blue bird, Woman 18; Les gaîtés de l'escadron 32; Koenigsmark 36; Katia 38; Volpone 39; La main du diable 42.

553 Toyoda, Shiro, Japanese director, b. 1906. At first scriptwriter. Assistant to Shimazu. Main films: Young people 37; Nightingale 38; Spring on Leper's Island 40; Young figure 43; Wild geese 53; Love never fails, Grass whistle, Love is shared like sweets 55; Madame White Snake (The bewitching love of Madame Pai), The cat Shozu, and two women 56; Evening calm, Snow country 57; The veil of sin, Makerare-masen katsumadewa, Hotelman's holiday 58; Hana noren, Pilgrimage at night, The curio master 59; Twilight story, East Side Street 60; The diplomat's mission 61; Till tomorrow comes 62.

554 Tracy, Spencer, American actor, 1900-67. 1922-30: stage actor. Main films: Up the river, Me and my gal, A man's castle, The power and the glory, Maria Galante, Fury, Captains courageous, The big city, Mannequin, San Francisco, They gave him a gun, Test pilot, Boys' town, Stanley and Livingstone, Northwest passage, I take this woman, Dr. Jekyll and Mr. Hyde (41), Keeper of the flame,

Tortilla Flat, The woman of the year, A guy named Joe, The seventh cross, Thirty seconds over Tokyo, The sea of grass, State of the Union (The world and his wife), Edward my son, Father of the bride, Father's little dividend, Adam's rib, Pat and Mike, The actress, Bad day at Black Rock, Broken lance, The old man and the sea, The last hurrah, Inherit the wind, Judgment at Nuremberg, How the West was won (narrator only), It's a mad, mad, mad, mad world, Guess who's coming to dinner.

555 Trauner, Alexandre, French set-designer, b. 1906. At first painter. Assistant to Meerson. "Artistic director" on: Love in the afternoon, The nun's story, Once more with feeling. Main films: Drôle de drame, Gribouille, Quai des brumes, Entrée des artistes, Hôtel du Nord, Le jour se lève, Remorques, Les visiteurs du soir (co. G. Wakhévitch), Lumière d'été, Les enfants du paradis, Voyage surprise, Les portes de la nuit, La Marie du port, Manèges, Les miracles n'ont lieu qu'une fois, Juliette ou la clé des songes, Les sept péchés capitaux (52), Land of the Pharaohs, Othello (52), En effeuillant la marguerite, Witness for the prosecution, The apartment, Romanoff and Juliet, How to steal a million.

556 Trnka, Jiri, Czechoslovakian animator, b. 1912. 1930-38: director of his own puppet theatre. See animation. All his films are puppet films except*. Films: Grandpa planted a beet* 45; Perak and the SS*, The gift*, The devil on springs*, The animals and the brigands* 46; The Czech year 47; The Emperor's nightingale 48; The song of the prairie, The story of the double bass

49; Prince Bayaya 50; The devil's mill, The golden fish*, The happy circus* 51; How Grandpa changed till nothing was left* 52; Old Czech legends 53; The two frosts*, The good soldier Schweik 54; Hurvinek's circus 55; A midsummer night's dream 59; Passion 61; The cybernetic grandmother 62; The hand 64; The Archangel Gabriel and Mother Goose 65.

557 Truffaut, François, French director, b. 1932. At first critic. See *nouvelle vague.* Also producer: *Paris nous appartient, Tire-au-flanc* (62), and all his own features. Co-scr.: *Mata Hari, agent H-21,* and all his own films. Shorts: *Les mistons* 57; *Une histoire d'eau* (co-dir. Godard) 58. Films: *Les quatre cents coups* 59; *Tirez sur le pianiste* 60; *Jules et Jim* 61; *L'amour à vingt ans* (one episode) 62; *La peau douce* 64; *Fahrenheit 451* (in Engl.) 66; *La mariée était en noir* 67.

558 Trumbo, Dalton, American scriptwriter, b. 1905. At first film critic. Also novelist. 1950: 10 months prison after appearing before McCarthy. Main films: *A man to remember, Kitty Foyle, Tender comrade, A guy named Joe, Thirty seconds over Tokyo, Jealousy* (co.), *Our vines have tender grapes, The prowler, The brave bulls, The brave one, Spartacus, Exodus, The last sunset, Lonely are the brave, The sandpiper, Hawaii* (co.), *The fixer.*

U

559 Ustinov, Peter, British director and actor, b. 1921. Since 1939 also stage actor and producer, playwright,

and novelist. Scripted: *School for scoundrels, The way ahead* (co.), and all his own films. Main films as actor: *The goose steps out, One of our aircraft is missing, The way ahead, The true glory, Quo vadis? We're no angels, Lola Montès, Un angel pasò por Brooklyn, Les espions, Spartacus, The sundowners, John Goldfarb, please come home!, Topkapi, The comedians, Assassinio a Sarajevo,* and*. Films as director: *School for secrets* 46; *Vice versa* 48; *Private Angelo* 49; *Romanoff and Juliet* 61; *Billy Budd* 62; *Lady L* 65.

560 Vadim, Roger, French director, b. 1928. 1944-47: stage actor. Then journalist. Assistant to M. Allégret. Scripted: *Futures vedettes, Cette sacrée gamine, En effeuillant la marguerite.* Also producer. Films: *Et Dieu créa la femme* 56; *Sait-on jamais?, Les bijoutiers du clair de lune* 57; *Les liaisons dangereuses* 59; *Et mourir de plaisir* 60; *La bride sur le cou, Les sept péchés capitaux* (one episode) 61; *Le repos du guerrier, Le vice et la vertu* 62; *Château en Suède* 63; *La ronde* (remake) 64; *La curée* 66; *Histoires extraordinaires* (Metzengerstein ep.), *Barbarella* 67.

561 Valentino, Rudolph, American actor, b. 1895 in Italy, d. 1926. From 1913: U.S.A. At first dancer. Main films: *The married virgin, The delicious little devil, The four horsemen of the Apocalypse* (21), *The young Rajah, Monsieur Beaucaire, Cobra, The eagle, The son of the sheik.*

562 Valli, Alida, Italian actress, b. 1921. Since 1956: also stage actress. Main films: *Piccolo mondo antico, Noi vivi, The Paradine case, The miracle of the bells, The third man, Les amants de Tolède, Senso, Il grido, Les yeux sans visage, Les bijoutiers du clair de lune, Le dialogue des Carmélites, Ophélia, Une aussi longue absence, Four women for one hero, Edipo Re.*

563 Vallone, Raf, Italian actor, b. 1916. Since 1958: also stage actor. Main films: *Bitter rice, Non c'è pace tra gli ulivi, Cuori senza frontiere, Il cammino della speranza, Il Cristo proibito, Anna, Roma ore 11, Camicie rosse, Thérèse Raquin, Guendalina, La venganza, Two women, Roses for the prosecutor, Recours en grâce, El Cid, A view from the bridge, Phaedra, The cardinal, Nevada Smith.*

564 Van Dyke, W. S., American director, 1899-1943. Child vaudeville actor. 1916: assistant to Griffith on *Intolerance.* Main films: *Gentle cyclone, War paint* 26; *Winners of the wilderness, White shadows of the South Seas* (co. Flaherty) 27; *Trader horn* 30; *Tarzan the ape man, Never the twain shall meet, Cuban love song* 32; *The prize fighter and the lady* (Everywoman's man), *Eskimo (Mala the magnificent)* 33; *Manhattan melodrama, The thin man, Forsaking all others, Laughing boy, Hide out* 34; *I live my life* 35; *His brother's wife, San Francisco, Love on the run, After the thin man* 36; *They gave him a gun* 37; *Marie Antoinette* 38; *It's a wonderful world, Andy Hardy gets spring fever, Another thin man* 39; *I love you again, I take this woman* 40; *Rage in heaven, Shadow of the thin man* 41.

565 Van Dyke, Willard, American director of documentaries, b. 1906. At first still photographer. Since 1965: Director of Department of Film, Museum of Modern Art, New York. Co-dir. of photogr.: *The river* (37), *The city.* Also produced: *Toby and the tall corn* and*. Main films: *The city* (co. R. Steiner)* 39; *Valleytown, The children must learn, To hear your banjo play* 40; *The bridge* 42; *Steeltown* 43; *Journey into medicine* 46; *Terribly talented* 48; *Mount Vernon* 49; *Years of change* 50; *New York University* 52; *Cabos blancos* (in Puerto Rico) 54; *Skyscraper* (co. S. Clarke) 58; *Land of White Alice* 59; *Ireland, the tear and the smile* 60; *Search into darkness** 61; *Harvest* 62; *Depressed area* 63; *Rice, Frontiers of news* 64; *Frontline cameras* 65.

566 Van Parys, Georges, French composer, b. 1902. Main films: *Le million, Abus de confiance, Le bienfaiteur, Le silence est d'or, Jean de la lune* (48), *Casque d'or, Fanfan la tulipe, Les belles de nuit, Madame de . . ., Avant le déluge, Les diaboliques, French Cancan, Le grand jeu* (54), *Les grandes manoeuvres, Les carnets du Major Thompson, Charmants garçons, Les fêtes galantes.*

567 Vanel, Charles, French actor, b. 1892. 1908-20: stage actor. Main films: *Ame d'artiste, La proie du vent, Les croix de bois, Les misérables* (33), *Le grand jeu* (34), *L'équipage, La belle équipe, Jenny, Abus de confiance, La loi du Nord, Le ciel est à vous, In nome della legge, Si Versailles m'était conté, L'affaire Mauritzius, To catch a thief, La mort en ce jardin, Le salaire de la peur, Les diaboliques, La vérité, La steppa, Du* *rififi à Tokyo, L'aîné des Ferchaux, Les tribulations d'un Chinois en Chine.*

568 Varda, Agnès, French woman director, b. 1928. Also still photographer. Shorts: *O saisons, ô châteaux* 56; *Opéra-Mouffe, Du côté de la côte, La cocotte d'Azur* 59; *Salut les Cubains* (in Cuba) 63. Films: *La pointe courte* 55; *Cléo de 5 à 7* 61; *Le bonheur* 65; *Les créatures* 66; *Loin du Viêtnam* (in coll.) 67.

569 Vasiliev Brothers, The, Russian directors. **Sergei:** 1900-59, and **Georgi:** 1899-1946. They were not in fact brothers. From 1928: editors. Films: *The sleeping beauty* 30; *A personal affair* 32; *Chapayev* 34; *Volochayevsk days* 38; *Defence of Tsaritsin* 42; *The front* 43; (Sergei Vasiliev alone) *The heroes of Shipka* 55; *October days* 58.

570 Vávra, Otakar, Czechoslovakian director, b. 1911. Main films: *Virginity* 37; *Cech panen Kutnohorskych* 38; *The enchanted house* 39; *Rozina sebranec* 47; *The silent barricade* 48; *The Hussite trilogy* 55-57; *The golden rennet* 64; *Romance for the cornet* 66.

571 Veidt, Conrad, German actor, 1893-1943. From 1913: also stage actor, at first under Reinhardt. 1938: France, England, then U.S.A. Main films: *Es werde Licht, Satanas, The cabinet of Dr. Caligari, Der Januskopf, Sehnsucht, Abend . . . Nacht . . . Morgen, Der Gang in die Nacht, Lukrezia Borgia, Waxworks, The hands of Orlac, The man who laughs, Menschen im Käfig, Tempête sur l'Asie, Dark journey, Contraband, The thief of Bagdad* (40), *A woman's face* (41), *Nazi agent, Casablanca.*

572 Vertov, Dziga, Russian director, b. 1896 in Poland, d. 1954. Real name: Denis Kaufman, brother of Boris. From 1915: Russia. In 1924 Vertov stated his theory of 'Kino-Eye' and laid the basis of the documentary film: "All 'Kino-Eye' films are made outside the studio without actors, sets or a script. They are documentary films, intended to give new directions to the development of the cinema. 'Kino-Eye' films are *written* by the camera in the purest cine-language; they are completely *visual*." Vertov's theories influenced Grierson (q.v.) and are the basis of *cinéma-vérité* (q.v.). Main films: *History of the Civil War* 21; *Kino-Pravda* (series of 12 newsreels) 22; *Kino-Eye* 24; *Leninist Kino-Pravda* 25; *Stride Soviet!, A sixth of the world* 26; *The eleventh year* 28; *Man with a movie camera* 29; *Symphony of the Donbas* 31; *Three songs of Lenin* 34.

573 Vidor, King, American director, b. 1896. At first newsreel cameraman. Assistant to Griffith and Ince. Also scr.† and produced* many of his own films. Films: *The turn in the road*† 18; *Better times*†, *The other half*†, *Poor relations, The jack-knife man** 19; *The family honour** 20; *The sky pilot*, *Love never dies*, *Conquering the women*, *Woman, wake up** 21; *The real adventure*, *Dusk to dawn*, *Alice Adams*, *Peg o' my heart* 22; *The woman of bronze, Three wise fools, Wild oranges, Happiness* 23; *Wine of youth, His hour, Wife of the centaur* 24; *Proud flesh, The big parade** 25; *La Bohème** 25; *Bardelys the magnificent** 26; *The crowd*, *The patsy* 27; *Show people* 28; *Hallelujah*†*, *Not so dumb* 29; *Billy the Kid** 30; *Street scene, The champ** 31; *Bird of paradise,*

Cynara 32; The stranger's return* 33; Our daily bread*, The wedding night 34; So red the rose 35; The Texas Rangers*, Stella Dallas 37; The citadel (in Engl.) 38; Northwest passage 39; Comrade X 40; H. M. Pulham, Esq.* 41; An American romance* 44; Duel in the sun 46; On our merry way, The fountainhead 48; Beyond the forest 49; Lightning strikes twice 50; Japanese war bride 51; Ruby Gentry* 52; Man without a star 54; War and peace 55; Solomon and Sheba 59.

574 Vigo, Jean, French director. 1905-34. Films: A propos de Nice 30; Taris 31; Zéro de conduite 33 (all shorts); L'Atalante 34.

575 Visconti, Luchino, Italian director, b. 1906. At first set-designer. 1936 and 1940: assistant to Renoir. Since 1945: also stage and operatic producer. Scripted all his own films in collab. See neo-realism. Films: Ossessione 42; La terra trema 48; Bellissima 51; Siamo donne (one episode) 53; Senso 54; Le notti bianche 57; Rocco e i suoi fratelli 60; Boccaccio '70 (one episode) 62; The leopard 63; Vaghe stelle dell' Orsa 65; Le streghe (one ep.) 66; Lo straniero, La vita di Giacomo Puccini 67.

576 Vitti, Monica, Italian actress, b. 1933. Also stage and TV actress. Films: I dritti, L'avventura, La notte, L'eclisse, Les quatres vérités, Château en Suède, Dragées au poivre, Deserto rosso, Alta infedeltà (Salce ep.), Il disco volante, Modesty Blaise, Le bambole (Rossi ep.), Fai in fretta ad uccidermi . . . ho freddo!, Le fate (Bolognini ep.), La ragazza con la pistola.

577 Vlady, Marina, French actress, b. 1938. At first ballet dancer. Main films: Dans la vie tout s'arrange, Avant le déluge, Le infedeli, Giorni d'amore, Les salauds vont en enfer, La sorcière, Pardonnez nos offenses, Crime et châtiment, Toi le venin, La sentence, La ragazza in vetrina, La princesse de Clèves, Adorable menteuse, Les sept péchés capitaux, Climats, Les bonnes causes, La cage, La steppa, Dragées au poivre, Ape regina, Le meutrier, Le voleur de la Joconde, Chimes at midnight, Deux ou trois choses que je sais d'elle, Mona, l'étoile sans nom.

578 Wagner, Fritz Arno, German director of photography, 1889-1958. From 1914: newsreel cameraman. See expressionism. Main films: Schloss Vogelöd, Der müde Tod, Nosferatu, Der brennende Acker (co. Freund), Schatten, Zur Chronik von Grieshuus (in collab.), The love of Jeanne Ney, Spione, Die Frau im Mond, Westfront 1918, Skandal um Eva, The threepenny opera, Brand in der Oper, Kameradschaft, M, The last will of Dr. Mabuse, Flüchtlinge, Der Herrscher.

579 Wajda, Andrzej, Polish director, b. 1926. Film school. 1953: assistant to A. Ford. Also stage and TV producer. Films: A generation 54; Kanal 56; Ashes and diamonds 58; Lotna 59; The innocent sorcerers 60; Samson, A Siberian Lady Macbeth (in Jugosl.) 61; L'amour à vingt ans (one episode; in France) 62; Ashes 64; The gates of paradise (in Engl.) 67.

580 Wakhévitch, Georges, French set and costume designer, b. 1907. Also painter. Since 1927: also stage set designer. Main films: *Baroud, L'homme à l'Hispano, Madame Bovary* (33), *La grande illusion, La Marseillaise, Pièges, Les visiteurs du soir* (co. Trauner; also costumes), *L'éternel retour, L'homme au chapeau rond, La danse de mort, Dédée d'Anvers, L'aigle à deux têtes, Miquette et sa mère, The beggars' opera* (also costumes), *Ali Baba, La femme et le pantin, Marie-Octobre, Le crime ne paie pas, Le journal d'une femme de chambre, Les fêtes galantes.*

581 Walbrook, Anton, Austrian actor, 1900-67. From 1920: stage actor. From 1937: England. Main films: *Walzerkrieg, Maskerade, Die Ratten* (36), *Gaslight, Victoria the Great, 49th Parallel, The life and death of Colonel Blimp, The red shoes, The queen of spades, La ronde, Oh! Rosalinda!, Lola Montès, Saint Joan, I accuse!*

582 Wallis, Hal, American producer, b. 1899. 1944: founded Hal Wallis Productions. Main films: *Little Caesar* (co. Zanuck), *I am a fugitive from a chain gang, A midsummer night's dream* (34), *The go getter, Green pastures, The life of Emile Zola, Jezebel, The adventures of Robin Hood* (38), *The private lives of Elizabeth and Essex, Yankee doodle dandy, Casablanca, The affairs of Susan, Saratoga trunk, Sorry wrong number, My friend Irma, Rope of sand, The furies, That's my boy, Sailor beware, The stooge, Jumping jacks, Scared stiff, Come back little Sheba, The rose tattoo, Artists and models* (55), *Hollywood or bust, The rainmaker, Gunfight at the O.K. Corral, Wild is the wind, Rock-a-bye baby, Don't give up the ship, Visit to a small planet, Last train from Gun Hill, Career, Becket, The sons of Katie Elder.*

583 Walsh, Raoul, American director, b. 1892. Assistant to Griffith. Acted: *Birth of a nation.* Also produced and scripted most of his films. Main films: *The thief of Bagdad* 24; *What price glory?* 26; *The loves of Carmen* 27; *Sadie Thompson* 28; *The big trail* 30; *Me and my gal* 32; *The Bowery* 33; *Klondike Annie* 36; *Artists and models* 37; *St. Louis Blues, The roaring twenties* 39; *Dark command, They drive by night* 40; *High sierra, The strawberry blonde, Manpower, They died with their boots on* 41; *Desperate journey, Gentleman Jim* 42; *Objective Burma!* 45; *Pursued* 47; *Colorado territory* 49; *White heat* 50; *Captain Horatio Hornblower, The enforcer (Murder Inc.)* (begun by B. Windust), *Distant drums* 51; *Glory Alley, The world in his arms, The lawless breed* 52; *Gun fury* 53; *Saskatchewan (O'Rourke of the Royal Mounted)* 54; *Battle cry, The tall men* 55; *The king and four queens* 56; *Band of angels* 57; *The naked and the dead* 58; *The sheriff of Fractured Jaw, A private's affair* 59; *Esther and the king* 60; *Marines let's go!* 61; *A distant trumpet* 63.

584 Walters, Charles, American director. Dancer on stage from 1934 and on screen from 1942. Choreographer: *Girl crazy* (co. Berkeley), *Best foot forward, Meet me in St. Louis, Weekend at the Waldorf, Ziegfeld Follies, Summer holiday and*.* Main films: *Good news* 47; *Easter parade* 48; *The Barkleys of Broadway* 49; *Summer stock (If you feel like singing)* 50; *The belle of New York*

51; *Lili* 52; *Dangerous when wet, Easy to love, Torch song** 53; *The glass slipper* 54; *The tender trap* 55; *Don't go near the water, High society* 56; *Ask any girl* 59; *Please don't eat the daisies* 60; *Two loves (Spinster)* 61; *Jumbo (Billy Rose's Jumbo)* 62; *The unsinkable Molly Brown* 63; *Walk, don't run* 66.

585 Warm, Hermann, German set designer, b. 1889. Also painter. Often collab. with Röhrig*. See *expressionism*. Main films: *The cabinet of Dr. Caligari* (*and Reimann), *Die Spinnen, Der müde Tod*, Schloss Vogelöd, Phantom, Gräfin Donelli, Der Student von Prag* (26), *The love of Jeanne Ney, La passion de Jeanne d'Arc, A night in London, Vampyr, Mazurka, Le corbeau, Wozzeck.*

586 Watt, Harry, British director, b. 1906. 1931-38: worked under Grierson (q.v.). 1934: assistant to Flaherty. Main shorts: *Six thirty collection* 34; *Night mail* (co-dir. Wright) 36; *North Sea* 38; *The first days* (co-dir. Jennings and P. Jackson) 39; *London can take it* (co-dir. Jennings) 40. Films: *Target for tonight* 41; *Nine men* (also scr.) 42; *Fiddlers three* (also scr.) 44; *The overlanders* (also scr.) 46; *Eureka Stockade* 49; *Where no vultures fly (Ivory hunter)* 51; *West of Zanzibar* 54; *The siege of Pinchgut* 58.

587 Wayne, John, American actor, b. 1907. Main films: *The big trail, Overland stage raiders, Stagecoach, Dark command, The long voyage home, Reap the wild wind, Flying tigers, They were expendable, Red River, Fort Apache, Three godfathers, She wore a yellow ribbon, The sands of Iwo Jima, Rio Grande, The quiet man, Jet pilot, The conqueror, Blood Alley, The searchers, The wings of eagles, Legend of the lost, Rio Bravo, The barbarian and the geisha, The horse soldiers, The Alamo* (also dir., 60), *The longest day, How the West was won, Hatari!, The man who shot Liberty Valance, Donovan's reef, North to Alaska, Circus world, The sons of Katie Elder, In harm's way, El Dorado, The green berets* (also dir., co. M. Le Roy).

588 Wegener, Paul, German actor, 1874-1948. Worked under Reinhardt. 1906-48: also stage actor. See *expressionism*. Main films: *The student of Prague, The Golem* (also co-dir. with H. Galeen, 14), *The pied piper of Hamelin* (also co-dir. with R. Gliese 17), *The Golem* (remake; also dir., 20), *Vanina, One Arabian night, The loves of Pharaoh, Lukrezia Borgia, Alraune, Der grosse König, Der Fall Molander.*

589 Weiss, Jiri, Czechoslovakian director, b. 1913. 1934-41: dir. shorts. 1939-45: England. Scripted many of his own films. Main shorts: *The rape of Czechoslovakia* 39; *Eternal Prague* 41. Main films: *John Smith wakes up* 41; *Dravci* 48; *Poslední vystrel* 50; *New heroes will arise* 51; *No middle road* 56; *The wolf trap* 58; *Appassionata* 59; *Romeo, Juliet and darkness* 60; *Robinsonka* 61; *The coward* 62; *The golden fern* 63; *31 degrees in the shade* 64; *Murder Czech style* 66.

590 Welles, Orson, American director and actor, b. 1915. Since 1925: also stage actor and producer. Also novelist, playwright, radio producer. Since 1947: Europe. Also scr. all his own films. Main films as actor: *Jane*

Eyre, Follow the boys, Tomorrow and forever, Prince of foxes, The third man, Return to Glennascaul, The black rose, Trent's last case (53), Si Versailles m'était conté, Napoléon, Trouble in the glen, Moby Dick, The long hot summer, The roots of heaven, Compulsion, David and Goliath, Austerlitz, Crack in the mirror, The V.I.P.s, Rogopag (Pasolini ep.), Paris brûle-t-il?, A man for all seasons, The sailor from Gibraltar, Casino Royale, and all his own films, except The magnificent Ambersons where he speaks the commentary offscreen. Films: Citizen Kane 40; The magnificent Ambersons, Journey into fear (completed by N. Foster), It's all true (unfinished) 42; The stranger 46; The lady from Shanghai, Macbeth 47; Othello 52; Confidential report (Mr. Arkadin), Don Quixote (unfinished) 55; Touch of evil 57; The trial 62; Chimes at midnight 65.

591 Wellman, William, American director, b. 1896. At first actor and novelist. Also produced some of his films*. Main films: The boob (The yokel) 26; Wings 27; Ladies of the mob, Beggars of life 28; The steel highway (Other men's women), Public enemy (Enemies of the public) 31; Call of the wild 35; Small town girl, Robin Hood of Eldorado 36; A star is born, Nothing sacred 37; Men with wings* 38; Beau Geste*, The light that failed* 39; The great man's lady*, Lady of burlesque (Strip-tease lady) 42; The Oxbow incident (Strange incident), Buffalo Bill 43; The story of G.I. Joe* 45; The iron curtain, Yellow sky 48; Battleground 49; Across the wide Missouri, Westward the women 50; The high and the mighty, Track of the cat 54; Blood Alley, Goodbye my lady 55; Darby's

Rangers (Young invaders), Lafayette Escadrille (Hell bent for glory) 58.

592 Wendkos, Paul, American director, b. 1923. Also TV producer. Films: The burglar 57; The case against Brooklyn, Tarawa beachhead 58; Gidget, Face of a fugitive, Battle of the Coral Sea 59; Because they're young 60; Angel baby, Gidget goes Hawaiian 62; Gidget goes to Rome 63; Attack on the Iron Coast 67.

593 West, Mae, American actress and scriptwriter, b. 1893. Since 1900: stage and vaudeville actress. Also scripted most of her films*. Films: Night after night, She done him wrong*, I'm no angel*, Belle of the nineties, Goin' to town*, Klondike Annie*, Go West, young man*, Every day's a holiday, My little chickadee*, The heat's on.

594 Whale, James, Director, b. 1896 in England, d. 1957. At first cartoonist. From 1918: also stage actor, producer and set-designer. From 1929: U.S.A. Main films: Journey's end 30; Frankenstein 31; The old dark house 32; The invisible man 33; The bride of Frankenstein 35; Man in the iron mask, Green hell 40.

595 Wicki, Bernhard, German director and actor, b. 1919. From 1938: stage actor. Main films as actor: Die letzte Brücke, Kinder, Mutter und ein General, The jackboot mutiny, La chatte, La notte. Films as dir.: Why are they against us? 58; The bridge 59; Miracle of Malachias 61; The longest day (co-dir.) 62; The visit 63; The saboteur — code name Morituri 65.

596 Widerberg, Bo, Swedish director, b. 1930. At first novelist. Also edited most of his own films. Short: *The boy and the kite* 61. Films: *The pram* 62; *Raven's End* 63; *Love '65* 65; *Heja Roland!* 66; *Elvira Madigan* 67.

597 Widmark, Richard, American actor, b. 1915. 1943-45: stage actor. Since 1957: also producer. Main films: *Kiss of death, Street with no name, Night and the city, Panic in the streets, Yellow sky, No way out, Pickup on South Street, O.Henry's full house, Halls of Montezuma, Destination Gobi, Take the high ground, Broken lance, Hell and high water, The cobweb, Prize of gold, Backlash, The last wagon, Saint Joan, Time limit, The law and Jake Wade, The tunnel of love, Warlock, The Alamo, Two rode together, The secret ways, Judgment at Nuremberg, How the West was won, The long ships, Flight from Ashiya, Alvarez Kelly, Cheyenne autumn, Madigan.*

598 Wilcox, Herbert, British director and producer, b. 1892 in Ireland. Main films: (dir. only) *Whispering* 22; (dir. and prod.) *Chu-Chin-Chow* 23; *Madame Pompadour* 28; *Carnival, Goodnight Vienna* 32; *Nell Gwyn* 35; *Victoria the Great* 37; *Nurse Edith Cavell* 39; *Irene* 40; *Odette* 50; *Trent's last case* 53; *Trouble in the glen* 55.

599 Wilder, Billy, Director, b. 1906 in Austria. Since 1934: U.S.A. Scripted: *People on Sunday* (in collab.), *Emil and the detectives, Adorable, Bluebeard's eighth wife, Ninotchka, Ball of fire, A song is born,* and all his own films. Films: *Mauvaise graine* (co-dir. A. Esway; in France) 33; *The major and the minor* 42; *Five graves to Cairo* 43; *Double indemnity, The lost weekend* 45; *The emperor waltz* 47; *A foreign affair* 48; *Sunset Boulevard* 50; *Ace in the hole (The big carnival)* 51; *Stalag 17* 52; *Sabrina* 54; *The seven year itch* 55; *The spirit of St. Louis* 56; *Love in the afternoon* 57; *Witness for the prosecution* 58; *Some like it hot* 59; *The apartment* 60; *One, two, three* 61; *Irma la Douce* 63; *Kiss me stupid* 64; *The fortune cookie (Meet Whiplash Willie)* 66; *The private life of Sherlock Holmes* 68.

600 Williams, Richard, Canadian animator, b. 1933. Since 1955: England. Credit titles: *What's new pussycat?, A funny thing happened on the way to the forum, The liquidator, The charge of the Light Brigade* etc. Also dir. of commercials (*Guinness at the Albert Hall* etc.). Films: *The little island* (full length) 58; *A lecture on man* 61; *Love me, love me, love me* 62; *Circus drawings* 64; *Diary of a madman, The dermis probe* 65; *Pubs and beaches* 66; *The sailor and the devil* (co. E. Le Cain), *I. vor Pittfalks* 67.

601 Winters, Shelley, American actress, b. 1922. Also stage actress. Main films: *To have and have not, A double life, Cry of the city, South Sea sinner, Winchester 73, A place in the sun, Untamed frontier, Executive suite, Mambo, The big knife, The night of the hunter, I am a camera, I died a thousand times, The diary of Anne Frank, Odds against tomorrow, The young savages, Lolita, The balcony, Gli indifferenti, The greatest story ever told, The moving target.*

602 Wise, Robert, American director, b. 1914. At first editor: *Citizen Kane, The magnificent Ambersons,* etc.

Main films: *Body snatcher* 45; *Born to kill* 47; *The set-up* 49; *Two flags West* 50; *The house on Telegraph Hill, The day the earth stood still* 51; *Destination Gobi* 52; *The desert rats, So big* 53; *Executive suite* 54; *Helen of Troy* 55; *Tribute to a bad man, Somebody up there likes me* 56; *Until they sail, Run silent, run deep* 58; *I want to live, Odds against tomorrow* 59; *West Side story* 61; *Two for the see-saw* 62; *The haunting* 63; *The sound of music* 64; *The sand pebbles* 66; *Star!* 67.

603 Wolf, Konrad, German director, b. 1925. 1949: U.S.S.R. (film school), then E. Germany. Assistant to Ivens. Films: *Once is nonce* 55; *Recovery* 56; *Lissy, Sunseeker* 57; *Stars* 58; *Men with wings* 59; *Professor Mamlock* 61; *Divided heaven* 64.

604 Wood, Sam, American director, 1883-1949. Drama studies. Main films: *Beyond the rocks* 22; *Bluebeard's eighth wife* 23; *The barbarian* 33; *Let' em have it, A night at the opera* 35; *A day at the races* 37; *Kitty Foyle, Goodbye Mr. Chips, Raffles* 39; *Our town, The devil and Miss Jones* 40; *King's Row* 42; *For whom the bell tolls* 43; *Casanova Brown* 44; *Saratoga trunk* 45; *Ivy* 47; *Command decision* 49.

605 Wright, Basil, British director and producer of documentaries, b. 1907. 1928-38: worked with Grierson (q.v.). 1939-45: dir. of Crown Film Unit. Main films as director: *Windmill in Barbados* 30; *O'er hill and dale* 31; *Country comes to town* 32; *Song of Ceylon* 34-35; *Night mail* (co-dir. Watt) 36; *This was Japan* 45; *The story of Omolo* 46; *The waters of time* 51; *World with-out end* (co-dir. Rotha) 53; *The immortal land* 58.

606 Wyler, William, American director, b. 1902. At first assistant. 1925-28: dir. many short Westerns. 1942-45: documentaries for U.S. Air Force. Main films: *A house divided* 32; *Counsellor at law* 33; *The good fairy* 35; *Come and get it* (started by Hawks), *Dodsworth, These three* 36; *Dead end* 37; *Jezebel* 38; *Wuthering Heights* 39; *The letter, The Westerner* 40; *The little foxes* 41; *Mrs.Miniver* 42; *The best years of our lives* 46; *The heiress* 49; *Detective story* 51; *Carrie* 52; *Roman holiday* 53; *The desperate hours* 55; *Friendly persuasion* 56; *The big country* 58; *Ben Hur* 59; *The children's hour (The loudest whisper)* 62; *The collector* 65; *How to steal a million* 66; *Funny girl* 67.

Y

607 Yamamoto, Satsuo, Japanese director, b. 1910. At first actor. Main films: *La symphonie pastorale* 38; *Hot wind* 43; *War and peace* (co-dir. F. Kamei) 47; *City of violence* 50; *Storm clouds over Hakone* 51; *Vacuum zone* 52; *The sunless street* 53; *To the end of the sun* 54; *Uproar over a typhoon* 57; *Oingen no Kabe* 60; *The song of the cart* 62; *A band of assassins* 63; *The power of gold* 64; *Freezing point* 65; *The great white tower* 66.

608 Yamamura, So, Japanese director, b. 1910. At first actor. Main films: *The crab-canning ship* 53; *The black tide* 54; *The mother and her children* 59;

Song of Fukagawa 60; *Maidens of Kashima Sea* 61.

609 Yordan, Philip, American scriptwriter. Also playwright. Producer of many of his own films*. Main films: *Dillinger, House of strangers, Reign of terror, Detective story, Johnny Guitar, Man crazy*, Broken lance, The man from Laramie, The last frontier, The harder they fall*, The wild party*, Joe Macbeth, Men in war, No down payment, God's little acre*, Day of the outlaw*, Studs Lonigan*, El Cid, King of Kings, 55 days at Peking, The fall of the Roman Empire, The day of the triffids*, Circus world* (co.), Battle of the bulge* (co.)*.

610 Yoshimura, Kimisaburo, Japanese director, b. 1911. Assistant to Shimazu. Main films: *Tomorrow's dancers, Warm current* 39; *The story of tank commander Nishizumi* 40; *South Wind* 42; *A bell at the Anjo house, The fellows who ate the elephant* 47; *The day our lives shine* 48; *Waltz at noon, Ishimatzu of the forest* 49; *About twenty years old* 50; *Clothes of deception* 51; *Violence, A tale of Genji* 52; *Cape Ashizuri* 54; *Women of the Ginza, The beauty and the dragon* 55; *Night river (Undercurrent)* 56; *Night butterflies, An Osaka story* (begun by Mizoguchi), *On this earth* 57; *The naked face of night, A grain of wheat* 58; *A design for dying, A woman of Kyoto, A woman's testament (Code of women)* (one episode) 60; *Their legacy, Marriageable age* 61; *Hiroshima heartache* 62; *Sonoyowa wasurenai* 63; *Mrs. Canary* 66; *A corrupt woman* 67.

611 Yutkevitch, Sergei, Russian director, b. 1904. Assistant to A. Room on *Bed and sofa* (27). Scripted: *The bold seven*. Main films. *Lace* 28; *The black sail* 29; *Golden mountains* 31; *Counterplan* (co-dir. Ermler) 32; *The man with a gun* 38; *Yakov Sverdlov* 40; *Fighting Film Album* (with others) 41; *New adventures of Schweik* 43; *Light over Russia* 47; *Three encounters* (co-dir. Ptushko and Pudovkin) 48; *Przhevalsky* 51; *The great warrior Skanderberg* 54; *Othello* 55; *Stories about Lenin* 58; *The bath house* (partly animated film) 62; *Lenin in Poland* 64.

Z

612 Zampa, Luigi, Italian director, b. 1905. At first vaudeville playwright, then scriptwriter. See *neo-realism*. Main films: *L'attore scomparso* 41; *Vivere in pace* 46; *L'onorevole Angelina* 47; *Anni difficili* 48; *Cuori senza frontiere* 50; *Processo alla città* 52; *Siamo donne* (one episode) 53; *La romana* 54; *Il magistrato* 59; *Il vigile* (also co-scr.) 60; *Frenesia dell' estate* 63; *Una questione d'amore* 65; *I nostri mariti* (one ep.) 66; *Le dolci signore* 67.

613 Zanuck, Darryl F., American producer, b. 1902. 1933: founded 20th Century, which merged with Fox in 1935. 1952: became independent producer. 1962: again dir. of 20th Century Fox. Main films: *Little Caesar* (co.), *The Bowery, The prisoner of Shark Island, Lloyds of London, The rains came, Young Mr. Lincoln, Drums along the Mohawk, The grapes of wrath, The return of Frank*

James, *The mark of Zorro, Tobacco Road, Western Union, How green was my valley, Blood and sand, Winged victory, Dragonwyck, Gentleman's agreement, Pinky, All about Eve, No way out, Twelve o'clock high, People will talk, The snows of Kilimanjaro, Viva Zapata!, Island in the sun, The sun also rises, The roots of heaven, Crack in the mirror, The longest day* (also co-dir.), *Cleopatra*.

614 Zarkhi, Alexander, Russian director, b. 1908. Main films: *Baltic deputy* 37; *Member of the government* 40; *Her name is Sukhe-Bator* 42; *In the name of life* (all co. J. Heifitz); *Pavlinka* 52; *Nesterka* 55; *The heights* 57; *Men on the bridge* 60; *My younger brother* 62; *Anna Karenina* 67.

615 Zavattini, Cesare, Italian scriptwriter, b. 1902. From 1934: journalist, film critic, theorist. See *neorealism.* Scripts usually in collab. Main films: *Darò un milione, Quattro passi fra le nuvole, I bambini ci guardano, La porta del cielo, Sciuscia, Il testimone, Un giorno nella vita, Caccia tragica, Bicycle thieves, Au delà des grilles, E primavera, Domenica d'agosto, Prima communione, Miracolo a Milano, Umberto D, Il cappotto, Roma ore 11, Buon giorno elefante!, Bellissima, Amore in città, Siamo donne, Stazione termini, L'oro di Napoli, Il tetto, La donna del giorno, Suor Letizia, Il rossetto, Two women, Il sicario, Le italiane e l'amore, Il giudizio universale, Boccaccio '70, Isola di Arturo, Il boom, I misteri di Roma* (series of shorts by various directors, 63), *Yesterday, today, and tomorrow, Marriage Italian style, Un monde nouveau, Controsesso, Caccia alla volpe, Le streghe.*

616 Zecca, Ferdinand, French director. 1864-1947. At first singer. From 1899: actor. From 1905: producer only. Main films: *L'histoire d'un crime, Tempête dans une chambre à coucher* 01; *Les victimes de l'alcoolisme, La catastrophe de la Martinique* 02; *La vie d'un joueur* 03; *Passion* 02-05.

617 Zeman, Karel, Czechoslovakian director and animator, b. 1910. See *animation.* Main shorts (puppet films): *The adventures of Mr. Prokouk* (series) 47-58; *Inspiration* 49; *King Lavra* 50. Films (which combine live shooting and animation): *The treasure of Bird Island* 52; *A journey into primeval times* 54; *An invention for destruction* 57; *Baron Munchausen* 62; *Two musketeers, The jester's tale* 64; *The stolen airship* 66; *The children of Captain Nemo* 67.

618 Zetterling, Mai, Swedish actress and director, b. 1925. Also stage actress since 1941. Since 1947: England. Main films as actress only: *Frenzy, Iris, The night is my future, Frieda, Knock on wood, Prize of gold, Only two can play, The vine bridge.* Shorts as director: *The polite invasion, Lords of little Egypt, The prosperity race, The do-it-yourself democracy, The war game* 60-63. Films as director: *Loving couples* 64; *Night games* 66; *Doctor Glas, The girls* 67.

619 Zinnemann, Fred, American director, b. 1907 in Austria. Since 1930: U.S.A. Scripted in collab.: *People on Sunday.* Main shorts: *The wave* (Redes) 35; *Crime doesn't pay* (series) 37-41; *Benjy* 51. Main films: *The seventh cross* 44; *The search* 48; *Act of violence* 49; *The men* 50; *Teresa* 51; *High noon, Member of the wedding* 52; *From here to* eternity 53; *Oklahoma!* 55; *A hatful of rain* 57; *The nun's story* 59; *The sundowners* 60; *Behold a pale horse* 63; *A man for all seasons* 66.

620   Zurlini, Valerio, Italian director, b. 1926. Scripted in collab.: *Guendalina,* and*. Main shorts: *Pugilatori, Il mercato della facce, Soldati in città, Il blu della domenica* 48-59. Films: *Le ragazze di San Frediano* 54; *L'estate violente* 59; *La ragazza con la valigia** 60; *Cronaca familiare* 62; *Le soldatesse* 64; *Vangelo 70* (one ep.), *Il giardino dei Finzi Contini* 67.

Guide to Technical Terms

back-projection: projection of film on to a transparency (a transparent screen) which serves as a background while the action is being shot. Most frequently used in car scenes, where the passing street is usually back-projected.

close-up: shot which takes in the actor from the neck upwards, or an object from a similarly close position.

crane: a piece of apparatus which can lift the camera vertically. A crane shot is any shot where the camera itself makes an upward or downward movement.

depth of field: depth of composition of a shot, i.e. where there are several planes, a foreground, a middleground, and a background.

depth of focus: a technical adjustment which insures that a shot with depth of field remains in focus in all its planes. The technique of depth of focus was pioneered by Gregg Toland (q.v.).

dissolve: a gradual transition from one shot to another (so that at a certain point both images are visible simultaneously). Often used to suggest the passage of time.

establishing shot: a shot, usually at the beginning of a sequence, which establishes the location of the action or the time of day.

fade in, fade out: the first is a device used at the beginning of a sequence, where the image gradually lightens from complete darkness; the second is used at the end of a sequence, where the image gradually darkens to complete blackness.

fast motion: a camera device whereby the movement of the action is speeded up; generally used for comic effects.

freeze: an optical effect whereby one image is held for a time and the action seems to "freeze", i.e. it becomes a still photograph.

general shot: any shot in which the entirety of the action can be seen and a large part of the set or location is visible; it may vary in scope from a medium to a long shot.

high angle shot: a shot from above which points down on the action.

insert: an inserted shot, usually a close-up, used to reveal something in greater detail.

intercut shots: any series of shots which is inserted at more or less regular intervals into another series of shots; for instance, shots of people running away from a bomb that is about to explode are often intercut with shots of the fuse burning.

irising: gradual opening up or closing down of the image from or to a pinpoint. Much used in silent films.

library shot: shot taken from a film archive or cinémathèque, either from another film or from a newsreel.

long shot: shot taken from some distance (usually not less than 50 yards from the action).

low angle shot: shot taken from below and pointing up at the action.

mask: a device for covering part of the screen with blackness, frequently used to create the effect of looking through binoculars or a keyhole.

medium shot: shot from 5 to 15 yards which includes a small group of people in its entirety.

montage film: film made up entirely of library shots; also known as compilation film.

overexposed: an overexposed shot is one where a more than normal amount of light has been allowed to reach the film, thus producing a blinding, glaring effect.

overlap: an overlap of dialogue occurs when two or more characters speak simultaneously.

pan: (or panoramic shot) a horizontal and circular movement of the camera on its pivot.

post-synchronise: (or postsync) to make a recording of the soundtrack (especially of the dialogue) in a sound studio (as opposed to on set), with the actors speaking their lines in accompaniment to the projected film.

reverse motion: a trick effect which reverses the movements of the characters and objects.

rushes: the sum of a day's shooting when it comes back from the laboratories after development and has not yet been edited.

shooting script: the final script used by the director, technicians, and actors, with the complete break-down of the scenario into separate shots.

soft focus: effect obtained by a special lens or gauze which creates a hazy, glittering effect, much used in films of the 'thirties.

stock shot: shot taken from a film company's library of useful material (for example, planes crashing, ships sinking etc.) which is inserted into a fictional film.

telephoto lens: lens which magnifies like a telescope. It has the effect of flattening the image and reducing perspective.

track in, track back: a movement of the camera on a trolley (a tracking shot) towards or away from an object or character.

underexposed: opposite of overexposed (q.v.), producing a dim, indistinct effect.

wide angle lens: a lens with a wide range of field which exaggerates perspective.

wipe: a device whereby a line moves across the screen erasing one image and introducing another.

zoom: a lens of variable focal length. It can, by gradually magnifying or reducing the image, give the effect of moving closer to or farther away from an object.

Index to Film Titles

When more than one entry number is given, the order of reference is as follows: director, actresses, actors, scriptwriter, director of photography, set-designer, editor, composer, assistant/second unit director, producer, and movements (e.g. cinéma-vérité or expressionism, except that this may come first if the director's name is mentioned only in that particular entry).

117

119

120

127

129

130

131

134

137

140

142

143

145

147

148

Mostri, I (D. Risi 64) 214
Mother (1914) 552
Mother (1926) 454
Mother (1952) 400
Mother (1956) 151, 37
Mother (1964) 508
Mother and her children, The 608
Mother and son 402
Mother-and-child grass 539
Mothering heart, The 225, 217
Mother's devotion 151
Mouchette 66
Moulin Rouge 259, 25
Mount Vernon 565, 315
Mountain eagle, The 249, 30
Mourir à Madrid 417, 267
Mourning becomes Electra 414, 152, 465
Mouse that roared, The (J. Arnold 59) 503
Mouth organ, The 237
Movie crazy (C. Bruckman 32) 334
Moving target, The (J. Smite 66) 412, 601
Mr. and Mrs. Smith 249, 336, 297
Mr. and Mrs. Swordplay 400
Mr. Arkadin 590
Mr. Deeds goes to town 81, 108
Mr. Magoo 17
Mr. Music (R. Haydn 50) 365
Mr. Moto takes a chance (N. Foster 38) 339
Mr. Moto takes a vacation (N. Foster 39) 339
Mr. Moto's last warning (N. Foster 39) 339
Mr. Skeffington (V. Sherman 44) 126, 460
Mr. Peabody and the mermaid (I. Pichel 48) 448
Mr. Poo 260
Mr. Smith goes to Washington 81, 462, 529, 545
Mr. Topaze 503
Mrs. Canary 610
Mrs. Miniver 606
Mrs. Parkington 213, 393
Mrs. Szabó 361
Mrs. Wiggs of the cabbage patch (N. Taurog 34) 181, 442
Mud and soldiers 539
Muddy waters 261
Müde Tod, Der 309, 232, 578, 481, 585, 169
Muiden circle lives again, The 229
Mujer sin amor, Una 74
Mulher de verdade 86
Mummy, The (1932) 201, 276
Mummy, The (1959) 184
Munakata sisters, The 426
Muraglia cinese, La 332
Murder 249, 363
Murder by contract 323
Murder Czech style 589
Murder Inc. 583
Murder in Dante Street, The 482, 521
Murder in Thornton Square 119
Murderers are amongst us, The 525
Murders in the rue Morgue 188, 343, 201

Muriel, ou le temps d'un retour 471, 65
Muro, El 549
Muscle beach 323
Musée Grévin 138
Music box, The (J. Parrott 32) 314, 478
Music in darkness 45
Music room, The 464, 388
Musical poster 15
Mussorgsky (G. Roshal 50) 94
Mutiny on the Bounty (1935) 333, 206, 313, 548, 326
Mutiny on the Bounty (1962) 384, 63, 255
My best gal 358, 71
My cousin Rachel (H. Koster 53) 131, 76
My darling Clementine 193, 190
My enemy the sea 260
My fair lady 119, 246, 235
My favourite wife 275, 221, 371
My geisha 82, 351, 479, 297
My grandmother's encyclopedia 58
My home is Copacabana 535
My learned friend 128, 240
My little chickadee (E. Cline 40) 181, 593
My man Godfrey (G. La Cava 36) 336, 448
My sister Eileen 455, 160
My sister my love (V. Sjöman 66) 10, 51
My universities 151
My way home 265
My wife the movie star 342
My wife's relations 282
My younger brother 614
Mystère Barton, Le (C. Spaak 49) 523, 484
Mystère de l'atelier 15, Le 362, 471
Mystère du château de dés, Le 27
Mystère Koumiko, Le 362
Mystère Picasso, Le 103, 469, 25
Mysterious lady, The 413, 209
Mysterious Mr. Moto, The (N. Foster 38) 339

N.U. 18, 204
Nadejda 215
Nail in the boot, A 274
Naïs 428, 174
Naissance du cinéma 317
Naked and the dead, The 583, 248
Naked city, The 124, 245
Naked face of night, The 610
Naked kiss, The 202
Naked maja, The (H. Koster 59) 210, 491
Naked night, The 45
Naked runner, The 203, 514
Naked spur, The 358, 529
Naked truth, The (M. Zampi 58) 503
Namu, the killer whale 43
Nana 470, 298, 65
Nanook of the North 185
Nanny, The 251, 126
Naomi and Rufus kiss 410
Napoléon (1927) 207, 75

151

153

154

156

157

161

163

164

169

171

174

175